The Relentless Question

The Relentless Question

Reflections on
the Paranormal

by
John Beloff

McFarland & Company, Inc., Publishers
Jefferson, North Carolina, and London

Frontispiece: John Beloff, ca. 1988, before
the University of Edinburgh Psychology Department

British Library Cataloguing-in-Publication data are available

Library of Congress Cataloguing-in-Publication Data

Beloff, John.
  The relentless question : reflections on the paranormal / John
Beloff.
    p.   cm.
  [Includes index.]
  Includes bibliographical references.
  ISBN 0-89950-417-5 (lib. bdg. : 50# alk. paper) ∞
  1. Parapsychology. I. Title.
BF1031.B328   1990
133.8—dc20   89-42704
                                                              CIP

Manufactured in the United States of America

McFarland & Company, Inc., Publishers
  Box 611, Jefferson, North Carolina 28640

To my graduate students
past and present

Acknowledgments

I wish, first, to thank Lisette Coly, vice president of the Parapsychology Foundation, Inc., for graciously allowing me to reprint the following papers: "The Subliminal and the Extrasensory," from *Parapsychology and the Sciences*, 1974; "The Study of the Paranormal as an Educative Experience," from *Education in Parapsychology*, 1976; "Backward Causation," from *The Philosophy of Parapsychology*, 1977; "Voluntary Movement, Biofeedback Control and PK," from *Brain/Mind and Parapsychology*, 1979; and "What Is to Count as Good Evidence for the Paranormal," from the *Parapsychology Review*, March-April, 1989.

I would also like to thank Paul Kurtz of Prometheus Books for kindly allowing me to reprint the following two papers: "Science, Religion and the Paranormal," from *Free Inquiry*, 1985 (Vol. 5), and "What Is Your Counter-Explanation? A Plea to Skeptics to Think Again," from *A Skeptic's Handbook of Parapsychology*, 1985.

I am likewise grateful to the following: to J. Neville of Gordon & Breach Science Publishers for permission to reprint "Is Normal Memory a 'Paranormal' Phenomenon?" from *Theoria to Theory*, 1980 (Vol. 14); to Mary C. Rose, editor, permission to reprint "Parapsychology and Radical Dualism," from *Journal of Religion and Psychical Research*, 1985 (Vol. 8); and to Colin Spooner of Prism Press, Ltd., for permission to reprint "Extreme Phenomena and the Problem of Credibility" from *Exploring the Paranormal: Different Perspectives on Belief and Experience*, edited by G.K. Zollschan, J.F. Schumaker and G.F. Walsh, 1989.

Of the remaining papers that were previously published, these appeared in either *Research in Parapsychology 19– *, published by Scarecrow Press for the Parapsychological Association, Inc., whose permission to reproduce I have obtained, or in the publications of the Society for Psychical Research, Inc., where it is my prerogative, as editor, to grant myself permission.

Contents

Autobiographical Introduction

I am an unlikely subject for biography. My life has been uneventful and inglorious and such adventures as have come my way have been no more than adventures of the mind. One of the temptations that a biographer must resist is the use of hindsight to give a spurious continuity to the life in question and thereby ignoring the part played by sheer chance. Parapsychology is such a deviant pursuit in our society that it is nevertheless proper to inquire how someone gets drawn into it. Perhaps the two most common explanations, in this connection, are the following. The individual in question may at some stage of his or her life have had intimations of the paranormal so impressive or disturbing that thereafter the topic became a consuming passion. Alternatively, and less dramatically, an interest in the paranormal may have been so strongly embedded in that person's family background and traditions that the seeds were sown from an early age.

Neither explanation, however, fits my particular case. Never at any time, alas, have I been favored with one of those inexplicable incidents which so many people I have met can recall from their past and which have played their part in the lives of so many of my fellow parapsychologists (Pilkington 1987). Indeed, I wonder sometimes whether I might not be specially deprived in this respect. Am I, perhaps, tone deaf to the promptings of my psyche? Has my right hemisphere — that half of the brain that is said to mediate our intuitions and our psychic functioning — become atrophied from neglect? I do not know, but I remain a stranger to such experiences. Still less can the answer be found in my family background. My family were all, without exception, stolidly impervious to what my friend, Stanley Krippner, has so aptly called the "song of the siren" (Krippner 1977). A much simpler, if less charitable, explanation in my case is my lack of success in any of the conventional pursuits. Deviants, after all, are generally misfits.

1

My Family Background

My parents were Russian Jews who settled in London shortly before the First World War. It was a time when Jews were leaving Russia in large numbers to escape discrimination and conscription into the Tsarist army. Most of them settled in the United States. As readers of the stories by Bashevis Singer will know, there was a rich vein of supernatural and mystical beliefs among the small Jewish communities of Eastern Europe. My parents, however, could be described as assimilated Jews. Their links with traditional Judaism were of a sentimental rather than pious nature. Indeed they prided themselves on their modern emancipated outlook—this was especially so with my mother, the more educated of the two. We children were given a mildly conventional Jewish upbringing but it never went very deep with any of us. I went through a typical phase of adolescent piety but before I was out of my teens I had lost completely my faith in a deity and nothing that has happened to me since has caused me to change my mind. Hence I was cut off thereafter from one traditional avenue to the supernatural, one that has meant a great deal to many of my friends and contemporaries.

It was our good fortune that my father prospered. He started an export business in the City of London trading in chemicals and sundry products with Eastern Europe and was in fact one of the first to do business with the newly established Soviet Union. We were thus brought up in comfortable circumstances in a large house near Hampstead Heath. I was born in 1920, the fourth of five children. We were a boisterous bunch and it was an invigorating nursery in which to grow up. Each of us, one could say, eventually made some mark on the world in our very different ways but, in the best Jewish tradition, we have remained a fairly closely knit family. My brother, Max (now Lord Beloff), is the eldest and I have three sisters whom I love dearly: Renée, Nora and Anne.

Max, ever since I can remember, was scholastically brilliant. He became an historian and later an authority on comparative government and international affairs. He attained the heights of British academic eminence when he gained his chair at All Souls, Oxford. Later he became president of Britain's only independent university at Buckingham, which he helped to found, and now, in his retirement, has become a Conservative life peer. As can be imagined, it was not easy to grow up in his shadow. My poor parents were fond of me in their own way and patient enough with my waywardness but there was no disguising their disappointment in me and they would teasingly call me their *schlemiel* or, more charitably, a "dreamer."

My eldest sister, Renée, after an abortive attempt at a career on the stage, settled for school teaching where she specialized in dramatic art. She married young and proved the most fruitful of the family by producing six children in fairly rapid succession. Unhappily her husband, a businessman, died while they were still young and, as she never remarried, she had to bear the burden of bringing them up on her own. A woman of exceptional energy, she has never truly retired and now runs her own school in Milton Keynes in Bedfordshire.

Anne, the baby of the family, was our one real scientist. It was to be her fate to marry Ernst Chain whom she met at Oxford when he was busy with the research that was to win him the Nobel Prize for his part in the discovery of penicillin. But she was a good biochemist in her own right and, after Chain's death, she was promoted to a chair at Imperial College, London.

It was my middle sister, Nora, however, with whom I had my closest ties. This was partly due to the fact that she did not marry until very late in life, but, more, to the fact that she was such good company. She served as foreign correspondent of the *Observer* newspaper in Paris, Moscow, Washington and elsewhere and won for herself an international reputation as a political journalist. Although a small person, she was surprisingly tough and combative and was often feared by politicians for her outspokenness. Since retiring from the *Observer* her main interest has been Eastern Europe. She published one book about her travels in the Soviet Union and another about the situation in Yugoslavia with a strong anti–Titoist slant. She has the proud distinction of having been expelled from both countries by the security police for spreading hostile propaganda.

Such, then, in brief, was my family but I can say that neither my parents nor my siblings nor their spouses shared my increasing interest in the paranormal and my brother, like most of his fellow Oxford academics, was openly dismissive.

My Career

It was obvious from an early age that I was not the bookish type. I am still a very slow reader — an immense handicap for someone in academic life. On the other hand I have always taken a keen interest in art. My parents, therefore, decided that a career in architecture might be the answer for my future. It was to prove a costly mistake. I never showed much skill even for drawing and painting, in which I liked to dabble, but I certainly lacked the concrete imagination, practical sense and grasp of detail that is so essential to the making of an architect. However, as I approached the age of leaving school, I still had not the least idea as to what I wanted to do with my life and so had nothing to counter my parents' wishes. And so, in 1937, I enrolled at the Architectural Association School of Architecture in Bedford Square, London. My studies there did nothing to allay my own misgivings but, after two years, war broke out and I went into the army.

By the time my battalion was ready to be sent abroad Dunkirk had fallen.

Later I fell ill and was invalided out of the army after two and a half years without ever having gone into action. It turned out that I had contracted Crohn's disease, a rare abdominal disorder whose etiology is, I gather, unknown but which can be cured by surgery as mine eventually was. I regard it as one of the many ironies of my life that the only time I have had a serious bout of illness in my adult life, which has been mercifully free from medical complications, it was, in all probability, my salvation since I learned later that my battalion had been sent to join the Allied campaign in Italy where casualties were very heavy. But my providential escape from the horrors of war exacted a price and left me with permanent feelings of inferiority towards those of my contemporaries who had a good war record to their credit.

I had managed to get through a good deal of reading while still in the army — there was always so much waiting around — including a fair amount of psychology. I had also picked up at a local library a copy of Rhine's *Extra-Sensory Perception,* which left a strong impression on me. When, therefore, I was fit enough to resume my education I wanted to make a clean break with architecture although I was still very vague as to my alternative. My mother pleaded with me to complete my architectural studies, warning me that, otherwise, I would become a drifter all my life (what today we would call a "drop-out"). I was still too docile and too dependent to thwart my parents' wishes so I stuck it out and, by 1946, had completed my professional qualifications. There followed a number of menial jobs in architectural offices which, owing to my incompetence, I could never hold for very long and which are among the unhappiest memories of my life. Eventually I decided that there was nothing for it but to go back to square one and I enrolled as a student of psychology at London University, at first at evening classes at Birkbeck College and, later, full time at University College.

One of the attractions of University College at that time was the weekly philosophy seminar I could attend under the late A.J. Ayer. Although I never succumbed to his logical positivism that was then much in vogue, his acute and trenchant intellect made a lasting impression on me and to this day I always strive to model my own writing on his taut prose style. By the time I graduated from University College in 1952 I had reached the advanced age of 32 with no firm prospects as yet of being able to make a living. However, the very first thing I did on graduating was to marry a fellow student of psychology, Halla, who was ten years my junior. Her parents, like mine, were immigrants though of a more recent vintage. They were refugees from Hitler who had managed to get out of Germany only just in time before the war came.

Halla soon became the most important person in my life and we have stayed together ever since. She was the better psychologist of the two, social psychology was her area of expertise. She eventually became active in the affairs of the British Psychological Society and served as president one year. She is the author of *Camera Culture,* a study of the part which photography plays in our

Halla and John Beloff in 1953, a year after their marriage.

lives (H. Beloff 1985). Our marriage produced two children, a girl in 1958 and then, five years later, a boy. Both have chosen their own path in life which they are now busily pursuing. My son, Bruno, is a computer scientist who already earns more than I ever did and whose facility with machines and grasp of technology is something that I can only envy. My daughter, Zoe, is striving toward a career as a filmmaker in New York and is endowed with the artistic abilities which the gods denied to me. Although our marriage was, in many respects, a marriage of minds — we are both devotees of the arts — I think I can truthfully say that neither my wife nor our children nor any of my many nephews and nieces were ever troubled by my "relentless question."

Straight after graduating we both went to work for Raymond Cattell at the University of Illinois. His main claim to fame was to have devised what is still one of the most widely used tests of personality. It was an exciting new experience for us as well as being our introduction to the American way of life. But, after a year, we had had enough and we returned to Britain where I had been offered a job in the Department of Psychology of Queen's University, Belfast, under George Seth. Neither of us had ever set foot in Ireland before but we found Belfast a pleasant enough place in which to make our home. The 1950s were the halcyon days before the advent of terrorism and, when the

troubles did eventually erupt, in 1969, we had long since moved on to Edinburgh. In those more carefree days one could still get a job as a lecturer without
having a Ph.D. I was able to work for it while doing my teaching and so, by
1956, I had managed to obtain my doctorate from Queen's University, as did
Halla at the same time. Visual perception was the area of psychology that then
interested me. It had grown naturally out of my interest in the visual arts which
had led me into the byways of experimental esthetics and psychophysics, but
I never had the patience one needs to become a first rate experimentalist.

By this time I was well acquainted with the literature of psychical research
and I made a point of trying to find out all I could about one very famous
episode that had taken place in Belfast during the First World War. It involved
Dr. W.J. Crawford, a lecturer in mechanical engineering, and the young
physical medium, Kathleen Goligher (Barham 1988). But I still never thought
that I might take an active role in experimental parapsychology unless I were
to be lucky enough to encounter a gifted subject. My initiation eventually
came about as the result of a talk I gave to the student physics society at
Queen's. A bright young physics student, Leonard Evans, persuaded me that
it might be possible to demonstrate PK using the emission of particles from
a radioactive source. I liked the idea and was taken with his youthful enthusiasm and we devised an experiment using equipment made available to
us in the Department of Chemistry with volunteers drawn from the local
spiritualist society. Alas, we obtained only null results (Beloff & Evans 1961) — a
presage of things to come — but we somehow had contrived to anticipate a new
development in PK research that was soon to reach fruition, thanks to the
genius of Helmut Schmidt, with the result that our paper has been cited more
often than any other experimental paper that I have published.

A crucial step in my career was the publication of my first book, *The Existence of Mind* (1962). It was a contribution to the philosophy of mind, rather
than to psychology as such, and it represented my outraged reaction to Gilbert
Ryle's *The Concept of Mind* (1949). Ryle's book had become enormously
popular and influential but my purpose was to show that it was utterly
misguided. Ryle propounds the doctrine known as "analytical behaviorism,"
that is to say the view that all mental concepts, without exception, can be ex-
plicated without residue in terms either of overt behavior or of the disposition
to behave in a particular way. My book attempted to show that mind was, on
the contrary, a cause of behavior and the subject of conscious experience. More
passionate, perhaps, than profound, it had little effect on the subsequent
course of British philosophy but I drew some comfort from the fact that it
caught the attention of some eminent thinkers who, for one reason or another,
were themselves at loggerheads with the philosophical establishment, including Michael Polanyi, Karl Popper, John Eccles and Arthur Koestler. I was
also very gratified to get a fairly favorable review in *The New Statesman,* by
"Freddie" Ayer (as he was known).

At FRNM, summer 1965; *left to right:* Cynthia Weaver, Wayne Whitfield, Betty Newton, J.B. Rhine, Fay David (back with glasses), B. Kanthamani (woman, front), John Freeman (back with glasses), John Beloff (front), Rex Stanford (glasses, rear center), Martin Johnson (bow tie), Harold Avery (glasses), Louisa Rhine (front, holding glasses), Charles Honorton (back), Dorothy Pope (middle, with glasses), Lynne Guyor, James Carpenter, Marie Avery (striped dress), David Rogers, Reid Creech.

More important, however, for the direction my career was later to assume, was J.B. Rhine's somehow getting wind of my book, the final chapter of which is devoted to "the paranormal," and inviting me to visit his laboratory in Durham, North Carolina. This I gladly did in the summer of 1965. I had argued in my book that parapsychology alone provides the empirical evidence needed to vindicate the autonomy and efficacy of mind, a view that I have adhered to ever since. Gaither Pratt, then Rhine's right hand man (Pratt 1987), also befriended me and it was he who invited me to give the banquet address when the Parapsychological Association met in Oxford, in 1964, for their annual convention. (Beloff 1964). I was further patronized by that other dominant figure of the parapsychology establishment, Eileen Garrett, and was in due course rewarded with invitations to her fabulous conferences at Le Piol near St. Paul de Vence in the south of France. I remained persona grata with the Parapsychology Foundation after she died when her daughter, Eileen Coly, became president.

Rhine showed, I think, some perspicacity in urging me to continue writing about parapsychology rather than practicing it. I was already acquiring the reputation, which has clung to me ever since, of being a negative or psi-inhibitory experimenter and Rhine, of course, had no use for anyone who could not deliver positive results.* I did not heed his advice because I did not wish to become a mere commentator from the sidelines nor was I a sufficient scholar ever to become one of the historians of the field. Nevertheless, I would have to agree that experimentation was never my strong suit whereas I do believe that I have an ability to write, an ability that has stood me in good stead ever since my schooldays.

In 1962 James Drever II offered me a job† in the Department of Psychology of the University of Edinburgh although he made no secret of the fact that he was an avowed skeptic with regard to parapsychology. We moved there in the winter of 1963 and Edinburgh has been my home ever since. At Edinburgh I was required to teach psychology on a broad front but no objection was ever raised, either by my superiors or by my colleagues, to my making parapsychology my primary research area, a fact which, I think, speaks well for British tolerance. Moreover, Drever's successor, the late David Vowles, though himself a neuropsychologist, took a benign attitude towards the paranormal. I was lucky in obtaining some private funding that enabled me to hire a research assistant.

Our first systematic research program was an attempt to replicate the work of Milan Ryzl of Prague who was then claiming to be able to train ESP using hypnosis. What gave substance to these claims was the presence of his star subject, Pavel Stepanek, who, after having undergone this training, was scoring consistently in a nonrandom way on a test of clairvoyance to the satisfaction of parapsychologists from several different countries who went to Prague for the sake of testing him. Stepanek, I may say, performed in the waking state, not under hypnosis. In 1964, with help from the British Council, I went to Prague myself to test Stepanek and make contact with Ryzl. Although the results I obtained with Stepanek were disappointing (Ryzl and Beloff 1965), I was favorably impressed with Ryzl himself and we duly went ahead with our program at Edinburgh. It eventually became clear, however, that, for whatever reason, we were getting no learning effect (Beloff & Mandleberg 1966). A few years later Ryzl defected from Czechoslovakia and went to live in the United States, at first to work for J.B. Rhine, then later settling in California. He has never subsequently furnished convincing proof that he has found a method of

---

*In the end, it proved to be his undoing. He could not desist from heaping favors on the young W.J. Levy who produced positive results, time and again—until he was caught cheating (Rhine 1974).

†Even better, he offered both Halla and me jobs. He was powerful enough to ignore the anomaly of a husband and wife in the same department.

training ESP which remains one of the supreme unfulfilled goals of the parapsychologist. Later we tried other training techniques such as the "waiting" technique, as described by Rhea White (1964) but with no better success (Beloff & Mandleberg 1967).

At Edinburgh I made the acquaintance of John Smythies, then of the Department of Psychiatry, now at the University of Alabama. Smythies already had a long-standing interest in parapsychology and and we even collaborated on an experiment he wanted to try using his brain-damaged patients (Smythies & Beloff 1965) but we had no luck here either. Smythies had been commissioned to edit two books for Routledge, *Brain and Mind* (1965) and *Science and ESP* (1967), and I was invited to contribute to both volumes. It was, once again, Smythies who proposed me for the Council of the Society for Psychical Research, to which I was elected in 1964 and to which I have been reelected continuously ever since. Much later, after Smythies had migrated to the United States, he invited me to coedit with him a volume of solicited articles defending the dualist position on the mind-body problem, a position to which both of us in our different ways adhered. By then, however, times were harder for the publishing trade and Routledge turned us down. Eventually, however, the University Press of Virginia came to our rescue (thanks to the good offices of Ian Stevenson) and our book, *The Case for Dualism,* has now at last appeared.

Our first doctoral student to do a dissertation in parapsychology was Adrian Parker, who had graduated from our Department but had then done a clinical training at the Tavistock Institute in London. The title of his dissertation was "The Experimenter Effect in Parapsychology" (Parker 1977). While engaged on it he also managed to write a book dealing with ESP in altered states of consciousness (Parker 1970), to which I wrote an introduction. Following Parker we had a succession of graduate students keen to work in parapsychology. Some of them, such as Richard Broughton, Brian Millar and Michael Thalbourne have become well known to the parapsychology community. Thalbourne, too, managed to produce a book while working for his Ph.D. (Thalbourne 1981), a very useful little glossary of parapsychological terms (Thalbourne 1982). More recently Julie Milton and Deborah Delanoy obtained their doctorates from this department on aspects of the ganzfeld technique and they are now employed as research associates by our new "Koestler Professor of Parapsychology," Robert Morris. I have always felt that I owed a special debt to my graduate students on whom I came increasingly to depend for the experimental output of our parapsychology unit and it is to them that I dedicate this book.

My second book, *Psychological Sciences* (1973), was, essentially, a distillation of my lecture courses but, again, I included a chapter on parapsychology. The title of the book was to convey the message that psychology never was and never could be a single unified science but at most a conglomerate of more or less related sciences. Not that the idea was new, indeed my old antagonist, Gilbert Ryle, had already said as much in his *The Concept of Mind* but perhaps not so many psychologists had made the point so explicitly. At all events, I took the view that parapsychology had the same right to be considered a "psychological science" as any other even if it seldom figured in the curriculum at the university or in the standard psychology textbooks. I was also at this time commissioned by Elek Science, a London publisher, to edit a volume of solicited papers in parapsychology, which duly appeared in 1974 under the title *New Directions in Parapsychology*. Arthur Koestler did me a great favor on that occasion by contributing an "Afterword" to the volume for which he demanded no payment. Quite recently this book has resurfaced in a Japanese edition.

Such honors as have come my way in the course of my career I owe entirely to my fellow members of the small but worldwide parapsychological community. I was once even awarded a money prize by a Swiss Society thanks to the recommendation of the late Anita Gregory. I was elected president of the S.P.R. for the period 1974–1976 and I have twice served as president of the Parapsychological Association, in 1972 and again in 1982. It was in 1972 that the P.A. met in Edinburgh for their annual convention. In 1982 it met in Cambridge to join forces with the S.P.R. to celebrate the centennial of the latter and the jubilee of the former. My presidential address for the Edinburgh convention is included in this volume (see "Belief and Doubt") but my presidential address for the Cambridge meeting ("Three Open Questions") has been omitted as the themes I touch upon there are dealt with more fully elsewhere. In Edinburgh it was Arthur Koestler who gave the banquet address while in Cambridge it was Hans Eysenck. Although these two intellectual titans disagreed on most issues, both were good friends of parapsychology.*

One particular honor conferred upon me descended from on high like a bolt from the blue. In March 1983 I received a telephone call from Koestler's solicitors informing me that I had been nominated in Koestler's will as one of four executors (the others being his solicitor, his publisher and his literary agent). The double suicide of Arthur and Cynthia Koestler that had just taken place had attracted wide publicity throughout the world. As myself a keen supporter of the cause of voluntary euthanasia, I admired Arthur's courage and rationality in deciding to choose the manner and moment of his death rather than waiting passively for the fatal diseases that were ravaging him to take their toll. But it was, of course, tragic that Cynthia, who was herself in good health, should have decided to die with him rather than go on living without him. Even after reading their joint posthumous autobiography (Koestler & Koestler

---

Both have shown goodwill towards me. Eysenck wrote a favorable review of my Psychological Sciences and Koestler cited it in the Observer, that Christmas, as among his choice of books of the year!

1984), it is still hard for me to understand how any woman could love a man to that extent but I may be unduly cynical. Anyway, as far as parapsychology is concerned, the consequences were wholly favorable since Koestler had bequeathed his entire estate for the establishment of a chair of parapsychology at a British university. As the only one of the executors with any knowledge of parapsychology, it thus devolved on me to find a British university that would accept his gift, which many might regard as something of a Trojan horse.

The experience brought home to me the distrust and suspicion that still surrounds the mere mention of parapsychology in academic circles. In the event, the one university that, from the outset, was fully supportive was my own at Edinburgh. This was due very largely to the then principal, John Burnett, and the then dean of social sciences, an architect, Barry Wilson. Perhaps my example in keeping a low profile all those years had paid off by convincing my colleagues that parapsychology could not be so scandalous as some averred. Anyway, I was delighted when the Koestler bequest was finally awarded to Edinburgh. It had saddened me to think, as I was reaching retirement age, that parapsychology would soon disappear from the Edinburgh scene had it not been for this turn of events. Fortunately I was allowed a place on the selection committee and could thus use my influence in the choice of a candidate to become the first Koestler professor and I was delighted when the appointment was conferred on Robert Morris, a youthful American who had won universal respect in his country from both parapsychologists and their critics.

The fact that I take seriously phenomena that have clearly failed to impress most of my contemporaries forces me to ask whether, in all honesty, I have some special *need* to believe? By the laws of cognitive dissonance the longer you commit yourself to some cause and the more effort you devote to it the harder it becomes to renounce it. My friend, Susan Blackmore, is one of those rare individuals who succeeded in swapping horses in midstream. Following a prolonged bout of failure to elicit psi she threw her lot in with the skeptical community (Blackmore 1986). But she was still in the early stages of her career while I am a veteran. Could it be that I no longer dared yield to doubt? There have been times when I have been assailed with the thought that, perhaps, the whole field had been misconceived from the start and was now running into the ground. The Levy scandal (Rhine 1974) was a bitter pill and even more traumatic for me was the final dismemberment of S.G. Soal (Markwick 1978). Another unsettling episode was when I thought I had discovered a remarkable medium on the Isle of Wight. But she turned out to be fraudulent and it was largely thanks to the help I received from friends, including my sister Nora, that I realized this just in time to prevent my making a fool of myself in print (Stevenson & Beloff 1980). However, I survived these various shocks and setbacks as did my basic conviction that psi is real.

John Beloff, September 1985 (photo by Sean Hudson).

Whatever the psychodynamics of my own personality, I cannot be accused of ignoring the skeptical literature. On the contrary I am always anxious to read what the critics have to say. I subscribe to the *Skeptical Inquirer* and to the *Zetetic Scholar*. I attended a CSICOP conference, the year it met in London, and I have engaged in lengthy correspondence with the amazing James Randi and the eminent Martin Gardner. I have come to realize that my own ignorance of conjuring techniques may have misled me in assessing the veridicality of some of the cases of strong phenomena. But, when all that is granted, my impression is still that the skeptics are, for the most part, too facile and too complacent. They dwell too often on the weaker cases while ignoring or glossing over the really awkward evidence. For example, they are far too ready to assume that, if a medium or psychic has been caught cheating, this disposes of their claim, as if it was their character that was at issue rather than the phenomena. Whereas, if K.J. Batcheldor is to be believed, there may be something inherent in the psychodynamics of producing strong phenomena that predisposes one to cheat. All one can say for certain is that, whatever the answer may be, it is by no means simple or straightforward. In our common desire to unravel the truth, I find the skeptics much less ready to see things from our point of view than we are from theirs.

I retired in October 1985. Never having occupied a chair, I could not then become "emeritus" but thanks to the good offices of our new head of department, Robert Grieve, I have been made an "honorary fellow" of the department and am allowed to retain a room there and use the university facilities. Hence, though I no longer teach, I am not cut off from my natural community of scholars. I still keep a fatherly eye on what goes on in the department and help, where required, with the supervision of graduate students. I am still editor of the *Journal* of the S.P.R. but, more than anything else, I have an urge to write. Always conscious of the inordinately long time it took me to find my feet in life, I am anxious to have my say before it is too late. Meanwhile I also like to keep up with my large international correspondence.

* * *

Such, then, has been my life, at least as I perceive it. What now follows are my thoughts about the topic that has occupied me for so long. They offer no revelations and no bold new theories of psi but I am hopeful that they may strike a chord with readers who share my curiosity and my puzzlement. I would describe myself as, basically, a conservative thinker. I mean by this not that I regard commonsense as sacrosanct but that I demand very good reasons before relinquishing a commonsense position. My main aim in these papers has been to do justice to the evidence while, at the same time, seeking to do the least violence to our reason and our general knowledge.

In this brief introduction it has not been possible to mention the names of all who have helped me or have influenced my outlook. Suffice it to say that they are not forgotten and that they have my sincere gratitude.

Explaining the Paranormal

The fact that the paranormal has to be defined in negative terms is still a constant refrain of the skeptical community. They argue that, if psi phenomena were real, they would, by now, have found a place in an acceptable framework that would allow some positive definition. In this paper I offer reasons for thinking that this skeptical argument is unsound. I discuss five possible explanatory frameworks to which psi phenomena might be assigned but, in the absence of any consensus, a purely negative definition remains necessary.

The paper was given as a public lecture under the auspices of the Society for Psychical Research in Kensington, London, on May 14, 1963. Francis Huxley, the anthropologist, was in the chair. I had then only recently joined the Society and felt duly honored at being invited to address it. Rereading it now, after a quarter of a century, I am struck at how little my basic views on the nature of psi phenomena have changed since then. Whether this demonstrates my incorrigibility or whether it betokens prescience on my part is for the reader to judge. This paper was chosen by the philosopher, Jan Ludwig, for inclusion in his anthology Philosophy and Parapsychology *(Ludwig 1978). However, at my suggestion, an updated addendum was included so that the full title became "Explaining the Paranormal — With Epilogue 1977." Here, however, I have reverted to the original paper plus a few updated notes.*

The field of psychical research must be unique in one respect at least: no other discipline, so far as I know, has its subject matter demarcated by exclusively negative criteria. A phenomenon is, by definition, paranormal if and only if it contravenes some fundamental and well-founded assumption of science. This alone is what makes it of interest to this Society [for Psychical Research].

Now, one would need to be almost perversely fond of mystification to sustain an interest in anything for any length of time for no other reason than that it was odd and inexplicable. Most psychical researchers, I feel sure, are drawn to their pursuit *because* they intuitively feel that these phenomena represent an important riddle about the nature of things which they want to decipher. Of course, there can be no logical guarantee that paranormal phenomena will turn out to possess anything in common beyond their negative qualifications, but there is plenty of precedent for trying to find some overall guiding principle which might embrace at least the major phenomena. In this talk I want, therefore, to discuss what such a guiding principle might be. Now, there are, on my reckoning, no more than five possibilities that are still seriously worth considering. I propose, therefore, to describe briefly each of them in turn and then weight their respective claims on our allegiance.

The first of these basic positions which immediately confronts every student of the psychical is the purely negative one of total disbelief. On this view there are no paranormal phenomena, there are only phenomena mistakenly believed to be paranormal. If they are of any interest this can be only to the student of human credulity and self-deception. This is the simplest and most clearcut of my five alternatives and if we can accept it it would certainly save us a great deal of bother. We should then no longer have to explain the paranormal, instead we should simply explain it away. What, however, we shall later have to decide is whether in the face of the evidence the mental gymnastics required to sustain this position is worth the effort.

The second answer I shall discuss is much less familiar. Indeed, it seems to have had so little appeal that in most discussions of psychical research it is overlooked altogether and, yet, logically, it is perfectly sound. According to this line of argument there are phenomena that are genuinely paranormal but they have absolutely no other significance. They are, in fact, the exceptions in an otherwise well-ordered universe. They occur from time to time and we may take note of the fact but nothing whatsoever follows from their existence. The laws of nature still stand, everything goes on as before, only maybe a few scientists feel chastened at the discovery that their theories have not quite the universal application which, in a more self-confident mood, they might have claimed for them.

The earliest reference I have come across to this interpretation of the paranormal as a sort of natural anomaly is in the writings of William James. In a paper he wrote in 1909 he half playfully puts forward the suggestion that perhaps the lawfulness of nature, that we had so come to take for granted, might, itself, like everything else be the product of a gradual, and still incomplete evolution.[a] Initially there might have been nothing but absolute chaos and, conceivably, the queer goings-on that we sometimes stumble up against in psychical research may be nothing more than the vestiges of this "primordial irrationality" as James calls it. There is not much to suggest that James himself ever took his idea very seriously but one can find an echo of it in a recent work "A New Approach to Psychical Research" by Prof. Antony

Flew, the philosopher (Flew 1953). Flew is at pains in his book to present the paranormal in as unmysterious a guise as possible without being forced to deny categorically all the evidence. Accordingly, he suggests that the phenomena are best regarded as weak anomalous effects devoid of further scientific or philosophical implications.[b]

Both the positions we have considered so far offer reasons why *no* explanation of the paranormal is called for. My third, however, does not allow us to preserve the *status quo*. If paranormal phenomena are genuine, it asserts, so much the worse for a science which declares them to be impossible. What we must now do is to reformulate science so that they will no longer lie beyond the bounds of scientific explanation. If necessary we shall introduce new postulates into physics, bring in additional dimensions of space and time, propose new psychic fields of force, but eventually we shall arrive at a new model of the universe, a synthesis where the distinction between normal and paranormal will no longer appear permanent and absolute. This is a point of view which is, I am sure, familiar to you all. It is one which can generally count upon a sympathetic response nowadays, especially among those who pride themselves on an enlightened and progressive outlook. The prospect of such a reconciliation between science and psychical research appears more hopeful, many now think, than it did in the early days of our Society. To the Victorians, orthodoxy in science presented a much firmer outline than it does to us. We have already witnessed a number of major revolutions in physics and this has shaken our complacency about the immutability of even the most sacred assumptions of science.

Nevertheless, if we turn to those who have actually most to further the cause of psychical research, we shall find that, by and large, they were inspired by quite a different outlook. They did not usually think of themselves as engaged in pushing the frontier of natural science one stage further forward; they believed, on the contrary, that they were using the methods of natural science to demonstrate the existence of phenomena that testified to an entirely different order of reality: namely to a psychic or mental reality. So far from apologizing for the inexplicability of their findings from a scientific point to an aspect of human personality that did not seem to belong to the world of mere objects where physical necessitation is paramount. They combined, in fact, what might be described as a transcendental or even religious attitude to man with a wholly scientific attitude towards factual evidence, a keen appreciation of the strength of scientific materialism with a sensitivity towards its implications.

My fifth and final position is one which I hesitated to present to you. In the first place it sounds ridiculous and I am not at all sure yet whether it is even logically defensible, and, secondly, it is the brain-child of one particular individual rather than the view of a group of thinkers. However ours is a field where we cannot afford to be too "choosy" but must gratefully accept any insight that offers the least possibility of an escape from our present perplexities. I refer, then, to the theory of meaningful coincidences or "synchronicity" (to give it its technical though somewhat misleading designation) which was first propounded by the late C.G. Jung in a small book which came out in Zurich in 1952.* I may add that my hesitation seems to have been shared by its author who waited many years before finally deciding to publish.

The crux of Jung's thesis lies in this curious phrase "meaningful coincidences." At first glance one might well suppose that we were faced here with a plain contradiction in terms. As the word is ordinarily used a coincidence implies a purely fortuitous conjunction of two or more events of a specific sort. How, then, can a coincidence be meaningful? Well, you may point out that we can always invest any set of events with a significance of our own devising, as when, for example an artist descries a profound aesthetic significance in some purely haphazard juxtaposition of assorted objects, or when we like to attribute to destiny or providence the accidents of fortune. But this would be to misunderstand Jung who explicitly denies that he is talking about any merely subjective significance. Synchronicity, he insists, is an objective fact about the universe, or, at any rate, is no less objective than those other fundamental categories such as space or time or causality by means of which we apprehend the external world. Indeed, there are, according to Jung, precisely four ways in which any two events may stand in relation to one another: (1) in spatial relationship (2) in temporal relationship (3) in causal relationship and finally (4) in a relationship based on what he calls an "a-causal connecting principle" or synchronicity (Jung 1955).

Now, if we adopt Jung's schema the interpretation of the paranormal becomes clear: paranormal events are demonstrably not based on the causal principle that appears to hold in the case of ordinary physical events, but neither are they based on some kind of para-mechanical causation such as the dualist would like us to imagine when he speaks of mind-matter interactions. The concept of causation, Jung argues, is indissolubly linked up with the transmission of energy in space and time, and it is just this that is lacking in paranormal phenomena, which can, therefore, only be manifestations of synchronicity.

I think you will recognize that we have here an idea which, however audacious and even preposterous it may appear to us educated westerners, is, in fact, of very ancient provenance. If we cast our minds back to the prescientific and magical past, or even if we stop to consider some of the popular superstitions and occult practices in our midst, we shall be forced to admit that synchronicity has always been acknowledged implicitly by mankind even if we

* C.G. Jung & W. Pauli Naturerklärung und Psyche Rascher, Zurich, 1952. It was reviewed in J.S.P.R. 673(1953), 26–35. An English translation has since appeared under the title The Interpretation of Nature and the Psyche, Routledge & Kegan Paul, 1955.

had to wait for Jung to give it a name. Take, for example, the many different arts of divination that one finds in almost every age and culture and which Jung, with his fantastic erudition, is able to discuss with remarkable authority. Now, a striking feature of so many of these practices is that the oracle is induced to yield its answer following the application of what we nowadays call a randomizing procedure. Jung describes some of the elaborate procedures recommended in the "I Ching" or "Book of Changes," that semimagical, semiphilosophical, ancient Chinese treatise that has recently come out here in a paperback translation; but we are all familiar with the idea from such homely examples as telling fortunes from the tea-leaves. Now, this random element shows that those who took such practices seriously realized perfectly well that there could be no conceivable causal connection between the disposition of the signs and the events which they portended, and nevertheless they treated it as a meaningful not a chance connection. Indeed, the whole logic of astrology, insofar as it can be said to have a logic, is the logic of synchronicity. Astrology is peculiarly repugnant to people of a rational cast of mind just because the lack of any causal connection between a man's fate and the configuration of the solar system at his birth is so glaring; but to those who think astrologically this absence of causality is no impediment. The same is true of alchemy, which was not simply a more primitive version of chemistry but was governed by the once universal belief in a natural and meaningful bond of sympathy between the external world and the world of personal private events, between what was called the macrocosm and the microcosm.

Now, Jung's point is that we would be wrong to dismiss these ancient beliefs as so much primitive rubbish. There is, he maintains, a definite tendency discernible in nature for meaningful coincidences to occur in conjunction with certain psychic states of the individual. Certain emotional states, in particular, are conducive to their appearance especially those that reflect subconscious attitudes. Jung then attempts to apply his theory to the results of Rhine's ESP experiments which he does, to his own satisfaction, despite the relatively unemotional atmosphere in which such experiments are conducted.

This completes my survey of the five basic interpretations of the paranormal which it was my intention to deal with. If I may refresh your memory these were first, the skeptical interpretation, according to which the paranormal had no more significance than attaches to any other species of delusion; secondly, the theory of natural anomalies, according to which paranormal events, if they don't actually prove any rules, at any rate don't disprove them; at worst they constitute a mild nuisance to those engaged in legitimate scientific pursuits; thirdly, a view which, to give it a label, I would call scientific monism because it seeks to preserve the unity of science by accommodating the paranormal within the scope of an extended physics; fourthly, the view which is I think most aptly described as substantial dualism. And fifthly and lastly Jung's theory of synchronicity.

I do not claim that my list is, by any means, exhaustive. I have said nothing at all about any of the various supernaturalist and spiritist accounts, or about any of those other occult doctrines of an esoteric kind that still have their adherents. The fact is that I find I already have my work cut out trying to convince some of my academic colleagues that there is still a case to be made for even a relatively straightforward dualism, without my getting involved with any of these more exuberant speculations.

For the remainder of this paper I propose, with your permission, to drop the mask of the impartial expositor and attempt a critical evaluation of the rival viewpoints I have been describing. First, then, need we explain or can we explain away? Explaining away will probably always be an important part of psychical research, because we deal with matters where the sham article so often masquerades as the real thing. A great deal, as you know, has already been explained away; the question is, given a bit more time and patience, will everything in our field be eventually explained away? Here, I am afraid, there is no right or wrong answer, there is only the evidence and one's personal judgment in evaluating that evidence. It is not enough, unfortunately, to point to the excellent credentials behind some of that evidence, for, in the last resort we are all of us fallible human beings, so that even so staunch a friend of psychical research as Gardner Murphy, the American psychologist, had to confess in his latest book that he could not, "in good conscience accept the simple statement that men of integrity and good will do not deceive themselves, do not get caught in ethical traps, do not withhold data, do not give false impressions (Murphy 1961). Nor is it enough to point out, what is undoubtedly the case, that most diehard skeptics are notoriously ignorant of the evidence; there are some authorities who are both intelligent and well versed in the literature who are still not persuaded that there is anything in the alleged phenomena.

In the circumstances, therefore, I can only give you my personal opinion, and it so happens that I am convinced that there *are* paranormal phenomena. I say this, not on the basis of firsthand experience or firsthand research, however, but simply because I cannot entertain the supposition that everything which has transpired since our Society was founded in 1882 is just so much smoke without even the flicker of a fire. But what will, I believe, eventually settle the issue, regardless of our personal beliefs, is whether the evidence will go on accumulating, and whether, as a result, psychical research will move towards a better understanding of the paranormal. If this does *not* happen, then sooner or later serious investigators will give up out of sheer boredom and the topic will slowly die a natural death, whatever its past history; just as many pseudosciences have perished already, despite whatever initial successes they may have gained. Although, like some of these pseudosciences, it may continue indefinitely to captivate the popular imagination. If, on the other hand, this *does* happen, then the arguments of the skeptics will soon become irrelevant and obsolete.

The great mistake which the skeptics have made, in my view, is to treat psychical research as if it were an historical issue that was at stake, like, for example, the authorship of the plays of Shakespeare. As a result, after failing to invalidate parapsychological experimentation, once for all, on some general grounds like hyperaesthesia in the subjects or recording errors on the part of experimenters or fallacious statistical analyses and so on, they have been forced into mounting a separate *ad hoc* attack against each new major investigation as it came along, even where this involved accusing reputable scientists of downright fraud. This being so, the only sensible thing to do, I would suggest, if you are a confirmed skeptic about the paranormal is to ignore it altogether. To set up as a psychical researcher with no other intention than to debunk the phenomena strikes me as about on a par with becoming a professional art critic with the intention not merely of castigating what is bad or mediocre but of proving that there never has been and never could be any such thing as good art!ᶜ

But, if we agree that we cannot entirely explain away, do we still need to explain? Can we not rest content just to acknowledge these as "wild phenomena" that defy explanation? Certainly some of the alleged facts that we are called upon to consider exhibit a degree of waywardness and absurdity which leaves us almost no option. What, for example can you make of the following incident that is recounted by the Swedish psychical researcher Dr. John Björkhem in a book of his which was reviewed in the *Journal* of the Society a few years ago by Professor Broad*:

In October 1948 a certain Swedish textile worker suffering from emaciation was admitted to the hospital at Lund, where Dr. Björkhem was working as a physician. While in there the patient confided to Dr. Björkhem that for some months previously he had been persistently haunted by the ghost of an elderly English gentleman. Although the patient understood very little English he had managed to gather that his ghostly visitor had during his lifetime been very active in psychical research and the name he gave was Price. Now, in point of fact, although Björkhem himself, please note, did *not* know this at the time, Harry Price had died in March of that year.

Was the patient pulling the doctor's leg? It seems most improbable. Is Björkhem pulling our leg? Again it seems most unlikely. Was Harry Price, then, really making a posthumous comeback in psychical research? And, if so, why on earth should he do so in such an incredibly devious fashion? No wonder even Prof. Broad confesses that he is baffled.

However, although this digression may illustrate the fact that one needs a sense of humor in psychical research, I do not think that an element of the

---

* *John Björkhem* Det Ockulta Problemet, *Lindblads Förlag, Uppsala, 1951. It was reviewed in* J.S.P.R. *673(1953), 35–8. A German translation has since appeared under the title* Die Verborgene Kraft, *Olten, 1954.*

absurd is by any means a necessary feature of psychical phenomena. Sometimes these phenomena make very good sense from a psychological point of view, especially if we bring to our aid a knowledge of unconscious psychology. Perhaps even the incident I mentioned, if we are to take it seriously, is not quite so lacking in rhyme or reason as may at first appear. Perhaps a condition of emaciation is conducive to seeing hallucinations. Perhaps the disembodied Harry Price exploited this chance to put in an appearance. We are told that it was at Price's instigation that the patient registered at the hospital at Lund instead of in his own district, with the result that this episode came at last to the ears of Dr. Björkhem. At any rate there is plenty of evidence of purpose in this story, if that is what you demand, although it would be a strange irony of fate if, ultimately, Harry Price as a ghost should carry more conviction than he ever did as a ghosthunter!

At all events, to make a policy of bewilderment is surely the worst form of defeatism. I regard this solution therefore as probably the most unsatisfactory of the five and one that should be accepted only as a last resort.

I would like next to deal with, and if possible to eliminate, the much more serious proposal put forward by Jung. Before I criticize it, I will confess that I am not without a certain sneaking sympathy for it. I say "sneaking" advisedly, because I heartily despise superstition; and yet, if there is one irrational belief which, before I ever read Jung's book, I might, if really pressed, own up to, it is a belief in what I would call the nonrandomness of runs. By this I mean that I have often been struck by the fact that, if some unusual or remarkable event occurs once, it often occurs several times more in close temporal succession, but independently on each occasion, and then never perhaps occurs again. Now I have never attached much significance to this casual observation, assuming it could really be explained on conventional lines as an allowable bunching effect, but I mention it to show that far from starting with a prejudice against Jung's theory I was quite ready to cock my ears when someone came along with the suggestion that the nature of things is such that we must revise our assumptions not only about causality but also about randomness.

Nevertheless, as I understand it, Jung is here guilty of a fallacy and it is, to be precise, the fallacy of identifying the concept of causation with what should properly be called "mechanistic causation." Now, in mechanics, that is to say classical mechanics, if an event A is causally connected with event B it follows that there must be an intervening chain of spatiotemporally contiguous events. Jung quite correctly points out that in ESP, information is transmitted without any such intervening chain of events, and he then concludes erroneously that causation is inapplicable to the psychic realm. Indeed, he even goes so far as to favor a Leibnizian theory of preestablished harmony to account for the normal mind-body relationship, rather than be forced into acknowledging any kind of causal interaction between mind and body. Yet the truth is that nothing in post–Humean philosophy obliges us to interpret the causal relationship in this way. Logically, an event A may be regarded as the cause of an event B provided it can be shown that an event of class A is sufficient condition for the occurrence of an event of class B. It is immaterial whether this implies action at a distance, action across a time interval or whether A is a mental event and B a physical event. It is useless for Jung to describe such a possibility as a case of magical causality; it would still be a matter of empirical investigation whether such magical causality ever in fact occurred. And the whole evidence of the ESP work points to the fact that it *does* occur. If the concept of synchronicity implied no more than the existence of certain peculiar correspondences in nature, then one could either take it or leave it. But the whole point about the experimental method is that a deliberate attempt is made to produce certain effects. If the attempt is successful, and the possibility that the result was due to chance can be ruled out as too remote to be worth considering, then the logic of science leaves us with no option but to postulate a *causal* connection between the result and the experimental situation.

My verdict then is that, *if* Jung is right in subsuming all paranormal phenomena under the principle of synchronicity, then experimental parapsychology becomes a contradiction in terms. This seems to me a good enough reason for thinking he must be wrong.[d] In fact, I suggest that synchronicity is a concept which has wandered by mistake into psychical research and that it belongs, if anywhere, to the field of literary criticism. In fiction meaningful coincidences abound, they are for example the basis of "dramatic irony," but they make little sense applied to real life, unless we are going to regard our lives as preordained by a supernatural dramatist, an idea that is conspicuously absent from Jung's theorizing.

We are thus left finally with only two serious contenders: scientific monism and substantial dualism. This, as I see it, is the central issue for the philosophy of psychical research, and my final task now will be to explain where I stand on this issue. The first thing which, I think, needs to be said on this point is that, if I believed that there was any prospect at all of the kind of integration of physics and psychical research, such as the scientific monist has in mind, I would regard it as no less than an act of intellectual sabotage not to take his part. After all, ever since we abandoned the older teleological interpretation of nature, every important scientific advance has come about by holding fast to the assumption that every new phenomenon, no matter how puzzling or how intractable it may at first have seemed, would eventually be comprised within the all-embracing framework of a deterministic science. What justification have we therefore for supposing that the paranormal will constitute an exception?

Now, there is one peculiarity of paranormal phenomena that tends, sometimes, to be overlooked: they almost invariably occur in connection with a human person. Now there is no *a priori* reason why this should be the case. One could conceive of a world in which inanimate objects took an occasional paranormal holiday during which they behaved entirely capriciously. But as it is, with the dubious exception of certain phenomena of a so-called poltergeist type and with perhaps the marginal exception of animal ESP, paranormal events are always bound up with people.[c] Thus whatever else they may be paranormal phenomena are always psychological phenomena and it is hardly surprising that the terms paranormal and psychical have become virtually synonymous.

The question we must ask ourselves, then, is in what way does a human being, considered as a physical phenomenon, differ from other physical phenomena? And the only answer appears to lie in the complexity of the human brain and nervous system. Accordingly, if the scientific monist is to make his case, everything will depend on how much he can squeeze out of this one critical difference.

Consider first the problem of telepathy, perhaps the best attested of all psychical phenomena. There was a time when the idea that telepathy might turn out to be some form of biological radio communication looked quite promising. This idea was further strengthened when in 1929 Berger discovered that every living brain emits a continual sequence of rhythmic fluctuations of electrical potential, and indeed Berger himself encouraged this conjecture. To-day, however, I do not think that anyone, not even Soviet parapsychologists, would pin much hope on this solution. There are a number of sound technical reasons for this, but perhaps I need only mention one: the electrical activity of the brain is much too feeble to enable it to function as a transmitter. Thus, according to Dr. Grey Walter, one of the foremost authorities on electro-encephalography, even the most pronounced of these brain-waves, the so called alpha rhythm, falls below "noise level" — that is to say below the theoretical threshold for detection — a mere few millimeters from the surface of the head.

But actually the situation is much worse than this, because the evidence for other ESP phenomena such as clairvoyance or precognition can hardly be considered much inferior to the evidence for telepathy. Consequently it would be arbitrary to accept the one while rejecting the other. The possibility of explaining ESP, therefore, in terms of any hypothetical brain mechanisms or unknown forms of radiation is, to say the least, quite unrealistic. What scientific monism requires, if it is to work, is something far more radical than this: nothing less, in fact, than a new physics, a physics which can dispense entirely with the postulates of mechanistic causation.

Such a step would be revolutionary but not, we may note, wholly unprecedented. Indeed, one could point out that quantum physics long ago abandoned mechanistic causation, and in general we may observe that new physical laws and new systems of physics have arisen during the present century as a result of studying what we may call extreme states. This, at any rate, would seem to be true of relativity physics where extreme velocities are involved, it would seem to be true of the physics of fundamental particles where extremely small magnitudes are involved, to some extent it would seem to be true of low-temperature physics. Consequently it might not seem too wildly implausible to suppose that when matter reaches a certain critical stage of complexity — and we must not forget that functionally speaking the human brain ranks as by far the most complex structure in nature — a new set of physical effects might, under certain conditions, become observable and that these effects would account for the so-called paranormal phenomena.

Now it would be foolish, after all that has happened, to rule out any future development in science as unthinkable, merely on account of its novelty. Nevertheless we must preserve a sense of perspective and not let ourselves be completely carried away. The development of such a "physics of complex systems," as I have hinted at as a minimal program for scientific monism, would be a stupendous undertaking, one that would far outclass any previous revolution in our conceptions of the physical world. For one cannot simply create a new physics by introducing certain verbal formulations, one has got to give it a rigorous mathematical structure which one can then use to make precise verifiable predictions. And finally one has still to show how conventional physics can be derived from it as a special case. Now, if your thinking takes you in this direction, I am the last person who would wish to disillusion you. However, if you are at all inclined to talk glibly about a new synthesis, or a new unified cosmology, I would beg you to remember that nothing short of these demands can possibly foot the bill.

In view of these considerations I hope that none of you will denounce me as a reactionary mystagogue if I declare that I would prefer to put my money on a horse of a very different color. The fact is I can see no future in the attempt to force the paranormal into the conceptual framework of systematic science. To me, on the contrary, the whole significance of psychical research, the very core of its positive content, lies in what it can tell us about mind as an autonomous principle in nature. It has become a cliché among a certain school of modern philosophers and psychologists to insist that the human person is *of necessity* a mind-body unity and is inconceivable in any other sense. I am afraid I cannot accept this as an ultimate truth about reality. Man in his natural state *is* such a unity, and it is the single psychophysical organism that forms the subject-matter of psychology; but there are, I believe, methods by which we can hope to isolate the psychic component in man, and it is just *this* that parapsychology, as an experimental science, is concerned to do. In support of my view I would remind you that a mere century ago it was still thought that the atom was the indissoluble unit of matter, indeed the very origin of the word pointed to its indivisibility. And yet today, while it still remains true that matter insofar as ordinary chemistry is concerned has an atomic constitution, we have learned to live with nuclear physics as well as with electronics. Paranormal phenomena I maintain mark the boundary conditions beyond which we can no longer treat the individual as a psychophysical atom; just as, to pursue the analogy, radioactivity in heavy metal marks the boundary conditions beyond which it is no longer possible to treat matter along conventional chemical lines.

I do not agree with those who regard such an approach as a betrayal of science. I have no wish to interfere with the work of a physiologically oriented psychologist like Prof. Hebb who takes his stand on an automaton theory of mind (Hebb 1949). On the contrary I consider that the only way in which we can arrive at a better understanding of psychical phenomena is by finding out how far behavior can be explained in purely mechanistic terms. Neurophysiological psychology is the obverse of the parapsychological medal. Nevertheless for many scientists and philosophers of science the very concept of explanation has become identified with explanation as understood in the exact sciences, where a phenomenon is said to have been *explained* only when it can be deduced from some general theory together with a set of specified initial conditions. In this sense, admittedly, I am asking you to abandon the attempt to explain the paranormal. But I would remind you that there is another weaker sense of explanation, which has a very respectable basis in common usage, and that it may be of more relevance to our purpose.

In this sense to explain something means essentially to conceive of it, not as an isolated fact, but in terms of some broader perspective. This is what we mean for example when we talk of a critic trying to explain some new movement in the arts or of an historian who is trying to explain some controversial historical episode. In this sense, too, we are forever trying to explain one another's behavior, meaning by this not of course deducing it from a general theory as a scientist would try to do, but trying to make it intelligible to ourselves in the light of our practical knowledge of our fellow men, as a biographer or novelist would try to do. Now, when we come to the paranormal our first task should be to see if we can make the phenomena intelligible in straightforward human terms. Our second task, I suggest, is to try to make the fact of paranormality, as such, intelligible in relation to our philosophical presuppositions. And on this latter point only some form of substantial dualism can, I believe, meet this requirement.

This, then, is my conclusion. I do not claim for it any originality; on the contrary, I would be content to think it would have gained the approval of the founding fathers of our Society, of men like Myers or Sidgwick.

Notes

a. Rupert Sheldrake has recently pointed out (Sheldrake 1988, Chapter 1) that the laws of nature might themselves have been subject to evolution, was being seriously canvassed at the turn of the century by thinkers as diverse as C.S. Peirce and Friedrich Nietzsche. "But then," says Sheldrake, "this entire line of thought more or less fizzled out." With the help of his theory of formative causation Sheldrake is trying to reinstate the idea so that lawful regularities in nature could be seen as evolving natural habits.

b. Flew has written extensively over the years on the problem of the paranormal but his position has oscillated between an outright dismissal (i.e., the skeptical theory) and this pure anomaly theory which I have occasionally referred to, in his honor, as "Flewism." For a recent statement of his position see Flew 1985.

c. There are, at the present time, a number of individuals who have made their reputations as critics of parapsychological claims and there is, in the United States, a prestigeful organization to back them up, best known by its acronym CSICOP (Committee for the Investigation of Claims of the Paranormal). I would not want to deny that such critics may serve a useful purpose. Being highly motivated to find fault with the parapsychological evidence, they may well help to keep us parapsychologists on the path of scientific rectitude. There need be no reason in principle, however, why parapsychologists should not be their own best critics and do their own policing. Indeed, in the case of the two biggest scandals that have occurred since I became involved in the field, the W.J. Levy case in America and the S.G. Soal case in Britain, it was the parapsychologists themselves, rather than the outsiders, who discovered and exposed the deception.

d. By now, however, the term "synchronicity" has become firmly embedded in the language of parapsychology, though its use varies. Sometimes it is used, as Jung intended, as a new way of conceptualizing ESP or PK, but sometimes it is used as a distinct phenomenon in its own right. Koestler, following Kammerer, tended to use it in this latter sense; see "Seriality and Synchronicity" (Koestler 1972).

e. I was afterwards challenged on this point, from the floor, by Renée Haynes who accused me of belittling the psychic power of animals (see her chapter on "The Psi Function in Animals" [Haynes 1961]). What I should have said to avoid this misunderstanding is that the evidence for psi in animals is slighter than it is for human beings, and this is still true today. There is no a priori reason why psi should not operate at lower levels of the phylogenetic scale; it is not, after all, an intellectual faculty. The point I was here concerned to make was that psi is bound up with the presence of mind, animal or human. The test case that would disprove this assumption would be a psi effect associated with an inanimate system or, perhaps, with plants.

Belief and Doubt

In the summer of 1972, the Parapsychological Association, which makes it a rule to hold its annual convention in Europe every fourth year, met in Edinburgh. I had been elected president for that year and served also as chairman of the program committee, which has to select the papers for the convention. Our guest speaker that year was Arthur Koestler, who gave the banquet address: "Out on a Tightrope: Parapsychology and Physics." The paper that now follows was my presidential address and was delivered on September 3, 1972. It marks one of the highpoints of my career and I certainly tried hard to rise to the occasion and produce something that would be suitably lively and provocative. Recently, this paper was chosen for inclusion in an anthology of diverse parapsychological papers published in Japan under the title Sai no Senjo *[The Battlefield of Psi], edited by Tosio Kasahara.*

At last year's convention my distinguished predecessor in office, Dr. Gertrude Schmeidler, carried out an opinion poll among members of the Parapsychological Association. The first item of her questionnaire read as follows: "ESP is so well established that new research which asks only, 'Does ESP occur?' is uninteresting." It turned out that almost 90 percent of our membership agreed with this statement (Schmeidler 1971). When I read this I was amazed. Had we now become such a tight little in-group, I wondered, that we had lost all touch with reality? Or had our recent admission to the American Association for the Advancement of Science gone to our heads?[a] For how was it possible to talk of ESP being "so well established" when the official organs of science and psychology are still extremely reluctant to publish any positive findings, when the standard textbooks of psychology rarely bother to mention ESP unless it be in a derisory manner, and when the national research foundations which, in effect, control scientific policy are not as a rule prepared to subsidize research on the topic?

Extrasensory perception may well exist, we may have excellent reasons for thinking that it does, and its existence may prove to be a fact of supreme importance; but, clearly, if words are to retain their meanings, we cannot talk about ESP being well established. And if this is true of ESP, it is presumably even more true of any other paranormal phenomenon. Yet I can scarcely suppose that my fellow members of the Parapsychological Association are ignorant of the facts of scientific life. What, then, could have prompted them to endorse this item? One can only surmise, but perhaps they reasoned somewhat as follows: "There is by now a vast body of evidence which points to the existence of ESP. If this has so far failed to carry conviction then accumulating further evidence of the same sort is unlikely to make any difference. In any case, only when we can offer scientists a plausible explanation for ESP will they begin to take notice. Our research should be directed to this aim rather than to the mere demonstration that ESP occurs."

This all sounds reasonable enough, though I should have thought that, in a field such as ours, one just *could* not have enough good evidence. Moreover, I have my doubts, personally, whether anything that we shall ever discover about ESP will be more extraordinary and more exciting than the sheer fact of its existence. But what really worries me when I hear talk of this sort is that it betrays a certain complacency about our situation vis-à-vis the scientific community as a whole. For I feel strongly that if ever we give up trying to win the support of the uncommitted and decide to go it alone we shall very quickly degenerate into an insignificant clique of tiresome pseudoscientists. Accordingly, I decided to devote my Presidential Address to an attempt to dispel the illusions and misconceptions which I believe to be rife among parapsychologists about the reasons which lead people to reject our evidence. I did not imagine that such an address was likely to enhance my popularity with members but since, unlike President Nixon, I shall not be running for a second term, I am free to speak my mind.

The first illusion which I want to challenge is the idea that there is some merit in being a believer. We naturally like to think of ourselves as somehow more imaginative, more finely attuned to nature's mysteries than other scientists and we look upon the skeptic as, by contrast, a dull dog, hidebound in his narrow and outdated materialism. Such an attitude, I submit, is a hangover from religion and has no place in science. Theologians have argued that the reason why God does not reveal Himself to us more plainly is that, if He did so, He would deprive us of the splendid opportunity we now have to exercise our faith in Him. The proudest boast of the faithful was to be able to exclaim, with Tertullian, *"credo quia absurdum,"* which freely rendered might be translated as "I believe, not because of, but in spite of the evidence!"

In science, on the contrary, there is no merit in belief and, equally, there is no merit in disbelief. If merit is anywhere involved it lies in following the implications of the evidence even when these run directly counter to one's fondest beliefs and expectations. The idea that the skeptic is prejudiced because he differs from us in his interpretation of the evidence finds little support in reality. Take the case of the late E.G. Boring of Harvard, the eminent historian of psychology. His long career encompassed in its span practically the entire history of modern psychology and his writings showed him to be a man of the widest sympathies who could discuss with understanding and appreciation the most diverse schools of psychology. Yet, for whatever reason, he drew the line at parapsychology. Almost the last thing he ever wrote was an enthusiastic introduction to Professor Hansel's book on ESP (Hansel 1966) in which he contrived somehow to appear even more negative and destructive than the author himself!

I can well understand how infuriating it must be when, after great efforts, you have succeeded in obtaining evidence that would undoubtedly be regarded as conclusive in any other branch of science only to find that your colleagues either ignore your results or, worse still, question your credibility. But before you dismiss the skeptic as willfully obtuse, consider how it looks from his point of view. If we did not have evidence that ESP exists, nothing in all of science would have suggested it; on the contrary everything we know would tell against it. Is it therefore *so* unreasonable if the skeptic prefers to think that there must be some flaw in your evidence even if he cannot spot it, some factor X which you have forgotten to control for which would allow for a normal explanation of your findings? I have come to the conclusion, after reading and talking to large numbers of parapsychologists, that there are in fact very few experiments, if any, which they would all accept as conclusive. What satisfies one, another will find wanting. We can hardly blame the skeptic, therefore, if he refuses to accept some piece of evidence at its face value even though he cannot think of a plausible counterexplanation.

My friend Dr. Robert Thouless has pointed out that, as more people carry out parapsychological experiments, conviction must grow, because, however, suspicious you may be about the honesty of other experimenters, you can scarcely doubt a result which you yourself have obtained (Thouless 1972, page 97). Certainly, I imagined that a successful investigator, one who had, so to speak, been touched with the wings of glory, would forever after be freed from the doubts that assail his less fortunate brethren. As I shall proceed to show, however, even this is not enough. Unless success can be sustained belief will sooner or later yield to doubt. Consider first two experiments which must surely rank among the most remarkable in the whole of our experimental literature.

In the year 1935 Dr. B.F. Riess, then of Hunter College, New York, was one of many psychologists of that period who were highly skeptical of the claims being put forth by the Duke University Parapsychology Laboratory. He decided very sensibly to try a card-guessing experiment for himself. Indeed J.B. Rhine personally encouraged him to do so. He found himself a suitable subject in the person of a young woman music teacher who had some reputation among her friends for being psychic. Every evening at 9 p.m. Dr. Riess, in his study at home, would go through two packs of ESP cards, with himself as agent, while his subject, in her home a quarter of a mile away, would record her guesses. The outcome, which is now a matter of history, is that, at the end of 74 runs, the girl had scored an average of 18 hits out of 25 trials (Riess 1937). I wonder how many of you here have ever witnessed even a single run of 18 out of 25 under strict conditions. Yet here was a girl who could average 18 out of 25 on 74 successive runs! What happened next was as follows. The girl fell ill and, when she recovered, she was dismayed to find that she was no more capable of scoring above chance than any of the other 67 students whom Riess had tested.

What was the effect of these events on Dr. Riess himself? At a meeting of the American Psychological Association the following year he had the candor to declare publicly that, although this finding outraged his own scientific philosophy, nevertheless he could see no possibility of explaining it away. The score-sheets had been kept locked in his desk at home, Gardner Murphy had inspected the records and had been able to spot only a single instance of a recording error and, in short, the only person who could have cheated was himself (Pratt 1964, page 65; Pratt, Rhine et al., 1966, pages 167–9). To the best of my knowledge Dr. Riess has never recanted or disowned the experiment as being invalid and yet, for some reason, he quietly backed away and from that day to this has never so far as I know evinced the remotest interest in parapsychology.

My second example concerns an experiment carried out in 1919 at the University of Groningen in northern Holland by Dr. H.I.F.W. Brugmans, Dr. G. Heymans, and Dr. A.A. Weinberg. Drs. Brugmans and Heymans were, incidentally, two of the earliest pioneers of the modern statistical approach to the study of personality. The subject was a student of mathematics and physics at the university named A. van Dam. The set-up involved a modified chess board and the subject's task was to point to the particular square which had been randomly selected as the target for that trial. The experimenters, who were also the agents, were situated in a room above from which they could observe the board through a glass panel in the floor, although they could not be seen by the subject. Under these conditions van Dam was correct on 32 out of 80 trials — i.e., 40 percent of the time — as against a chance expectation of about 2 percent. On those sessions when he was given alcohol his scoring rose to 22 out of 29 trials — i.e., 76 percent correct. In his published report of 1921 Brugmans wrote: "We can therefore say without any reserve that the existence of a transfer of thoughts under circumstances which completely exclude communication by sense organs is proved by this" (translated from the original by Zanstra, 1962, page 107).[b]

One might have thought that this declaration would have signalled the start of a great era of experimental parapsychology in the Netherlands before the Duke Laboratory had yet been thought of. Nothing of the sort happened. The incredible van Dam, like all his kind, soon lost his ability and Dr. Brugmans drifted away from parapsychology. He died not long ago and by then, so I gather from my Dutch friends, his position was one of open contempt for the whole field.*

There is one more example I would like to mention which is perhaps the most revealing of all, for it concerns two of the most learned men who have ever devoted a considerable portion of their lives to the study of the paranormal. They are Dr. Eric Dingwall and Dr. Theodore Besterman. The name of Dingwall is probably familiar to most of you here unless you happen to be newcomers to the field. Besterman, however, is less likely to be known to you since he abandoned parapsychology in the 1930s. Since that time he has become an authority on the literature of the French Enlightenment, has recently published a big biography of Voltaire, and has edited Voltaire's letters in an edition which, I gather, runs to 106 volumes!

Now the relevant facts which I want to bring to your attention are as follows. Both men were at one time research officers of the Society for Psychical Research. In this capacity both had an opportunity to test the celebrated Polish clairvoyant, Stefan Ossowiecki (Besterman 1933; Dingwall 1924). They used very similar techniques: both prepared a crude little drawing which they then elaborately packaged and sealed. In both cases Ossowiecki succeeded, under observation in reproducing the drawing with almost perfect fidelity. Both men duly published statements saying that they were satisfied on all counts with the results and that the precautions they had taken ruled out any possibility of a normal explanation.

Eventually, and the point of my story, both men developed doubts. I thought it would be instructive to discover why; so, not long ago, I wrote to them and asked them. Dingwall replied that for a few hours prior to the critical session the target-packet had been in the possession of Dr. von Schrenck-Notzing, the well-known German parapsychologist. Since he no longer had any confidence in Schrenck-Notzing he could no longer vouch for the experiment. I must explain at this point that, at the time, it was thought important to demonstrate that Ossowiecki's powers were clairvoyant rather than telepathic and so, although Dingwall travelled to Warsaw, he could not be present at the critical session. This was how Schrenck-Notzing came into the picture; Dingwall had deputed him act in his place. This was methodologically the right thing to do in any case. If Dingwall had been present himself it would now be impossible to know how much information he might unwittingly have transmitted to the subject through facial expressions, lip-movements, and so on.

---

* I have since been informed by Dr. H.C. Berendt of the Israel Parapsychology Society, Jerusalem, that A.A. Weinberg emigrated to Israel where he recently died. Unlike Brugmans his interest in parapsychology seems to have persisted to the end.

Because of this consideration, Dingwall's attempt to shift responsibility to his erstwhile colleague struck me as somewhat disingenuous, and I wrote to him again pressing him to be more specific. I inquired, in particular, whether he was suggesting that Schrenck-Notzing had conspired with Ossowiecki to fool him, or whether he thought that Ossowiecki had somehow outwitted Schrenck-Notzing. I asked how, on either hypothesis, he proposed to explain his own published statement to the effect that the day after the critical session the target-packet was returned to him intact, with all its seals and private code-marks undisturbed. To this Dr. Dingwall replied that it was obvious that, like most parapsychologists, I adhered to what he called "the magical way of look-ing at the world" and, this being so, it would be a mere waste of his time to answer any more of my silly questions. So that was that.[c]

Dr. Besterman, though he was not peevish, like Dingwall, was a good deal less forthcoming. He confirmed that he had developed reservations but he wanted to make it clear that these in no way reflected upon his coex-perimenter, Lord Charles Hope. This, I may say, is a crucial point because, in this instance, it was Lord Charles Hope who both supervised the test and opened the target-packet at the session in Warsaw while Besterman stayed behind in London. Thus to me, at least, it was clear that neither of these two great scholars really had any reason whatsoever for changing their minds, otherwise why would they have been so evasive? Yet their doubt was quite sincere.

You may say that this only goes to prove what unreasonable people skep-tics really are. This may be so; certainly skeptics are just as capable of being irrational as believers. Yet, can we altogether blame them? The point is that, when he perished in the Warsaw uprising of 1944, Ossowiecki, arguably the greatest sensitive on record, left behind him no successors. The law of cognitive dissonance suffices to explain the sequel; in the fullness of time every miracle, no matter how incontrovertible it may once have appeared, will lose its luster.

No discussion of the problems of belief and doubt would be entirely frank without touching upon the distasteful and embarrassing question of experi-menter fraud. There are some of you, I know, who feel strongly that this whole question is so outrageous that we should outlaw it from all our deliberations. While respecting the sincerity of your feelings, I cannot agree with this opinion. Of course, no worse calamity could befall a person in academic life than to be suspected of fraud. But, in the circumstances, this is an occupational hazard that we must accept. If you are too worried about it you would be better sticking to some safer occupation. I believe that I have a reputation for honesty and yet I have no illusions that, if ever I were to make a claim that was worth doubting, a smear campaign would soon be mounted to suggest that I was a person of unsound mind. When all is said and done parapsychology is too im-portant, too much is at stake, for it to be left entirely in the hands of gentlemen.

During this past year one of the ablest critics of parapsychology, who rightly believes that truth is more important than anybody's feelings, has been carrying out a minute examination of the famous Soal-Shackleton series of 1941–1943. I prefer not to divulge his name until he is ready to publish his own account, but I may say that the primary object of the exercise was to see whether there was any substance in the allegation made by a certain woman, who had been an agent in some of the sessions, to the effect that she had seen Soal altering figures on the score sheet. As part of his investigation, this critic initiated a multiple correspondence with six Council members of the Society for Psychical Research, including myself, who shared his interest in this particular episode of our history. Whenever any of us had any comment to make we would post copies of it to all the other members of the group. The experience gave me a unique glimpse into the mind of a highly sophisticated skeptic.[d]

It eventually became apparent that no agreement could be reached. For although there were indeed some suspicious statistical irregularities in the data these might represent a peculiar pattern of the subject's ESP scoring. Only if this possibility were ruled out would the evidence be sufficient to condemn Soal. Hence, ultimately, the verdict was going to depend on which of the two alternatives you found the more incredible: that Soal was a fraud or that Shackleton was genuine. My critical friend did not pretend that it would have been particularly easy for Soal to have cheated throughout, to have hoodwinked everybody including his lynx-eyed coexperimenter Mollie Goldney, but he *did* quite sincerely believe that this was more than likely than that Shackleton possessed ESP. And, from one point of view, the logic of his position was unassailable. We know for a fact that people *do* lie and cheat but, as I have said, it still remains for us to prove that there are people who have the gift of ESP. I realized that the only argument which would have carried any weight with my friend would be for me to produce for him another Shackleton whom he could test for himself, but that is precisely where I was completely powerless.

The special irony of this particular case is that the Soal-Shackleton series is among the few major investigations that was deliberately designed to be proof against experimenter fraud and yet, over the years, it has been a constant focus of suspicion! There is, however, one lesson we have learned as a result of this unfortunate affair and it is this: if you have a good subject do not keep him to yourself; let someone else test him before it is too late. Good subjects are so rare that you are naturally tempted, when at last you find one, to monopolize him. However, if you loan him out, as Dr. Ryzl did with Stepanek, for example, or Dr. Eisenbud did with Serios, then you avoid having to bear alone the whole onus of suspicion.

It may strike some of my forward-looking American colleagues as strange, not to say preverse, that we British parapsychologists should be so obsessed with our past. I think this is a reflection of the fact that, when it comes to the phenomena, the Atlantic does seem to represent some kind of a divide. There have been occasions this year when, getting together with my friends at the Society for Psychical Research in London, we have asked one another, in mournful tones, whether perhaps ESP is not just something that happens in America! Certainly, since Soal retired from the field some twenty years ago there has been precious little sign of it in these parts, at any rate in the laboratory. Of course part of the explanation lies in the sheer magnitude of the American research effort relative to our own, as this conference so strikingly illustrates; and yet I wonder whether this can be the whole story.

I must beg my American friends to believe me when I say that we have not been entirely idle over here. I do not wish to cite my own paltry efforts in this context (I may just be an incompetent investigator), but I cannot help recalling my indomitable friend, Dr. George Medhurst, who unhappily died about a year ago of an illness.ᶜ In addition to a distinguished career as an electrical engineer, Dr. Medhurst devoted practically all his leisure hours to parapsychology. Over the years he tested literally thousands of individuals, always hoping that another Shackleton might turn up or, at the very least, that he would obtain some firm evidence for the reality of ESP. He died, alas, a disappointed man. Yet his experience was so common by British standards that it never evoked any comment; no one suggested, for example, that he had a negative effect on the phenomena. I do not know why it is that British parapsychology, which once led the world, has sunk to such a low ebb. Presumably there is a tide in all these things and, hopefully, the tide may one day turn again. Meanwhile, however, I think it is important to understand that there are these unexplained national differences within our field. No doubt the situation on the Continent is different again.

Perhaps, in view of all that I have been saying, we should start to pay more attention to that growing body of opinion which believes that we should strive to gain a better theoretical understanding of the phenomena rather than to continue piling up evidence. Supporters of this view often take their stand on the Kuhnian interpretation of scientific history according to which science goes through a succession of revolutionary transformations. The implication is that, after the next revolution in science, parapsychology will fall naturally into place and what now appears to us as anomalous or "paranormal" will then become an integral part of the scientific world view. Sometimes reference is made to an Einstein-figure whose genius will bring order out of chaos. No one could deny that this is an alluring prospect, and I do not wish to deflate it, but I must confess that I can see no sign that such a revolution is imminent and if it means that parapsychology must mark time until the revolution arrives, I fear that the outlook is very bleak indeed.

Fortunately, there is another way; and if it is less grand, at any rate it is a good deal more practical. I refer to the search that has been going on for a repeatable parapsychological experiment. To avoid cavil, let me quickly add that, by "repeatable," I mean that the predicted effect must work at least 50 percent of the time and, even more important, must not depend on the availability of a particular individual as subject.[f] Now, it may be optimistic to think that such an experiment is even possible, but I do not think that anyone could call it utopian. Though it may never come about it may alternatively be lurking just round the corner. It may, indeed, be implicit in one or another of the papers we shall be hearing at this conference. I am thinking especially of the exciting recent developments in the field of animal experimentation[g] as well as of the possibilities inherent in Dr. Schmidt's ingenious machines.

Once such an experiment became knowledge things really would start to move. In one university after another research workers and Ph.D. students would be clamoring to try it out; journals like *Nature* and *Science* would open their columns to them; psychology textbooks would hurriedly be revised and the national research foundations would loosen their purse-strings. At the end of it all we might still not understand ESP but, then, do we understand any psychological phenomenon in any fundamental sense? At any rate, ESP would at last have become a demonstrable phenomenon along with hypnosis, conditioning, the reminiscence-effect and even subliminal perception.

Such an outcome might, of course, have some rather disconcerting repercussions. It is conceivable that this organization of ours would be swept aside. What became, I sometimes wonder, of the Interplanetary Travel Society of my youth when the space age actually arrived and NASA came into being? One parapsychologist with whom I once discussed the point told me that so far as she was concerned a repeatable experiment would take all the fun and adventure out of parapsychology and it would then become just another routine science. Undoubtedly progress always exacts a price, but of one thing we can be certain: when that day arrives the long-drawn-out struggle between belief and doubt will at last be over.

While preparing this address it occurred to me that the city of Edinburgh forms a fitting backdrop to my theme. For not only is Edinburgh the city of David Hume, the great philosopher, but it also has associations with his near namesake Daniel Home who was born in the village of Currie just outside. David Hume, whose life fell wholly within the eighteenth century, was the author of a famous essay on miracles which is still one of the best statements of the skeptical position ever written and ought to be compulsory reading for every aspiring parapsychologist. Daniel Home, whose life fell wholly within the nineteenth century, was a man of mystery. A scion of the noble house of Home (of which the present British Foreign Secretary[h] is the most illustrious living representative), he was, by all accounts, the greatest miracle-monger in the history of the human race. We have heard something about this unique individual earlier in this convention in Mr. Fraser Nicol's paper "A Psychic Tour of Historic Edinburgh." Later on we shall be hearing more from my friend

Dr. Zorab of the Hague who has spent many years researching his life (see "ESP Performances of D.D. Home"). And so, poised betwixt the twin pillars of belief and doubt, of Hume and of anti–Hume, I must now take my leave of you and it only remains for me to wish you all every success in all your enterprises and a very pleasant conference.

Notes

a. This historic event occurred in 1969 some twelve years after the P.A. was founded. Douglas Dean represented the P.A. on this occasion and steered us to a victorious conclusion. A speech by the late Margaret Mead was, I gather, a key factor in turning the tide in our favor.

b. I have discussed this case more fully in my "Seven Evidential Experiments" Zetetic Scholar *6(1980), 91–120. S.A. Schouten and E.F. Kelly had recently published a detailed analysis of this experiment in the* European J. of Parapsychology *2(1978), 247–90, which strengthened a positive evaluation. Nevertheless, I was duly challenged by Christopher Scott, who acted as one of the peer commentators for the Z.S. article. He put forward the ingenious hypothesis that an ambiguity as to exactly where or when the subject's finger had come to rest might have been sufficient to account for the extrachance scoring. Whatever the merits of this counterexplanation, which presupposes an extraordinary degree of ineptitude on the part of the three experimenters, it would hardly account for the striking differences in scoring between the alcohol vs. no-alcohol conditions.*

c. Eric J. Dingwall died on August 7, 1986, at the age of 96. I never knew him well but he was, by all accounts, a tortured soul in whom an irresistible fascination with the paranormal alternated with an abject disillusionment compounded by a deep contempt for his fellow investigators. A good example of Dingwall in one of his more depressed moods is the paper he gave to the conference of the Parapsychology Foundation at Amsterdam earlier that summer which I attended. It was called, innocently enough, "Is Modern Parapsychology a Science?" but concluded with these words: "The outlook is gloomy. I see no rent in the clouds and little likelihood of one in my lifetime" (Parapsychology Foundation 1973). Yet Dingwall could also be good fun; see the obituaries by Donald West, Alan Gauld and others in J.S.P.R. 54(1987), January, April and July issues.

d. The individual in question was none other than Christopher Scott (see note b above). The upshot of this exchange was "The Soal-Goldney Experiments with Basil Shackleton: A Discussion with Christopher Scott ... [and others]," Proc. S.P.R. *56(1974), 43.131. The controversy was still unsettled in 1975 when Soal died but when Betty Markwick published the findings of her computer analysis in* Proc. S.P.R. *56(1978), 250–81, it became impossible to doubt that Soal had indeed perpetrated spurious results. I wrote a letter to the* J.S.P.R. *acknowledging my misplaced confidence in Soal's integrity but pleading that, prior to these latest revelations, my position was by no means irrational. For a comprehensive review of this entire controversy, see B. Markwick "The Establishment of Data Manipulation in the Soal-Shackleton Experiments" (Kurtz 1985).*

e. See "Richard George Medhurst 1920–1971," an obituary by Mary Rose Barrington J.S.P.R. *46(1971), 124–6.*

f. Some years later I was reminded of this remark by Charles Honorton. By then claims were confidently being made that techniques such as the ganzfeld and remote-viewing were producing success rates approaching 50 percent. Unfortunately, success was still limited to a few favored experimenters. My students at Edinburgh were no more successful using these new techniques than they had been with traditional methods of testing for ESP.

g. At that time Walter J. Levy at the Institute for Parapsychology was still producing an unprecedented string of successes with his gerbils and other animal subjects who were required to influence a random-event generator in order to obtain some reward. The crash came in the summer of 1974 when Levy was detected by his colleagues fraudulently manipulating the computer.

h. That is, Sir Alec Douglas-Home. Recently, however, Hall (1984) has raised serious doubts as to whether Daniel Home was, in fact, related to the Earls of Home. It was thought that his father was an illegitimate son of the 14th Earl. D.D. Home, for understandable reasons, sought to foster belief in a relationship by adopting, as his middle name, "Dunglas." In the Currie register he is listed simply as Daniel Home.

The Subliminal and the Extrasensory

What follows was my contribution to an international conference at Amsterdam in August 1972 to which I had been invited by the Parapsychology Foundation of New York. The theme of the conference was "Parapsychology and the Sciences" (Parapsychology Foundation 1974) but the one science about which I had any qualifications to speak was, of course, psychology and it was the experimental study of visual perception that had been my special concern. While reviewing Norman Dixon's Subliminal Perception *(1971) for a psychology journal, I had been struck by the implications of his findings for parapsychology. At that time there had as yet been no empirical research linking subliminal with extrasensory perception but since then there have been a fair number of such studies (Roney-Dougal 1986; Nash 1986). Professor Dixon, himself, is one of the few distinguished British psychologists who has been consistently friendly to parapsychology. He has himself speculated since then on the relationship that I here discuss (Dixon 1979; 1987) and provided valuable assistance to Serena Roney-Dougal when she was working on her doctoral dissertation on this topic (Roney-Dougal 1987).*

From the earliest days of parapsychology it has generally been acknowledged that, whatever part of us is responsible for mediating extrasensory information, it is not the part that we associate with our conscious or rational intellect. The concept of the unconscious became a commonplace of nineteenth-century thought long before it reached fruition in the work of Freud and, as can be seen from the writings of Frederic Myers or of William James, the phenomena of the séance-room played a part in its development second only to those of the clinic. Indeed both depth psychology and parapsychology can trace a common ancestor in the mesmerist movement of the early 19th century. But, although parapsychologists have never ceased to borrow freely from the treasure house of psychoanalytic ideas, these ideas for the most part were lacking the rigorous experimental basis that was necessary if they were to be integrated into an experimental parapsychology. There was, however, one concept of a psychodynamic nature that right from the start was firmly grounded in laboratory experiments rather than in clinical observations. Such was the concept of subliminal perception. In this paper I want to consider what implications, if any, the findings on subliminal perception may have for the study of extrasensory perception. Is there, in short, a useful parallel to be drawn between SP (Subliminal Perception) and ESP (if you will allow me this play on words or on letters)?

My interest in this question arose from reading a recent book by Dr. Norman Dixon of University College, London, entitled *Subliminal Perception* (Dixon 1971), which I had been asked to review. Dixon, I should say, is the foremost authority on this topic in my country and his extensive researches have done as much as anything to establish, on a secure scientific footing, a concept that not long ago was still being treated with suspicion, if not derision. It is noteworthy that Dixon subtitles his book "The Nature of a Controversy." As I read the book I was struck repeatedly by the fact that what he had to say about SP seemed to apply equally to ESP, and the analogy seemed the more telling inasmuch as Dixon nowhere makes it explicit. In fact, though I gather that he is open-minded on the question, he has no special interest in and no definite views about paranormal phenomena. To make my intentions quite clear from the beginning, however, let me declare straight away how far I propose to press my analogy and what I take to be its necessary limits.

Obviously, no amount of knowledge that we may acquire about the working of SP will account for the existence of ESP. There is, after all, an absolute difference between a stimulus of very low intensity and a target that, being isolated from all sensory contact with the subject, is, in effect, a stimulus of zero intensity. Thus, whereas Dixon devotes a considerable portion of the book to arguing that there is nothing in the physiology of the brain or nervous system that should preclude the existence of SP, this, of course, is just what we cannot argue with respect to ESP. For, whether or not one believes that ESP may eventually be assimilated within the framework of an expanded physics and physiology, the obdurate fact that we have to face is that, as of now, the problem of how a subject might acquire information about an extrasensory target remains a total and absolute mystery.

Hence my analogy can begin only at the point at which we may suppose that, somehow or other, the target has been apprehended. But, from that point on, what happens to the information, how it is decoded and processed, how the transition is effected from unconscious to conscious awareness, to questions of this order, Dixon's evidence and interpretations are, I maintain, relevant and illuminating. Following Dixon I am going to assume that we all possess two distinct cognitive systems, each mediated by its own set of brain mechanisms. There is, on the one hand, a primary system whose main function is to subserve selective attention and logical thought. This always involves consciousness, a relatively high state of arousal and the mediation of the ascending reticular activating system of the brain. There is, on the other hand, a secondary system that may operate in the absence of consciousness, is associated with a relatively low state of arousal and is mediated by limbic and midbrain mechanisms. The function of this secondary system is less easy to define but it appears to be a kind of cognitive safety valve that allows us to access to a wide range of information that would otherwise be entirely excluded by the inhibitory mechanisms of the primary system. It is, we may suppose, involved in dreaming, in free-association and spontaneous imagery, in intuitive thinking and, no doubt, in those "games of the underground" that Koestler has described for us so graphically in connection with the bisociative leaps of his creative thinkers (Koestler 1964). It is to this secondary system that Dixon ascribes our capacity for subliminal perception and it is my thesis that it is this system that is involved in the psi process.

In the classical or Cartesian tradition of European philosophy "mind" and "consciousness" are interchangeable concepts so that events or processes that are not conscious cannot be mental and must therefore be physical. According to a very different philosophical tradition, however, of which Bergson may here be taken as representative (Bergson 1911), our conscious self is nothing more than the residue that remains when awareness has been filtered of everything except that which pertains to the individuals' biological needs. Mind itself is conceived of as being potentially omniscient and all-embracing but this universality is sacrificed, according to Bergson, in the ego-centered struggle for survival. Now, just as Dixon regards SP as a compromise between the restrictive demands of selective attention and the need for the organism to monitor a much wider range of stimuli, so I am going to suggest ESP may be regarded as a compromise between the exclusiveness of the Bergsonian filter and this cosmic capacity of mind to transcend the limits of the senses. Both phenomena, however, seem to be of marginal importance in everyday life relative to normal perception.

So much for the general viewpoint from which I am approaching this question. Now let us take a look at some of the facts and findings that research on subliminal perception has uncovered. First we should note that SP is a special case of the more general phenomenon of discrimination without awareness. No one can deny that we constantly make all kinds of adaptive discriminations without being aware of what we are doing. Indeed, the more skilled we are at any given activity the less we need to be aware of the details of our performance. What is peculiar about SP is that in this case the cues are so feeble physically that they could never reach the threshold for conscious recognition however hard we might try attending to them. Now it is one of the key points of Dixon's argument that SP is not just a dilute form of ordinary perception. Provided (a) the stimulus is well and truly below recognition threshold and (b) that it still retains any efficacy at all, then it will be dealt with by the subject in quite a different way from one that is strong enough to elicit a conscious sensation.

This is best illustrated when the stimulus in question is a familiar word.

Suppose your subject is shown a word and asked to report, as best he can, what he sees. Then, provided the word is visible at all, however faintly or however briefly, the subject's response is likely to bear at least some structural resemblance to the actual word. But if that word is exposed at such a low intensity or for such a minute duration that it is in effect *in*visible, so that the subject can do no more than guess at it, as if it were an ESP target, then the evidence suggests that the response is unlikely to have any structural resemblance to the stimulus word but may very well have a semantic relationship. Sometimes the semantic processing involved, which, of course, all takes place at a purely unconscious level, seems to involve a rather elaborate symbolic transformation. This is particularly so if the word has some emotional or sexual significance for the subject. Dixon himself gives several examples of such responses that show a distinctly Freudian character. This qualitative shift in the response, which occurs when the intensity of the stimulus falls well below recognition threshold, is explained by supposing that it is then that our secondary system takes over from the primary system. Dixon further points out that subliminal perception is more likely to occur when the subject is in a relaxed or passive state, as when he is made to recline on a couch; in other words he functions best in a low state of arousal.

A special kind of subliminal perception that has long intrigued investigators is the so-called "Poetzl Phenomenon," after the Austrian neurologist, Otto Poetzl, who first drew attention to it in 1917 (Poetzl et al. 1960). Briefly, what he found was that if his subjects were shown a picture in a tachistoscope for about a 10m.s. duration, so that it was impossible for them to discern more than the most fragmentary features of the picture, much of the remaining content could still be recovered, even if in a somewhat disguised or symbolic form, if the subject was later asked to recall his dreams of the subsequent night. Although, needless to say, the validity of this phenomenon has been strongly challenged, there have also been some good confirmations of it from recent experiments using very carefully controlled experimental designs (Dixon 1971). However, recent work has also shown that the effect is not limited to dreams. It appears to be sufficient if, after being presented with the picture in the tachistoscope, the subject is merely asked to relax and describe any spontaneous images that may then emerge into consciousness. It surely requires no special pleading to find a parallel here with the Maimonides situation (Ullman et al. 1970). The Maimonides experiments exploit the same oblique approach in demonstrating an ESP effect in the way the picture target influences the dream imagery of the sleeping subject. Moreover, in this case, too, hypnotic dreams and waking imagery can be used as well as nocturnal dreams

(Krippner 1968). In general wherever free-response techniques have been used to test for ESP, as for example in token-object reading, the symbolic distortions noted by Dixon when testing for SP are liable to occur.

One of the main points of departure for the modern study of SP was a series of observations arising out of the work of a group of experimental psychologists in the late 1940s who came to be known as the "New Look School of Perception." Leo Postman and Jerome Bruner, two of its leading exponents, claimed that, in general, recognition thresholds for emotive words differed from those for neutral words. If the threshold was raised, i.e., recognition took longer, as might be expected when the word had unpleasant, alarming or distressing connotations for the subject, then one had a case of "perceptual defense." If, on the contrary, the threshold was lowered, i.e., recognition became easier, as might be expected if the word had positive connotations for the subject, then one had a case of perceptual sensitization. Actually, whether the threshold for a given word is raised or lowered relative to a neutral word may depend as much on the personality of the subject as upon the character of the word, so that a perceptually vigilant subject may be expected to respond sooner even to a distressing signal. The important point, however, is the existence of this differential effect as between emotionally charged stimulus words and neutral words.

A particular experiment by E. McGinnies (McGinnies 1949) in 1949 sparked off what may well qualify as the longest specific controversy in the history of experimental psychology (Brown 1961). In this experiment he exposed a series of words in a tachistoscope in which the critical items were so-called "taboo" words, i.e., words with a strong sexual flavor like "whore" or "rape." He duly reported that these critical items required longer exposure to reach recognition than control items of the same length. The interpretation was that a censorship was operating at an unconscious level to prevent identification of the forbidden words for as long as possible. Thus the concept of "perceptual defense" was postulated as a direct analogue to the Freudian concept of repression in the field of memory phenomena. Of course McGinnies' experiment was far too full of flaws to establish the validity of such a concept of its own accord. All kinds of reasons were put forward by critics to account for the fact that the taboo words took longer to recognize — subjects might have hesitated before pronouncing the words until they were quite sure, or the words might be less common than the control words, or perhaps less expected in the laboratory situation. Evidence and arguments both for and against the reality of perceptual defense continued to pile up during the 1950s and 1960s as supporters of the concept strove to meet each new criticism and counter-explanation. Eventually, however, though there still are doubters and waverers, perceptual defense does appear to have been vindicated as a genuine manifestation of the unconscious.

In a sophisticated modern demonstration of perceptual defense, of the kind we owe to Dixon, or to A.G. Worthington, a Canadian psychologist, the subject never, at any time during the experiment, suspects that there *are* any words involved, let alone that some of them may be obscene. All the experimenter looks for is whether the critical words will raise the recognition threshold relative to the control words with respect to some quite neutral stimulus such as a patch of light. Thus, in Dixon's set-up, the critical word is exposed continuously to one eye only and at a level well below that at which he could be aware that there *is* any kind of stimulus present. At the same time the other eye is presented with a visible spot of light whose intensity the subject himself can control. His instructions are to keep the spot of light from disappearing altogether while at the same time not to let it exceed in brightness a second spot of light that surrounds it. Dixon duly found that the mere presence of the taboo word was in itself sufficient to raise the threshold-setting for the spot of light; the implication being that resistance to seeing the taboo word raised the general threshold for form discrimination.

In an experiment of this kind which one of my own students carried out this year (Gregor 1972), the subject was required only to indicate when a certain luminous rectangle was visible against a uniform luminous background. Unbeknown to the subject the luminous rectangle was in fact a slide containing a word, either a sexually suggestive word or a carefully matched neutral word. Although great care was taken to guard against artifacts — for example the experimenter himself did not know which slide was being used on which trial — it duly transpired that the mean intensity necessary to discriminate the rectangle against its background was significantly greater when the word it contained was of an obscene nature than when it had no such emotional connotation.

Findings like these strike one as so bizarre, from a commonsense point of view, that one may be forgiven for wondering whether ESP might not be a more straightforward explanation for the results than one in terms of SP. Actually, Dixon himself has told me that one cannot rule this out as a hypothetical possibility since few experimenters have bothered to control for an ESP effect. Not that this would be difficult, all one would need would be for the stimulus to be present, as a target, on certain trials but completely screened from the subject. I do not think Dixon takes this possibility very seriously or he would already have done something about it. Neither do I take it seriously for that matter. Nevertheless, it is a nice stroke of irony that, for once, we should be discussing ESP as a potential explanation of an alleged case of SP instead of, as so often, SP as an explanation for an alleged case of ESP.

The acknowledgment of perceptual defense as a genuine psychological phenomenon should make it that much easier for us to accept the concept of "psi-missing" as a parapsychological phenomenon. For the point about perceptual defense is that it implies the possibility of identifying a stimulus at an unconscious level in order to prevent its recognition at a conscious level. Now it is true that in a case of psi-missing the targets are not usually of an intrinsically threatening or disturbing nature; negative scoring is more likely to occur if, for some reason, the subject is feeling anxious at the time or is acting under stress. Nevertheless, given that we all tend to be apprehensive about anything paranormal, that we instinctively recoil from anything that threatens to penetrate our safe Bergsonian filters, it becomes understandable that we sometimes consciously deny what our unconscious, so to speak, already knows. For methodological reasons, however, it is difficult to compare psi-missing at all directly with perceptual defense since the former can be clearly demonstrated only by using quantitative experiments of the forced-choice variety whereas the latter rely on qualitative free-response tests.[a]

A type of perceptual defense that has been studied exhaustively in Sweden is that which is observed in the so-called "Defense Mechanism Test" designed by the Swedish psychologist Ulf Kragh (Kragh et al. 1970). This test uses as a stimulus a TAT type of picture that invariably contains one threatening figure and one figure who is being threatened. A picture of this sort is then exposed in a tachistoscope at successive trials of increasing duration starting at a subliminal level, progressing through stages of preconscious recognition and ending when the entire picture is clearly visible. The assumption behind it is that an anxious subject will postpone for as long as possible acknowledging the threatening figure that he will contrive to see in various innocuous ways. Martin Johnson, a parapsychologist and a colleague of Kragh's at Lund University, using the Defense Mechanism Test (DMT) as a measure of anxiety, was able to demonstrate a very significant correlation between the subject's score on the DMT and his ESP score on a standard test of clairvoyance (his DMT protocols were of course scored blind, i.e., in ignorance of his ESP scores). In general the more anxious subject tended to be a psi-misser and the less anxious subject tended to be a psi-hitter (Johnson et al. 1967).

Philosophers who write about parapsychology like to point out that ESP is a misnomer, that really ESP is not a species of perception at all, or even of cognition, since the typical ESP test is assessed solely according to the proportion of guesses that coincide with the targets even though the subject himself cannot distinguish in any way between his correct and his incorrect guesses. This objection, however, stems from adopting the classic empiricist assumption that we cannot know anything unless we are consciously aware of knowing it. But it is precisely such an assumption that is challenged by the whole body of evidence that Dixon brings to our notice. Consider modern signal-detection theory as it has been developed by J.A. Swets and others as a branch of decision-making theory (Swets 1964). Here the concept of a conscious recognition threshold is abandoned entirely. The subject is asked simply to guess whether the signal in question is on or off for a given trial. Much of the time the subject behaves in the same sort of way as an ESP subject, that is to say he goes on guessing to oblige the experimenter but is not conscious either of the presence or absence of the stimulus. Yet the percentage of correct guesses can be shown to be a direct mathematical function of the intensity of the stimulus starting at the baseline of chance expectation, when the stimulus is at some very low level of intensity, and climbing to 100 percent accuracy when the intensity reaches some optimal level. Of course, somewhere along this continuum consciousness must supervene but from the standpoint of signal detection theory, which is behavioristic and operationist in its approach, this is quite immaterial.

Ultimately what terms we choose to employ is always a question of semantics and if a philosopher wants to insist that perception implies conscious perception he is free to do so and can no doubt adduce good precedents for his usage. The point I want to make here, however, is that the modern psychophysical study of sensation and perception provides us with a good analogue for describing extrasensory perception. The typical card-guessing demonstration of ESP corresponds to the subliminal zone of the perceptual continuum whereas an accurate clairvoyant ascertainment of pictures, objects and scenes, such as is occasionally reported with certain exceptional sensitives, corresponds to the superliminal zone. That, subjectively, there is no difference between ESP guesswork and subliminal guesswork was shown in an experiment that J.G. Miller published in 1940 (Miller 1940). He told his subjects that the task was one of telepathy and that they were to gaze into a mirror, as if into a crystal ball, and try imagining certain geometric figures that he was going to try and transmit to them. Actually, he projected very faint real images of the figures onto the back of the semitransparent mirror and the subjects duly scored well above the chance level but, and this is the point I wish to bring out, none of them suspected this ruse and all were surprised to learn that it was not after all a genuine test of telepathy.

Finally, are there any practical implications to be derived from the work on SP for research on ESP? One enticing possibility worth mentioning is that of using an SP set-up in order to disguise a test of ESP. The idea has gained currency lately that subjects perform better when they are unaware that they are using their ESP. For example, some success has been reported using an ostensible test of memory. Items on which the subject recalled one of the wrong alternative answers were analyzed to see whether these corresponded significantly with the alternatives which the experimenter arbitrarily designated as being the correct ESP target (Stanford 1971). It would not be difficult at all from a practical point of view to reverse J.G. Miller's procedure and make the subject think he was using his SP while in fact he was required to use his ESP. There is, in fact, one experiment in the literature which I have come across which does use this stratagem. This was an experiment by Jule Eisenbud published in 1965 (Eisenbud 1965). He presented the numerals 2, 3 or 4 in a tachistoscope and the subject had to guess at each trial which of these three different numerals had just been presented. On the critical runs, however, the same constant stimulus, consisting of an amalgam of all three numerals, was presented at *every* trial. Meanwhile, in the next room, an agent was synchronously watching a series composed of the numerals 2, 3 or 4 being flashed on a screen at superliminal durations, the idea being to influence the subject's responses. Unfortunately, however, this ingenious idea did not work and no significant scores were found on these critical runs, nor did it make any difference on the ordinary runs whether an agent saw the stimuli or not.

There are, however, other ways of combining the subliminal and the extrasensory that are worth trying. Here again Martin Johnson has been breaking new ground with promising results (Johnson 1972). In an experiment, which he has recently completed, he exposed his words subliminally but these words were in the Finnish language so that any effects that they might have on the responses of his Dutch subjects would have to be due to ESP over and above any SP . It has also been suggested that, in a telepathic experiment, it is the agent who should be presented with the targets on a subliminal basis. The idea being that if it is indeed our unconscious that mediates the information, the best results should be expected if the target directly enters the unconscious of the agent. But, as yet, I have come across no actual accounts of experiments using this procedure. Lastly, as I have already suggested, I hope the time will come when experimental psychologists will have sufficient respect for the ESP hypothesis to take the precaution of always introducing a set of ESP control trials in any future experiment on SP. It is not, however, my main concern in this paper to suggest how SP might be exploited in parapsychological research. My concern has been rather to consider how the advances that have been made in our knowledge of subliminal processes, both on the psychodynamic and on the physiological fronts, might contribute to advancing our knowledge of psi processes.

Note

a. *This was a mistake, as I later discovered thanks to Michael Thalbourne. If a ranking procedure is used in connection with some free-response target, as was the case in Thalbourne's own experiment on the paranormal reproduction of target drawings (Thalbourne 1981), then it is perfectly possible to demonstrate psi-missing.*

The Study of the Paranormal
as an Educative Experience

In August 1975 I participated in a conference in San Francisco to which I had been invited by the Parapsychology Foundation on the theme "Education in Parapsychology (Parapsychology Foundation 1976). The first speaker was, fittingly, J.B. Rhine, who had been the first to engage in parapsychology at a university and was the co-author of the first textbook of parapsychology. Among the speakers that followed were Stanley Krippner, already then installed at the Humanistic Psychology Institute (now the Saybrook Institute) in San Francisco; Martin Johnson, who, the previous year, had become the first holder of the newly created chair of parapsychology of the State University of Utrecht, in the Netherlands; Robert Morris, then teaching parapsychology to undergraduates in the interdisciplinary "tutorial program" of the University of California, Santa Barbara; and the veteran parapsychologist, Gertrude Schmeidler of City College, New York, to mention only some of the notable contributors. At Edinburgh we were already admitting graduate students to the Department of Psychology who wanted to work on a parapsychological topic for their Ph.D. under my supervision.

Since then, time has wrought its changes. J.B. Rhine died in February, 1980; I myself retired officially in 1985, though happily not before I had helped to set up the Koestler Chair of Parapsychology in our department under whose aegis students could continue to work in this area. Unfortunately, the Utrecht chair was terminated in 1988, the victim of a Dutch economy drive, and Martin Johnson returned to his native Sweden and to Lund University.

In the talk which follows, I point out that parapsychology can have little to offer at present from a vocational point of view and can make, at most, a modest contribution to other disciplines, notably to psychology and perhaps to physics. On the other hand, the study of the paranormal can, I argued, afford an excellent training in mental agility or, as I then put it: "There is no other discipline that I know which engages at the same time a person's critical

48

faculties and his imagination and then stretches them both to a comparable extent."

The question I want to raise in this paper is a very basic one, namely: What justification can we offer for the teaching of parapsychology at the university?

I presume that no similar defense is called for with respect to parapsychological research. If there *are* paranormal phenomena — and I take it that we are all agreed that there is an overwhelming case for supposing that there are — then, clearly, someone ought to be studying them and where better than at the university? In short, the pursuit of knowledge, the quest for truth is one of those unconditional values of our culture that requires no extraneous justification.

The same cannot be said, however, when it comes to our educational policies. We cannot teach everything and it is a matter for debate as to which options deserve a place on the undergraduate curriculum. Basically, two reasons can be advanced for the teaching of any particular topic: the one social, the other purely intellectual. The social reason is that there are certain sorts of knowledge and certain skills that a student needs to equip himself for his future profession. Hence the prominence we give at the university to such faculties as those of law, medicine or engineering. Since parapsychology can scarcely be described as a profession — the number of those who make it their career, in your country, is still negligible — we can hardly justify the teaching of it on vocational grounds.

The intellectual reason is the one that is presupposed in the idea of a liberal education. Philosophy, logic, pure mathematics, no less than history, literature and the study of dead languages and defunct civilizations have few social applications and they have vocational value only to those who will in turn be teaching them to others. Yet only the most hardened philistine would dare to suggest that we banish them from our seats of learning!

Could a case be made for parapsychology on the grounds that it contributes to a liberal education? We must admit that it seems sadly lacking in many of the qualities that we expect of those disciplines that are cultivated for their own sake. It lacks that majestic edifice of theory that has been the pride and delight of the physical sciences; it lacks an agreed body of facts such as gives the historical, geographical or social sciences a firm consensual basis; and it lacks, finally, both the aesthetic appeal and the cultural significance that attaches to the arts and the humanities.

Nevertheless, there are, I am going to suggest, three possible lines that our defense may take. First, we may argue that the demand for it already exists. That the young are eager to learn more about the paranormal and that, if we fail to satisfy this demand in a responsible academic manner, there are charlatans and vulgarizers enough to whom they can turn who will be only too willing to satisfy it in an irresponsible, commercial manner! Secondly, we may argue that, whether or not parapsychology has any intrinsic educational merit, it has by now shown itself to have sufficient relevance to other disciplines whose importance is not in question: to psychology, psychiatry, or anthropology, to philosophy and theology and finally to physics itself. Then, thirdly, we may argue — indeed I shall argue — that, over and above any relevance which it may have to these other disciplines, the objective study of the paranormal (which is how I would define parapsychology) may be credited with certain unique virtues as an educative experience in its own right. In what follows, I shall consider each of these arguments in turn before trying to draw some general conclusions.

Let us start, then, with the argument that, since the demand exists, it is incumbent on us to try and meet it. This is a recent development and it is still only marginally relevant to the situation that obtains in my country. Its urgency arises from growth of the so-called "counterculture" in the United States during the 1960s and, more particularly, of the "occult revival" which was one aspect of it.

I am not here concerned with the causes of the particular episode of our recent social history. It may be, as some have suggested, that too many people these days are educated beyond their intellectual means. When they find that they are incapable of grasping genuine scientific ideas or are bored by genuine scholarship they turn instead to the pseudosciences which, at the cost of a modicum of intellectual effort, enable them to enjoy the seductive feeling of being the possessors of a hidden knowledge and a superior wisdom. It is also the case that we are witnessing today a widespread disenchantment with official science, which is often blamed for the crisis through which our civilization is now passing. Anything, therefore, that serves to cast doubt upon the validity or at least the sufficiency of the accepted scientific world view is bound to be welcome to those who are struggling to promote an alternative world view. In these circumstances we have to think carefully before lending ourselves to what is essentially an antirational, anti-intellectual revolt.

Our traditional antagonist was the hard-headed skeptic who clung tenaciously to a dogmatic materialism. It was against his opposition that we strove to produce some small dent in the carapace of scientific orthodoxy. We were less concerned about those who believed too much too readily; we thought of them as the lunatic fringe whom we had to learn to tolerate. In the present intellectual climate, however, when the universities are no longer peaceful havens of reason and learning, we have a positive duty to restrain the credulity of the young and to counter the mass of information to which they are exposed, and to which they are so pathetically vulnerable. For, after all, is not one of the chief aims of all education that of helping the learner to distinguish between well-founded and ill-founded claims to knowledge? It is, I may say, unfortunate that, at such a time, too many among us who should know better are themselves being seduced by the ideals of the counterculture and are willing to lend countenance to the nonsense that is purveyed under its aegis, but it is all the more vital that the rest of us should not weaken in our resolve to uphold the highest critical standards.

We come now to our second line of defense, namely the relevance of parapsychology to established fields of inquiry. Here the two most promising openings are those afforded by (a) psychology and (b) physics. How you propose to integrate parapsychology with either of these two fields will depend, in the first instance, on what you conceive a paranormal phenomenon to be. If, like the late Sir Cyril Burt, or like J.B. Rhine, you believe that psi is essentially nonphysical, even though it may have physical manifestations, you will be more likely to want to assimilate parapsychology to psychology than to physics. If, on the contrary, like a number of parapsychologists of a new generation, you believe that everything that happens must ultimately have a physical explanation, you will look for an understanding of psi phenomena, not to the mind but to the brain, conceived as a purely physical system, and to the possibility that it may possess certain novel and unsuspected physical properties which we had not previously allowed for.

Physics, in any case, can never be left out of the equation if only because PK is, in effect if not in origin, a physical phenomenon. Today, in the post–Geller phase of parapsychology, when PK effects of a directly observable kind have once more come to the fore, we again find that physicists, in America, in Britain and in the Soviet Union, are being drawn to parapsychology in the hope that it may enhance our understanding of fundamental physical processes. There is some difference of opinion, however, among these physicists as to whether psi phenomena can be explained in terms of known physical principles or whether physics itself will have to undergo another transformation before it can encompass them. Only a little while ago it looked as if nothing could be more discredited than the idea that parapsychology could be reconciled with physics as it now stands. Yet, no less an authority than Gerald Feinberg, in his foreword to Edgar Mitchell's compendium *Psychic Explorations* (Mitchell et al. 1974), ventures the opinion that psychic phenomena may not, after all, be found to contradict "known physical laws" and may prove explicable "within the existing body of physical principle."

Again, it looked until quite recently as if nothing could well be more futile than to attempt an electromagnetic theory of ESP. Yet, today, we find several theorists independently coming forward with the suggestion that telepathy at least might turn out to be a form of telecommunication based on extremely low frequency electromagnetic waves, the idea being that this type of transmission is exceedingly penetrating and so cannot be arrested by faraday cages, long distances or other obstacles that interfere with other types of radiation. John Taylor (Taylor 1975), a theoretical physicist of King's College,

London, Michael Persinger (Persinger 1974) of the Psychophysiology Laboratory of the Laurentian University, Canada, and I.M. Kogan (Kogan 1969) of the Society of Radio, Electronics and Biocommunication of Moscow, have each, in their various ways, been toying with this idea. Taylor has gone further and suggests that this kind of radiation can explain the metal-bending performances he has observed with Geller and a number of mini-gellers.[a]

Personally, I do not take very seriously this line of speculation. It seems to me that if psi phenomena are ever reconciled with physics it will only be when physics has been transformed and extended out of recognition. But, of course, I am not a physicist and I may well be mistaken. Meanwhile the critical test of the physicalistic approach to psi, I suggest, will be whether the phenomenon can be simulated artificially. Thus, if low frequency electromagnetic radiation of the sort which the brain can emit can carry information of the sort that has been demonstrated in telepathic experiments, then it should be possible to design apparatus that can pick up this information in lieu of a living subject. Similarly, if such radiation is responsible for releasing stresses in metals so as to create bending, as Taylor suggests, it should be possible to design a gellerizing machine that would render Geller redundant. After all, we can, to a large extent, simulate artificially in this way the functions of our sense organs. We can even design artificial intelligences. We surely have a right to demand from those who believe that psi is physical, an artificial psi subject!

But, whatever the future may hold, there can be no doubt that the most concerted attempt so far to bring parapsychology into the academic fold has been via psychology. This is hardly surprising since, whatever else may be said about psychic phenomena, they seem only to occur in the presence of, or at least in connection with, a living subject, normally a human being. Hence, so long as we are content to ignore the question of the mechanisms by which information is acquired or transmitted, the only questions we can ask about psi are psychological ones, questions relating to the psychological conditions under which they occur and the characteristics of the individual who manifests them.

Historically speaking, the most famous attempt to domesticate parapsychology, with a view to affiliating it to academic psychology, was that associated with William McDougall and his disciple J.B. Rhine at the Duke University Parapsychology Laboratory. They were inspired in their endeavor by three ideas in particular: first, the idea that ESP was a universal property of mind, not just the freakish gift of a few exceptional individuals; secondly, that a statistical methodology would enable us to reveal even the small degree of ESP ability that ordinary individuals may possess; thirdly, that by making the test-procedure simple and rigorous it could be readily copied as a result of which independent confirmations would be forthcoming that would put an end to any lingering doubts about the question of authenticity. The same reasoning, of course, was applied to PK which entered the picture somewhat later. We may note here that, by introducing the term "parapsychology," McDougall hoped to delineate this quantitative and experimental approach from the broader field of psychical research which would continue taking care of spontaneous cases and uncontrolled phenomena but could not so readily be brought within the academic purview.

These were splendid ideas and by no means unreasonable at the time they were conceived. Yet, I do not think I am being provocative if I say that none of them has been fulfilled. Positive results still largely depend on having the right subject, and a good card-guesser is no less of a rarity than a good medium in the bad old days of psychical research. Independent corroboration is still the exception rather than the rule, and it is now beginning to look as if we need not only the right subject but even the right experimenter. Rhine, I gather, discourages young aspirants from embarking on a career in parapsychology if they cannot first demonstrate that they are the right sort of experimenter, that is one who can get positive results! In the event, so far from skepticism dissolving under the weight of accumulating statistical evidence from the laboratories, few other universities have felt encouraged to follow the example of Duke, which, on Rhine's retirement, itself severed its connection with parapsychology.

Yet, despite these setbacks, the aim of bringing psychology and parapsychology closer together is still very much alive. It is notably exemplified in the work of Gertrude Schmeidler and Ramakrishna Rao, who have done much to link parapsychology with personality theory, using unselected subjects. It is the point of departure for the work of Rex Stanford. His PMIR (Psi Mediated Instrumental Response) model of psi is based on the premise that, without knowing it, we utilize paranormally acquired information in the satisfaction of our immediate needs (Stanford 1974). Stanford has pioneered what I like to call the "surreptitious" approach to psi. That is to say, the subject is kept in ignorance of the fact that psi is involved in the ostensible task that he is required to undertake. In recent years at least three researchers have independently adopted the surreptitious approach with positive results: Stanford himself, using a pseudomemory task (Stanford 1970), the Kreitlers of Tel-Aviv University using a pseudosubliminal perception task (Kreitler et al. 1972) and Martin Johnson using a pseudoexamination task (Johnson 1973).

Others have sought a meeting point between psychology and parapsychology not in these everyday acts of cognition but rather in certain special states of consciousness. Perhaps the most notable exponent of this approach at the present time [1975] is Charles Honorton, currently president of the Parapsychological Association, but the approach has been so widespread that it may seem invidious even to single out any particular worker. An enormous number of different techniques and different states of mind have been explored from this angle and, although success has been sporadic, this approach continues to attract adherents.

Yet another avenue towards a rapprochement with academic psychology has been to explore the physiological substratum that may be assumed to be common alike to psychological and parapsychological phenomena insofar as both are mediated by the physical organism. Here, again, many names could be cited, but I do not need to look any further than our own laboratory at Edinburgh. Thus, Richard Broughton has been investigating the possibility that our ESP function may be mediated by the right hemisphere in the sort of way that language and, more generally, logical and sequential thinking seems to be mediated by the left hemisphere.[b] Brian Millar is pursuing an even bolder hypothesis. He is attempting to replicate the so-called "Lloyd effect (Lloyd 1973), namely, that if you stimulate the agent, in a telepathic set-up (Millar uses a stroboscopic lamp for this purpose), an evoked potential should be discernible in the subject's EEG record, if this is analyzed by a computer which averages the brain-responses on each trial. Both Broughton and Millar will be reporting on their work to the forthcoming Parapsychological Association Convention so I will not say more about it now and I mention it only to illustrate the new psychophysiological approach to psi. Perhaps, however, I should add that, in the best Edinburgh tradition, Millar got only chance results.

As a psychologist myself, as well as a parapsychologist, I naturally welcome these attempts to bring parapsychology into the psychological arena. Psychology is, in any case, far from being a unified science and I have myself elsewhere attempted to present parapsychology as one of the many distinct psychological sciences (Beloff 1973). Yet, for all that, I am bound in all honesty to admit that, so far, the influence which parapsychology has had on any of the other psychological sciences has been minimal. The one area where parapsychology has undoubtedly made a difference is that of philosophical psychology. It no longer seems possible to discuss the nature of mind, or the mind-body problem, as if the parapsychological evidence did not exist, although, amazingly enough, there are plenty of philosophers who are so purblind that they go on writing as if they were still living in the 18th century, when commonsense could always expect to have the last word!

But, if, as we have seen, the relevance of parapsychology to physics is still so controversial and its relevance to psychology is at best marginal, where does this leave us with respect to the question of justification that we set out to answer? I think that one thing we have got to recognize is that our field is much more erratic, anarchic and basically subversive than we like to admit when we are engaged in one of our public relations exercises. It is only by arbitrarily restricting the scope of parapsychology, as McDougall and Rhine attempted to do in their justly celebrated program, that we can give it even the semblance of being like any other conventional science. If there are any of you who are ever tempted to play down the sheer unruliness of our data, I would recommend the following salutary exercise to be performed once a day before breakfast until further notice: try repeating over to yourself the names of some of the more colorful psychic personalities who have left their imprint on our turbulent history: Daniel Home, Eusapia Palladino, Franek Kluski, Eileen Garrett, José Arigo, Ted Serios, Uri Geller . . . you may add or subtract as you please. I am not asking you to accept any or all of these at their face value, merely to acknowledge that they represent so many prodigious question marks. To contemplate the careers of these, or others like them, is to be confronted with the sheer impenetrable mysteriousness of the world which makes a mockery of our scientific pretensions.

This brings me to my final point, namely, what *I* conceive to be the most distinctive contribution which parapsychology can make to a liberal education, and the chief lessons that we can hope to learn from it. It teaches us, I suggest, not only that the world is a stranger place than we would otherwise suppose, but also how difficult it is to arrive at any definite conclusions about it. It raises for us, in its most acute form, the eternal question: "What can I believe?" This question is one that we encounter all through life whenever we are forced to consider some creed or religion that makes far-reaching claims on our credence. Unlike these other creeds or religions, however, parapsychology spurns any resort to propaganda or appeal to faith. On the contrary, it deliberately fosters skepticism by being hypercritical of every claim which it is called upon to ad-judicate and so keeps us in a particular state of uncertainty. At one instant it will open up for us exciting vistas of new worlds to be conquered; at the next, it will cause them to vanish again in a haze of doubts. It forces us to reckon with the almost bottomless duplicity of our fellow creatures, and yet it forbids us to take refuge in any easy cynicism no matter how fantastic the case under consideration. In a word, it plays tug-of-war with us so that we can enjoy neither the peace of mind of the committed believer nor the complacency of the skeptic.

From one point of view we have much in common with the lawyer, or even the historian, who is likewise concerned to reach a conclusion about some episode that can only be reconstructed on the basis of human testimony or, at most, documentary evidence. We, however, are in a much more perplexing situation than they are, in that we lack the canons of plausibility based on com-monsense experience to which they can appeal. One can see this when the law is called upon to pronounce on some paranormal claim that comes before the courts. The result is usually farcical. As we know, it is not easy to prove that an accused person is insane, but to convince a judge that an accused person has paranormal powers is almost beyond the wit of man! A celebrated trial took place in London, at the Old Bailey, during the last world war, of the notorious materializing medium Helen Duncan, who was indicted for fraud under the "Witchcraft Act" (Becchover Roberts 1945). Her defense counsel offered to stage a séance for the benefit of judge and jury in order to demonstrate their client's authenticity. The judge, however, declined the offer on the grounds that it would be demeaning to the dignity of the court!^{c} In spite of a score or more of witnesses who testified to the marvels which she had wrought, it took the jury only twenty minutes to return a verdict of guilty. Perhaps the jurors were all earnest disciples of the philosopher David Hume who, you will remember, argued that it was always more rational when in doubt to suppose that those who testify to a miracle are either lying or are deluded than that the miracle really happened as alleged. And, in the case of Mrs. Duncan's miracles, this may well have been the wisest maxim to adopt (West 1946). Unfortunately, the parapsychologist cannot settle for this simple Humean rule or for any other *a priori* principle of rationality. Or, perhaps, this is not a misfortune after all, perhaps it is this very absence of rule or precedent that makes the study of the paranormal such a unique educative experience. There is no other discipline that I know which engages at the same time a person's critical faculties and his imagination and then stretches them both to a comparable extent.

Notes

a. He later renounced this hypothesis but, having no other explanation to offer, declined to repudiate his own evidence along with all other evidence for psi phenomena. The upshot was a second book, Science and the Supernatural *(Taylor 1980).*

b. Broughton's dissertation, which won him a doctorate from the University of Edinburgh, was entitled "Brain Hemisphere Differences in Paranormal Abilities: With Special Reference to Experimenter Expectancies" (Broughton 1976 & 1977a). Broughton, who is now assistant director of the FRNM Institute for Parapsychology in Durham, North Carolina, found some evidence in favor of the right-hemisphere hypothesis but then ran into difficulties in trying to replicate his own results. This led him to concern himself with the "experimenter effect" (Broughton 1977). Since then empirical evidence for the superiority of the right hemisphere in psi tasks has been meager. Nevertheless, the link between psi ability and the right hemisphere remains, on general grounds, a plausible and seductive hypothesis (see Playfair 1985, chapter 3).

c. This is incorrect. The judge was willing to allow such a demonstration; it was the jury who declined! I discuss the Duncan case more fully in my "Extreme Phenomena and the Problem of Credibility" (see pages 175–190 below).

On Trying to Make Sense
of the Paranormal

My presidential address to the S.P.R. might be described as my "finest hour." At the same time nothing could have made me more aware of my own inadequacies than taking on that mantle which, in the heyday of the Society, had been worn by such luminaries as William James and Henri Bergson. I was anxious to put on as good a show as I could muster and I decided to discuss what I believed—and still believe—to be the essential characteristics of psi phenomena.

I was gratified when, at the subsequent reception, I was complimented on my efforts by Arthur Koestler. Later, however, I was taken to task by my friend, Gaither Pratt, who, in the course of correspondence, rightly pointed out that I had omitted to give credit to Robert Thouless although the ideas I was purveying were essentially his (Thouless & Wiesner 1947). However, if I was guilty of plagiarism this was certain uncertainly unintentional. The fact is that I had imbibed my lesson so well I no longer saw the need to go back to its source. I can only hope that I made amends to some extent when I wrote my obituary of Thouless for the Journal of Parapsychology *(Beloff 1985).*

Two questions, in particular, are considered in this paper. First, what properties must the mind possess if it is indeed the source of psi phenomena? I suggest two basic properties: it must be capable of transcending the known constraints of the physical world with respect to space, time and mater; and it must, itself, be capable of constraining the physical world to realize its purpose using whatever means may be available. Secondly, I consider where, in the history of ideas, do we find a ready made niche for the concept of the paranormal? I suggest that, as between the realms of magic, religion and science, it is with the traditions of magic, sorcery or witchcraft that, whether we like it or not, it has a natural affinity.

I would like to use this occasion to share with you some thoughts I have concerning certain fundamental questions that are of interest to us as members of this Society. I have used this phrase "sharing my thoughts" because I am anxious to avoid at the outset any expectation that I am about to deliver myself of some authoritative pronouncements. If there is one thing that I have learned from my many years of involvement in this field it is a lesson in humility. The problems we face are so vast and our understanding of them so slight that there could be no excuse for any sort of dogmatism. If at any point in my address I should sound dogmatic to you I must ask you to believe that this is solely in the interests of brevity and clarity and in no way reflects my attitude. On the contrary, in our present state of ignorance we should not merely tolerate but positively encourage a multiplicity of viewpoints — including even that of total skepticism. All I would ask is that whatever viewpoint you do adopt you should be prepared to follow through its implications if necessary to the bitter end. What I refuse to tolerate is the intellectual sloppiness that blurs all the critical distinctions and makes clear thinking an impossibility. We may not yet be able to achieve much precision in our thinking but we can always try to be logical.

My declared aim in this paper is to try to make sense of the paranormal. Now to make some sense of something, to make it intelligible, is not the same thing as explaining it. Explanation, as the term figures in scientific discourse at any rate, presupposes that we have some theory which can tell us why the phenomenon occurs when it does occur or fails to occur when it does not occur. In our field we have innumerable specific hypotheses, indeed all our experiments are designed to conform or refute one or other of these hypotheses, but any general theory, if it is ever to come, is still a long way off. In this respect we must not allow ourselves to be misled by the success of the physical sciences; our own problems, our own history, are so different that we can have no assurance that similar progress is inevitable. My concern today is with certain questions that must precede any attempt at theory construction, questions about the meaning or nature of the phenomena with which we deal, how best we can conceptualize them, in what context they can best be understood.

The first difficulty that one encounters in this connection is to know which phenomena one can take as authentic. There seems to be absolutely no consensus as to what constitutes our hard facts. What we have, instead, is a spectrum of belief. At one end we have those who refuse to take even the first step and would prefer to deny the evidence of their own senses rather than admit the reality of a single paranormal phenomenon. Next there are those who refuse to believe anything which they have not confirmed for themselves. Then come to those who dismiss anything that occurs spontaneously in real life but will acknowledge something if it has been established in a laboratory and the more so if it has been corroborated in another laboratory. And so on until finally, we have those who will cheerfully swallow almost anything they have read in print, especially, perhaps, if it is said to have been demonstrated by the Russians. This is not at all surprising given the unsatisfactory nature of the evidence. In the circumstances each of us brings to it a different criterion for evaluating it, a different range of background knowledge and, of course, a different degree or credulity. Today I propose to concentrate on the problem of meaning rather than on the problem of validity but, before I can do so, I must first indicate roughly where I stand on this spectrum of belief.

Let me say at once, therefore, that I would have to rate myself as someone who was moderately credulous. If I compare myself with my colleagues, and even more with my wife, I would have to admit that I do not seem to have as much difficulty as they do in believing that quite amazing things can happen. But credulity is only one dimension of belief, knowledge is another, and I have found that my own belief system has undergone some fairly drastic shifts over the years as new evidence came to my attention that I could not ignore. I am thinking now not so much of the classic manifestations of ESP or PK, where a greater measure of agreement can be found, but rather of some of the more far out paranormal phenomena such as psychic photography, materializations, teleportations or the more spectacular forms of psychic healing. Before I knew anything at all about psychical research I would assuredly have laughed in the face of anyone who had asked me to take seriously such obvious nonsense. Then you start to dip into the literature and you begin to wonder whether there might not be something in it after all. Then you read more deeply and learn how much fraud and self-deception are implicated in such phenomena and you start to doubt whether there ever was, indeed, a single authentic case. And so the dialectic of belief and doubt goes on without ever achieving finality. My own current position with respect to such phenomena is that, while we must suspend judgment, we cannot afford to treat them as if the evidence simply did not exist. Knowing all we now do about the conditions under which Ted Serios was tested, can we say categorically that we refuse to believe in psychic photography? Given Anita Gregory's monumental study of the Rudi Schneider mediumship (Gregory 1968 & 1985), can we dismiss all further thought of materializations? Dare we rule out the numerous accounts of teleportations that have been reported in connection with Uri Geller, including the many incidents which Professor John Hasted has observed in his own home? Given only the agreed facts about the career of the late Arigo, have we the right to affirm that there is nothing at all in psychic surgery? I must apologize to you for asking so many rhetorical questions but in each case the answer, it seems to me, must be no.[a] And yet if we believe too much we run the risk of what I would call the "house-of-cards effect." We might go on to build a beautiful theoretical superstructure only to see it come toppling down again because something which, in our enthusiasm, we mistook for a piece of solid evidence, turned out to be an insubstantial figment. To change the figure of speech we are like a group of archaeologists intent on reconstructing some vanished civilization but are constantly hampered, not just by the scantiness of the remains, but by the fact that none of them can agree as to which of the artifacts are genuine and which are fakes!

Some of you, I am sure, were privileged to hear my distinguished predecessor-in-office, Professor Mundle, when he delivered his presidential address which he entitled "Strange Facts in Search of a Theory" (Mundle 1973). He suggested, on that occasion, that there were two main types of theory competing for our allegiance, those which he called, respectively, the physicalistic and the mentalistic. The former sought to explain the paranormal in terms of physics, either existing physics or, if that was not possible, some sort of speculative futuristic physics. The latter took its stand on the traditional dualism of mind versus matter, explaining the paranormal as due to certain occult powers of mind. The dilemma that confronts us, he argued, was that neither type of theory had shown itself to be of much use. Some of the physicalistic theories were able to offer a plausible enough account of certain selected facts but were quite unable to meet certain other facts that had just as much claim to be taken seriously. The mentalistic theories, on the other hand, tended to lack testable implications and, in general, their metaphysical complexion tended to alienate scientific opinion. He concluded, therefore, by exhorting us, in the words of our first president, Henry Sidgwick, to "ascertain facts . . . without any foregone conclusion as to their nature."

Up to a point I agree with my predecessor. I would not want us to prejudge the issue and I think we are wise to adhere to as neutral a terminology as possible that does not commit us to one interpretation rather than another. I would agree that the primary task of a society such as ours must be that of "ascertaining the facts," as Sidgwick put it, letting ultimate explanations await the verdict of posterity. There is no more important service that we can perform, especially at a time like this when once more superstition is getting the upper hand, than to try and sift a few hard facts from all the welter of rubbish that would otherwise smother them. And yet I cannot emulate Professor Mundle's austerity in sedulously refraining from taking sides. If I am going to devote a large slice of my life to the study of the paranormal I want to be able to offer a better reason for doing so than that, at some unspecified time in the future, some scientist may be able to make some unspecified use of the puzzles and anomalies to which I now draw attention. After all, we have now been ascertaining the facts for nigh on a century and if we are still unwilling to venture an opinion as to their nature we deserve the rebuke that we are just trading in mysteries for the sheer hell of it. For my part I would rather be thought wrong than so guarded as never to expose myself to that risk.

For reasons which I hope will become increasingly clear as I proceed, I see no prospect whatever of making sense of the paranormal in purely physical terms however unorthodox. With respect, therefore, to Mundle's dichotomy I am bound to align myself with his mentalists. Mentalism may not necessarily be the best term to use here (dualism? transcendentalism?), the terminology is optional, the question is whether the phenomena we are considering are essentially manifestations of mind, whatever we understand by that very imprecise word. I, for one, am willing to make this jump from the concept of the paranormal, defined purely negatively as that which cannot be explained, to the concept of the psychical in the positive sense of belonging to the psyche or psychic component of the psychophysical organism that we know as a person. There may, for all we know, exist paranormal phenomena in the universe which are not mind-dependent in this critical way; indeed if we were to credit some of the stories about flying saucers we would have a case in point. But, with respect to the overwhelming majority of paranormal phenomena that have been of interest to students of psychical research, the paranormal makes sense, I would maintain, only in the context of the mind-body problem. There we are already confronted with the existence of consciousness, which has never been easy to assimilate to a purely materialist view of the world, and it is there we should look for the source of psychic or "psi" phenomena.

The thesis I shall try to defend in this paper is that what happens in cases of paranormal cognition or paranormal action, that is in ESP or PK, as the parapsychologist would call them, is essentially of the same nature as that which happens in our normal cognitive processes or in our normal voluntary behavior. The distinction is that, in the former case, something I am calling "mind" interacts directly with the external environment whereas in the latter, normal situation, this mental influence interacts directly with the brain alone and only indirectly with the outside world. Let us now look more closely at this idea and see whether it makes sense or not. The view I am putting forward is based on the supposition that, during a life cycle of the individual, mind and brain coexist in a unique and exclusive relationship of a causal kind whereby mind depends almost entirely upon the brain for information about the outside world as well as for its capacity to control the movements of the body when acting upon that world. Thus, in the case of perception, the brain, as a physical mechanism, must be credited with the capacity to process the messages relayed to it via the sensory channels but the mind must be credited with the final step that involves decoding the brain-processes in order to produce a meaningful conscious percept. Similarly, in motor activity, it is the brain that must be held responsible for coordinating the various muscle groups that are involved in the performance of some piece of skilled or adaptive behavior but it is ultimately the mind that must be held responsible for initiating or sustaining that activity by operating on the brain centers.

The question then arises as to how, if this is the normal situation, paranormal activity can ever come about? To answer this I have to make the further assumption that the mind-brain system is not a completely closed one. For reasons that are still quite obscure, a jolt to the brain perhaps or whatever it might be, the mind, we must suppose, can free itself from this dependence on the brain and set up an interaction with events or processes in the world at large. When this occurs we have either a case of extracerebral information processing that we refer to as ESP or we have a case of extracerebral control over objects that we call PK. It is conceivable, on this showing that, given the final jolt to the brain which constitutes death, the mind could be permanently liberated from its dependence on the brain and continue either as a store of conscious memories of its premortem existence or as an active agent communicating directly with the world and its living inhabitants. However, the survival evidence is, in my opinion, so equivocal and so open to a variety of interpretations, that I can come to no conclusion as to whether any such state of affairs ever actually occurs or not.

This view of the mind-body relationship that I have been describing is not, you will realize, the orthodox view as expounded by our contemporary neuropsychologists or psychophysiologists, although some of the most eminent brain physiologists of this century, Sherrington, Penfield, Sperry, Eccles, have all, in their own way, hankered after some form of dualist interactionism (Eccles 1970). According to the orthodox view, it is the brain and the brain alone that governs alike our cognitive processes and our motor activity. The mind, which orthodoxy equates, wrongly in my view, with consciousness, is no more than a subjective reflection of whatever brain state happens to obtain at the given instant. It has no autonomy of its own, from the functional standpoint it would make no difference if it did not exist, the world would go on exactly as it does now except, of course, that no one would ever know this. Many contemporary philosophers would now argue that the mind *is* the brain, meaning by this that mental processes are brain processes *as* they are known to the brain itself as opposed to the way they are known to the outside observer, namely as electrical impulses circulating in brain tissues. There is no denying that this formulation has a lot to commend it. It is parsimonious, it avoids the awkward questions that inevitably beset the dualist, questions about what sort of stuff is mind stuff, where it originally comes from, how it enters into a partnership with bodies and so forth. It is a formulation that is in tune with modern cybernetic ideas, the brain-body system can be thought of as a single self-regulating cybernetic machine or automaton. If it were not for the existence of paranormal phenomena it would, I think, be very hard to fault on scientific grounds alone.

There is no doubt, however, that the orthodox view does do violence to our commonsense intuitions. It asks us to believe that our thoughts, our feelings, our desires, intentions and so forth play no part at all in determining what we actually do or do not do. For these, as I have pointed out, can be no more than passive registers of what happens to be going on in the brain. What actually determines our behavior, in any given instance, are certainly purely impersonal physical facts having to do with electrochemical events, the patterning and positioning of neural circuits and the like. Clearly no one when engaged in a real life situation, or in an encounter with a fellow human being, will ever think in this way—we all think and act as if we had free will—but, in spite of all that may have been said to the contrary by the philosophers, there is really no getting away from this dilemma: either the mid-brain identity equation is incorrect or the commonsense view of human action is an illusion. Since the dualism that I am propounding also imposes a certain strain on commonsense, if for different reasons, it is important to bear in mind these consequences of a physicalistic monism.

Fortunately, we do not have to rely on commonsense to arbitrate between these alternatives. If paranormal phenomena do exist then the boot is on the other foot, as it were, for now, on strictly empirical grounds, it is the physicalist who is on the defensive. For I think I can confidently say that there is nothing in the whole of brain science that would lead us to expect, or even to suspect, that the brain would possess the capacity to acquire information from the environment without the use of any known sense organs still less than it could intervene physically in nature other than through the known bodily effectors. The skepticism with which official science regards paranormal claims confirms me in this judgment. The physicalist might object, however, that the dualist was in no better position when it came to the paranormal for, after all, is there anything we can point to in the whole of conventional psychology that would lead us to suppose that mind had the necessary powers implied by psychic phenomena? This is a fair question but my answer would be that while we know a great deal about matter, even about brain-matter, we know next to nothing, in a scientific sense, about mind and its potentialities and hence there are no *a priori* grounds either for expecting or not expecting what its scope might be. Conventional psychology, after all, concerns itself exclusively with the integral psychophysical organism, to generalize from this may be illegitimate. To use a very crude analogy, it is rather as if all that we could ever know about a certain person was what we could observe of him when he was driving his car. No doubt we would soon learn a great deal about his habits as a motorist, not to mention the performance of his car, but there is little else we could learn about him. My point here is that if we want to learn about mind as such, then psychology must be supplemented by parapsychology.

On one point my dualism diverges from the classical Cartesian or empiricist position. There it was assumed that our own mind was the only thing we could know with any sort of certainty; material objects and other minds could be known only in the weaker sense that depended on inference and induction. However, the empiricists, no less than the materialists, tended to equate mind with its conscious manifestations and constituents. It is certainly true that the way in which we know our conscious experience is of an immediacy that is very different from the abstract theoretical way in which we know about the physical world, Russell called it a knowledge by acquaintance; but, when I said that we know next to nothing about the mind, it was not this immediate qualitative kind of knowledge that was referring to but knowledge concerning the properties or "powers" of mind, to use an old-fashioned but telling term. I am a confirmed realist about mind, as I am about matter, and for me the reality of both resides primarily in their causal powers. I look to parapsychology to reveal the powers of mind. Let us define mind provisionally, therefore, as that which *animates* matter, normally the matter of a living brain. If this definition strikes you as circular, I must ask you to bear with me until later when I can make more explicit what is involved in this process of animation. In this way consciousness, though it be the most distinctive aspect of mind, need not be taken as its defining attribute. Mental activity could be regarded as in general unconscious, conscious activity being a special case. On the orthodox view, the unconscious aspects of behavior merely betoken the automatic functioning of the nervous system in the absence of any conscious concomitants; on my view, mind must be regarded as permeating behavior at all levels, at any rate above the purely reflexive or vegetative.

This is an important point for us to bear in mind if we are ever to succeed in carrying through my suggestion that we equate normal with paranormal mental activity. For the parapsychological evidence forces us to acknowledge the reality of an unconscious mental life in a much more literal sense than we are obliged to do even in depth psychology, where the Freudian type of unconscious can, in the last resort, always be conceived as a purely theoretical entity. The point is that consciousness does not appear to be necessary to the occurrence of psi phenomena. For, not only does the subject rarely have much conscious control over his psi abilities but, in some situations, he may even be unaware that they are being exercised. This is notoriously the case in a poltergeist disturbance where the putative poltergeist focus is usually quite ignorant of the role he plays in the production of the phenomena which, indeed, may sometimes persist even in his physical absence. A trance medium is, by definition, unconscious of his or her performance; one recalls that Rudi Schneider was totally oblivious throughout the séance of all the exuberant goings-on around him. Recently a number of experimental parapsychologists, Rex Stanford in the United States, Martin Johnson in Holland, the Kreitlers in Israel, have quite independently been conducting experiments, with some success I may add, in which the subject is never told until it is all over that any psi response was required of him. He is made to think that he is participating in some memory or problem-solving or perceptual type of task but may in fact be rewarded in some way if he produces certain arbitrary responses that are randomly selected to represent the psi targets.* Stanford has also coined the

---

* *Rex Stanford has been the most active proponent of the use of such disguised tests of psi and he has made these the cornerstone of his PMIR (Psi-mediated Instrumental Response) theory of the psi function (Stanford 1974). A disguised ESP test in the form of an exam for students was used by Martin Johnson (1973). The Kreitlers used a test of subliminal*

expression "release of effort" to refer to the effect he has obtained in PK experiments where the subject thinks that the run is over but, unknown to him, the randomizer is kept going. In this situation he may score significantly even though he is no longer attempting deliberately to influence the outcome (Stanford & Fox 1975). It was Dr. Thouless, incidentally, who first noted, a long time ago, when he was using himself as a subject, that he got his best scores at PK when he was reading a poetry rather than thinking about the dice! (Thouless 1951).

One objection that could be raised against the view that I have been putting forward, that a psi phenomenon represents a case of mind acting directly on the environment rather than through the brain, is the confused inaccuracy of the typical telepathic or clairvoyant ascertainment as revealed in a qualitative free-response type of test. Even when the correspondence is close enough to score a hit, it is likely to be distorted and garbled in devious symbolic ways that often reflect more the subject's own personal experiences and outlook. This has encouraged some theorists, e.g. H.H. Price, W.G. Roll, to suggest that ESP can only operate by exciting appropriate memory traces in the subject, that memory affords a better model for the ESP process than does perception (Roll 1966).

I have myself drawn attention to the many parallels between ESP and SP (Subliminal Perception) where we likewise find symbolic distortions of the stimulus (Beloff 1974). However, we must be careful not to confuse what is merely typical or habitual with what is necessary and universal. The mind may still have direct access to the external information and yet, in the course of converting this information into a conscious percept we may from sheer force of habit filter the information through our brain and memory store giving it in the process the characteristic personal bias. Nevertheless, there are plenty of hints in the literature, especially in connection with what is known as billet-reading, that accurate ascertainments of a clairvoyant nature are possible; witness the performances of such as Bert Reece, Ossowiecki, some of Tischner's subjects or even Geller at his best, assuming that any or all of these are valid. Here, as also in the case of some out-of-body experiences that have been reported, the analogy with direct perception does not seem misplaced.

A somewhat similar line of reasoning could be advanced against the objection that most manifestations of PK are so clumsy and haphazard that there can be no basis for a comparison with the way in which we normally move our limbs. Even such exceptional PK subjects as Geller or Mme. Kulagina will sometimes move an object other than the one on which they are concentrating. Indeed, one of the hazards of working with Geller, one that has also provoked so much suspicion, is precisely that it is usually the unexpected event that

perception in one of their experiments with an agent attempting to influence telepathically the subject's response (see H. Kreitler & S. Kreitler 1972).

happens. But, here again, we must not forget that we have had a lifetime of practice in moving our own limbs. An infant, however, is always liable to move an inappropriate limb, so is someone who is recovering from a paralysis. Can we wonder that when the mind makes an excursion into the external world that results should be so uncertain and lacking in skill? The brain, after all, is the only object in the universe that we are accustomed to manipulate directly and our reliance on the brain must rank as perhaps the most deeply ingrained habit that nature has implanted in us.

Yet this claim that psi is the result of mind reaching out into the environment and bypassing the brain may seem difficult to take seriously at a time when many enterprising parapsychologists are busy monitoring the brain's activity, using EEG or other apparatus, in the hope of discovering the physiological basis of psi. Not long ago I was lecturing to this Society on the search for a physiological index of psi and it is an approach that certainly inspires my own research team at Edinburgh. However, in the light of what I have been saying about the mind-brain link-up, it should not surprise us if the brain continues to reflect the relevant state of mind even if it is not itself critically involved in producing the psi effect. In the case of a telepathic situation, it is also feasible to suppose that the agent exerts a PK effect directly on the subject's brain, in which case it would make sense to try and pick up the signal directly from the brain in the form of an evoked potential or in some other way. Nevertheless, if my view of psi is on the right lines, it would be pointless to expect that we could ever find the source of psi however minutely we examine the brain; it would be like expecting to discover the cause of the Geller-effect by a detailed metallurgical analysis of the target object.

If it really is the mind, not the brain, that is critically involved in paranormal phenomena, what sort of properties or powers must we assign it in order to make this credible? There are, I am going to suggest, two principal properties that are crucial in this connection: first, the non-physicality or transcendence of mind, its potential freedom from the constraints of the physical world as expressed in the parameters of space, time and matter or energy and, secondly, its intentionality, i.e. the purposive nature of its commerce with the material world. Both of these call for careful discussion. The main reason for calling psi non-physical was the absence of any systematic relationship between the phenomena and the physical variables of the situation in which they were observed. It was never suggested that there is no relationship at all because psi is demonstrably highly sensitive to the psychological conditions involved and these cannot be wholly divorced from the physical conditions, if only because if the subject believes that certain physical conditions are necessary to his success there is a strong likelihood that they will become so. Thus one could show that in cases of spontaneous precognition the frequency of hit falls off as the time span increases (Orme 1974), but given our biological concern with the immediate rather than the remote future, this relationship is very understandable. But this sort of relationship is very indirect, there is no sound evidence that I know to suggest either a definite numerical law by which the magnitude of the psi effect could be expressed as a function of the physical parameters or a definite theoretical physical limit of some kind beyond which psi could not function at all.

Naturally, a physicalist will want to dispute this argument. He will protest that not enough systematic work has yet been done on the problem to warrant any such conclusion. He will also point out that not all the possible candidates that could serve as the physical carrier of the psi information have yet been explored. Thus, a number of scientists have recently been toying with the possibility that very low frequency electromagnetic waves could serve as the carrier of the information in telepathy; this type of radiation would be immune to most of the screening devices that have been used in such experiments. This possibility has been independently canvassed by John Taylor in this country, Michael Persinger in Canada and I.M. Kogan in the Soviet Union. I hope they will pursue this idea to the limit but I am confident that no such hypothetical physical carrier will be found. In terms of a Cartesian mind, on the other hand, the range of psi in space and time is perfectly intelligible. For it cannot be too strongly stressed that the relationship between mind and matter is an exclusively causal one; the only sense in which mind can be assigned a position in the space-time continuum is in terms of the material object with which it interacts. It is, I know, terribly tempting to think of mind as somehow located in the head, perhaps even just behind the eyes, and I have myself spoken earlier of the mind as "reaching out into the environment." But, of course, this is no more than a figure of speech. There is simply no distance to traverse and no time span to jump, the mind being actually nowhere is potentially, as a causal factor, omnipresent.

We come next to that other facet of mind which I mentioned, its intentionality[b] Although much less of it has been made so far by parapsychologists it is, I believe, even more significant and presents even more of a challenge to conventional physicalistic thinking. It is most clearly illustrated with respect to PK, especially in the recent work of Helmut Schmidt. In a typical Schmidt set-up the subject is required to try and influence a random number generator in such a way as to cause it to produce an excess of one out of the two possible digits from its binary output. All that the subject ever sees or knows of the set-up, however, consists of the feedback display in which a pointer moves now in one direction, now in another, depending on the success of the subject in achieving his aim. Thus the situation is very similar from the subject's point of view to that used in "biofeedback" training where the subject has to achieve control over some internal physiological process, his heartbeat or his brain rhythms etc. In the Schmidt situation, however, the system over which the subject has to gain some control is an external artificial machine, hence only this latter task would qualify as paranormal. Now the point that Schmidt has been at pains to emphasize is that it makes no difference to his results — which, I may say, are highly significant statistically though small enough in percentage terms — what he does at the business end of the set-up. It makes no difference where the random-number generator is placed, how it is triggered whether from a radioactive or some other noise source, whether he swaps machines half way through the experiment without informing the subject, even, in the last resort whether the output sequence has already been prepared on some previous occasion! All that matters is that the subject should intend a certain result and that he should have the necessary feedback to monitor his progress. Perhaps one should add to this that the subject's attitude and other similar psychological imponderables may be vital to success but certainly not the objective conditions at the randomizer.

But it is in the domain of macroscopic PK that we find the most conspicuous examples of a thought, an idea, an intention, translating itself into some physical embodiment. That is why we should not neglect some of these more far out phenomena which I mentioned earlier, however unsatisfactory the state of the evidence. The peculiar fascination of psychic photography, psychic healing and materialization phenomena is that here one seems to be confronted with mind in the act if imposing form and order on amorphous material. Consider what is implied by a genuine psychic photograph. The molecules of silver chloride, or whatever makes up the surface of the sensitive film, must organize themselves in such a way as to correspond with an image in the subject's mind (for the sake of simplicity I am here assuming the most straightforward case; in fact Serios worked with blind target pictures and the pictures that he produced never corresponded with anything that he was actually thinking about). What we have here may well be the paranormal analogue of what takes place in our own brain whenever we conjure up an image in our mind's eye, for I reject the orthodox view that our images are mere epiphenomena of the associated brain-processes and I suspect that, on the contrary, our brain processes organize themselves to correspond with the mental image and that, quite possibly, the storage and retrieval of conscious memories may well depend on this effect; at any rate we have as yet no satisfactory comprehensive physical theory of memory storage and retrieval. On this interpretation I would hypothesize that light was not an essential element in a psychic photograph (perhaps the term psychograph would be more apposite), the clicking of the shutter like the use of the gismo was, I presume, a mere concession to Serios' human frailty.

In psychic healing we can likewise find an analogue of the sort of processes involved in ordinary self-healing. LeShan has pointed out that healers do not claim to perform absolute miracles, they cannot restore a lost limb, for example; the paranormality of their influence lies in the extent to which it accelerates the regenerative, immunological and enzymatic reactions of the patient's body (LeShan 1974). We must here be careful to distinguish between paranormal healing as such and the various forms of faith healing that depend on suggestion. Experiments designed to demonstrate paranormal healing may use animals as the target objects or even, as in one celebrated case, a quantity of an enzyme *in vitro;** if human patients are used the healing procedure must be done at a distance without their knowledge. And yet, conceptually, there may well be a connection between the autosuggestive and psychosomatic effects we produce on our own organism during illness and the effects which the healer's mind can have on an alien organism. Moreover, insofar as paranormal healing can be authenticated it supports the assumption that self-healing is not purely an affair of self-regulating physiological mechanisms but likewise relies on a psychic factor.

Materializations are, perhaps, the most bizarre phenomena of the entire paranormal repertoire; there seems to be no parallel to them in normal life. It is as if the subjective idea of a body or part of a body could somehow take on an objective if ephemeral existence, whether by fashioning itself out of some peculiar ectoplasmic emanation from the subject's own body, as Richet believed, or in some other way. Alas, we no longer have any subjects who claim to possess this extraordinary phantom-forming power. Instead we have to be content with such as Geller. The trouble is that, apart from the repair of watches with which he is credited, his PK effects are more destructive than creative, a kind of psychic vandalism. In this respect they are still too close to the poltergeist phenomena to which they are surely allied. What we need next is a Geller who, out of a strip of metal, could, without contact, fashion a coherent work of art, a psychic sculpture. That would indeed be something worth watching!

How are we to understand this purposive-creative power which mind seems able to exert on matter? Traditional Cartesian dualism has little to teach us on this point. Descartes' categorical distinction between mind and matter is still, I would maintain, despite the heavy battering which Descartes has taken at the hands of modern British philosophers, the most important single insight in the entire history of philosophy. However, the way in which he formulated the distinction made it vulnerable to criticism right from the start. The trouble is that Descartes was mainly concerned to make the world safe for a mechanistic determinism, which, of course, was just what science at that time needed if it was to make progress. By encapsulating the mind inside the brain he accomplished this nicely while satisfying the dictates of his religion by providing one small loophole for the exercise of free will. But the only kind of action that mind was allowed to exert on matter was of a paramechanical sort: the demon-overseer, from his vantage point in the pineal gland, could control

* *See J. Smith (1968), "Paranormal Effects on Enzyme Activity." In this experiment Sister (Dr.) Justa Smith, a biochemist, working with the Hungarian healer, O. Estebany, demonstrated a PK effect on the enzyme extract similar to the effect of placing it in a high magnetic field.*

the flow of animal spirits by the opening or shutting of the sluices and so regulate the machinery of the body. But, if we are to make sense of the PK evidence, such a conception is quite inadequate; we need some much more global principle of a teleological sort.

In his much publicized essay, *Chance and Necessity,* Jacques Monod (1971) takes, as his point of departure, the fact that the universe is full of what he calls "teleonomic structures," that is objects and systems that appear to be purposive as if exemplifying some preconceived design. Being a materialist, however, Monod regards it as a scientific duty to explain away such structures as teleonomic in appearance only. As an eminent microbiologist Monod was, of course, particularly concerned to eliminate the teleological element from biology and evolution; his own career, after all, was a brilliant vindication of the reductionist approach. Now it is not my business to challenge Monod's interpretation of the biological evidence. In any case I am not a vitalist and I am not intent on reviving the notion of entelechies for the purpose of distinguishing living things from inanimate matter. But Monod, like so many contemporary scientists and philosophers, buys his materialism on the cheap, as it were, that is to say he never even discusses the paranormal evidence. If he had he might not have found it so easy to dismiss as the relic of prescientific superstition something which he calls, pejoratively, "animism" in favor of something which he calls, honorifically, the "principle of objectivity." What he seems to mean by this latter principle is that everything in the universe, and this includes ourselves and our behavior, must be explainable in terms of purely impersonal forces, there can be no third principle between those of chance and necessity. "The postulate of objectivity," he writes, "is consubstantial with science; it has guided the whole of its prodigious development for three centuries. There is no way to be rid of it, even tentatively or in a limited area, without departing from the domain of science itself."

What I want to do now is to propose, in direct opposition to Monod, that we adopt a postulate of animism. What I mean by this is that, under certain conditions, still to be established, an idea or intention in the mind can automatically constrain a physical system to act in such a way as to express this idea of intention. That this is, in the last resort, an ultimate fact about the world; there is no further "bridging mechanism" to be invoked to make this fact intelligible. I realize, of course, that this is a very shocking suggestion to make, it is uncomfortably reminiscent of the magical thinking that preceded our scientific era. However, I do not share Monod's alarmist fears that it would spell the end of science as a rational enterprise; I believe that, with patience, we shall be able to absorb it without having to jettison our hard won scientific knowledge. I am encouraged in this hope by some of the speculations to which we have been treated in recent years by some of the bolder spirits among our interpreters of quantum theory. What they seem to be telling us, insofar as I, as a layman, can follow their reasoning, is that physics must remain incomplete until we discover how to allow adequately for the role of the observer in the making of an observation, what they call the "measurement problem." Harris Walker, for example, proposes certain equations that incorporate a factor corresponding to Consciousness and another corresponding to Will (Walker 1974). Whether such speculations can lead to a meeting point between the view of mind that I have been advancing and the theoretical requirements of quantum physics, I do not know, but at least the rigid materialism of Monod's position would seem to be premature given the current state of fundamental physics.

Once parapsychologists have come to accept, in principle, my postulate of animism — as already PK experimenters accept it in practice — they will be rid of a lot of bogus problems that at present lead them into blind alleys. Thus, some theorists, especially since Kirlian photography became such a popular fad, like to explain psychic healing as due to a flow of "psychic energy" from the healer to the patient, a view, incidentally, that is encouraged by many healers themselves. Yet, unless there were independent evidence for the existence of such a psychic energy — and, despite the efforts of those calling themselves psychoenergeticists, no such evidence exists — such an assumption strikes me as grossly unparsimonious. Psychic healing of all things is a teleonomic process that beautifully exemplifies the postulate of animism. But, of course, this postulate must not be treated as an explanation obviating the need for further research. On the contrary it raises many exciting questions for which future research may be able to provide experimental evidence. For example, is the PK effect governed by a single end state initially determined by the subject who wills it, or is the process a gradual one which would suggest something like a clairvoyant feedback loop whereby the subject could guide the target system towards its goal by coordinating his ESP and PK? Or, perhaps, both possibilities are realized on different occasions as they are in the case of our normal skilled behavior where most of the time we rely on sensory feedback but where occasionally we perform a single ballistic movement that is preprogrammed to follow a particular course?

Up to this point I have striven hard to preserve, wherever possible, the analogy between normal mental functioning and psi phenomena. But now I must, in all honesty, confess that there comes a point where it is not easy to do so without very special pleading. The fact is that there is such a stark incongruity between the scope and power of the mind as implied by the existence of these psi phenomena and the obvious limitations of the normal mental capacities of the subject. Think, for a moment, of the extravagant incidents that have been quite reliably reported in some of the well known poltergeist cases and then think of the individual who, in some sense, is said to be responsible for them, typically a pathetic youngster. Or think of the great mediums and psychics of our history, so ordinary and humdrum in their personalities and private lives, so extraordinary in the powers they could command or the energies they could unleash. Is it any wonder that they saw themselves, for the most part, as no more than the passive vehicles—mediums in the literal sense—of occult and supernatural forces be they angels or demons, the spirits of the deceased or superior intelligences from outer space?

Consider, next, a typical test of clairvoyance. The subject, let us say, is attempting to visualize a picture target contained in a sealed, opaque envelope. In what sense can such a target be thought of as a visual stimulus seeing that light cannot reach it? And, suppose we were to substitute for the picture a strip of videotape on which it was recorded. Could we still expect the subject to identify it? For now the target is not even perceptible under normal conditions until it has been processed by a television apparatus. And suppose, finally, that we were to go one step further still and arrange our experiment in such a way that no one at any time could know what was contained inside a particular target envelope nor even where that particular envelope was located and that we also arranged for all the checking to be done by a computer which merely printed out the overall result of the test. Is it conceivable that such a test could still be successful? Some theorists, especially those who hope for a physicalistic explanation of ESP, balk at the concept of pure clairvoyance and suggest various more or less devious ways in which the evidence for it might be interpreted in terms of telepathy, precognitive or retrocognitive. It is of enormous theoretical interest to know whether pure clairvoyance is, indeed, a fact and it is to be hoped that further research may help to resolve the question even if it can never logically preclude all possible alternative explanations. But the point I want to make here is that even if pure clairvoyance is not a fact, the amount of information processing implied in the existing evidence of ESP, when one stops to think about what is involved when a subject has to search out and identify a given target, is already so far beyond anything that the psychologist would recognize in normal cognitive functioning that our analogy becomes frayed at the edges.

It may be, then, that, ultimately, we shall have to abandon the attempt to relate psi phenomena to the personal mind of the individual subject and fall back on something more like a universal cosmic intelligence or collective unconscious which the subject can somehow tap when engaged in a psi situation. But, having said this, I want to draw back as it would take me further in my speculations than I am at the moment prepared to venture.

This brings me to the final section of my paper. If we are ever to succeed in making sense of the paranormal we must, I believe, be prepared to bring to our task a broad historical perspective. If we focus on too narrow a range of phenomena and consider too narrow a range of interpretations we risk missing the essence of the problem. In any case, since the phenomena we are dealing with have, for the most part, been known at all times and in all places, it cannot be otherwise than instructive to look at the way in which our ancestors attempted to make sense of them.

There have, I am going to suggest, been three main systems of belief or

thought into which people have, with varying degrees of success, tried to ac-
commodate the phenomena. These are religion or mysticism, magic or sorcery,
and science. The view that I shall take—and I must beg you not to be too
alarmed—is that it is with the second of these, that is, with the traditions of
magic and sorcery, that the phenomena show their clearest affinity and it is
there they find their natural home. It is only with something of an uphill effort
that they can be assimilated to either of the other two categories and even then
they represent a permanently subversive element.

Consider first the religious angle which has always enjoyed a certain appeal among those who have been most active in our field. Only recently it has
been eloquently defended by our former president Sir Alister Hardy. He takes
the view that it should be possible to construct a natural theology on the basis
of (a) an empirical study of people's religious and mystical experiences and of
(b) an experimental study of psi phenomena, especially telepathy. Indeed, it
was precisely because of its potential implications for religion that Sir Alister
was bold enough to say that: "psychical research is one of the most important
branches of investigation that the human mind has ever undertaken" (Hardy
1965, 1966 & 1975).

It is not hard to understand why Hardy and others who share his approach
should take this view. Psychical research, after all, was born of the conflict of
science and religion that came to a head in the late 19th century. If ever
scientific materialism should win the day it is hard to see how religion, in any
meaningful sense, could survive. Such religious concepts as prayer, as divine
intervention in history, as an afterlife and so forth, all presuppose the possibility
of paranormal powers. It is, moreover, an historical fact that all the great
religious traditions made free use of a miraculous element. This is notoriously
the case with Catholicism, with its long list of miracle-working saints, many
of whom continued to work their miracles posthumously like St. Januarius.
Yet, when one looks closer one finds that there has always been a good deal
of ambivalence in the attitude of the truly devout towards the miraculous.
Miracles might be justified as an aid to faith among the weaker brethren but
they should never be cultivated for their own sake. I am very fond of the story
about St. Theresa of Avila who is reported to have been greatly embarrassed
when her nuns caught her levitating during her devotions. She considered it
vulgar and ostentatious and prayed to God to relieve her of this superfluous
grace.* A rather similar attitude is reported of the holy men of India who practice Yoga. A *siddhi,* such as levitation, is a natural concomitant of a certain
advanced stage of Yoga but it must not be allowed to distract the practitioner
from his search for *samadhi* or union with the cosmic consciousness. It is,
perhaps, significant that St. Joseph of Cupertino, whose levitations are, I

---

* *See Thurston (1952). Thurston was a Jesuit priest as well as a notable authority on psychic
phenomena.*

suppose, the best attested miracles associated with any religious figure in history, was never held in high esteem by the Church, indeed he was looked upon, no doubt for good reason, as a simpleton. Even the late Padre Pio, who was credited with a number of impressive miracles and was certainly a genuine stigmatic, was treated by the hierarchy with a certain coolness and reserve.

The reason for such ambivalence is not hard to find. The fact is that, by and large, psychic phenomena lack the one thing that is essential, from the religious viewpoint, a spiritual dimension. At best they may have practical importance for those concerned, like a telepathic distress signal or a premonition of disaster, at worst they may be malicious or destructive but, for the most part, they are trivial, ridiculous or preposterous. The one religious sect which did attempt to build a faith on the basis of paranormal evidence was, of course, the Spiritualists. But it cannot be said that they did a very convincing job of it. Their heaven was just a shade too secular, too like this life only without some of its discomforts and inconveniences. Indeed, "spiritualism" was a misnomer, "spiritism" was the more accurate name for this creed. Yet even the Spiritualists were sometimes embarrassed by the undignified pranks of the séance room, especially where physical phenomena were concerned. Moreover it soon became clear that some of the most powerful mediums were persons of a low moral calibre when they were not outrightly immoral. One of the more confusing aspects of the search for good mediums was that a readiness to cheat could never be taken as a sign that the medium lacked genuine psychic abilities — one has only to recall Palladino and she was by no means exceptional. In general, despite LeShan's recent attempt to find a common denominator in the vision of reality as apprehended through the eyes of the mystic and the medium, it has not been easy to represent paranormal phenomena as having any cosmic or spiritual significance.

But the attempt to divest the paranormal entirely of any supernatural or transcendental connotations has likewise met with dubious success. It is, of course, a rather recent development despite such interesting early precursors as Charles Richet. I have already discussed some of the difficulties connected with the so-called physicalistic approach to psi. It is true that many newcomers to the field, especially those who come to it with a background in the physical sciences and are steeped in quantum theory, are full of optimism that it can be made to work. J.B. Rhine imagined — he still imagines — that his work conclusively demonstrated the non-physicality of psi. What he overlooked was that physics itself is a much more protean system of thought than it used to be; it now allows for many more speculative possibilities and is much more hesitant about declaring any sort of phenomenon as absolutely unthinkable.* It would be wrong, therefore, to discount the efforts of a physicalistic school of parapsychologists, indeed I wish them well; I am sure there is a great deal

---

* Cf. Arthur Koestler "The Perversity of Physics" (Koestler 1972, Chapter 2).

that they can teach us concerning the interface of mind-matter interactions, but it will require a *tour de force* if they are to succeed in taking over the whole of parapsychology and converting it into paraphysics.

There remains, lastly, the tradition of magic. Perhaps the only societies where the paranormal has ever been fully integrated into the lives and beliefs of its members have been those tribal societies which the anthropologists have made known to us with their witch-doctors, shamans, seers and diviners, in other words societies that have a strong continuous tradition of magic. In Western civilization, at least among the educated strata if not always at the folk level, the concept of magic has long fallen into disrepute except where the word is used to refer to stage magic. But it was not always so. If we go back in history, beyond the Enlightenment, to the period of the high renaissance in Europe of the late 16th, early 17th centuries, we come across a remarkable flowering of magical thinking and practices. At that period, the challenge to orthodoxy in religion and philosophy, especially to Aristotelian scholasticism, had left something of an intellectual vacuum which science had not yet been able to fill. The result was a great upsurge of interest, not only in the two traditional occult sciences of astrology and alchemy, but also in all manner of old and new systems of magic: Hermeticist, Paracelsist, Kabbalistic, Rosicrucian and so forth. This murky terrain has recently been illumined by the work of the historian, Frances Yates, who has made it peculiarly her own (Yates 1972). It was, on the one hand, an age of gross incredulity. How else are we to explain that even learned men of that time could lend credence to the grotesque allegations of witchcraft which proliferated as the witch-hunting mania in Europe was reaching its frenzied climax? Yet, from another point of view, the interest in magic was a forward-looking one, inasmuch as it was inspired by the belief that a new era was at hand when powerful new knowledge would be used to improve the lot of man on Earth. We must remember that, unlike the occult revival of our own time, which makes its appeal mainly to the semieducated, this earlier movement attracted to its ranks some of the most advanced thinkers of Europe, men of the stature of Giordano Bruno, Johannes Kepler, John Dee, the Elizabethan mathematician, and even Francis Bacon, that apostle of the coming scientific revolution.

Such was the intellectual climate before it was forever swept away by the triumphant progress of the new science of Galileo, Descartes and Newton, although it lingered on until late in the century so that we find even the great Newton himself engaged in secret alchemical experiments at Cambridge. Or, perhaps, it might be truer to say that it was never completely swept away but only went underground to reemerge in some guise or other whenever discontent with the prevailing orthodoxies became too strong to contain. Thus it was that, during the Romantic revolt against the aridities of 18th century rationalism, we witness the rise of mesmerism as a popular cult with its strong paranormal overtones. Similarly, the occult revival of today grew out of the widespread disillusionment with official science and its associated technologies that was expressed by the "counterculture" of the 1960s. Now the point I want to make is that, despite the nonsensical and irrational ideas which these movements invariably generated, there may be something we can learn from this prescientific magical tradition.

The conception of nature which it propounded was, of course, a profoundly anthropomorphic and teleological one. Even inanimate processes were thought to exemplify symbolic and mentalistic concepts so that one could seriously discuss whether the iron filing was attracted to the magnet or dragged towards it against its will! But, for all its naivety, it did at least try to do justice to the existence of mind and it did try to come to terms with the paranormal. The revolution that dethroned it did neither. It sacrificed mind as an effective agent in nature and it could do nothing with the paranormal except to sit tight and hope that it did not exist. The time has now come, I suggest, when we must rethink the scientific enterprise. Our mistake, it seems to me, is that what, for the past three centuries, we have taken to be distinctive of science, namely its determinism and materialism, was never its most valuable feature; rather, as Popper has never tired of telling us, what we should be paying attention to is its openness and its fallibilism. Occult knowledge was essentially authoritarian, dogmatic and esoteric. The magus was one who came into the possession of hidden wisdom and secret doctrine. Scientific knowledge, on the other hand, is self-critical and hence self-correcting. Its teachings may sometimes harden into dogma but, in principle if not always in practice, nothing in it is sacrosanct except its obligation to submit its claims to evidence and argument. Science cannot, therefore, be damaged, as Monod seemed to fear, even if we were to drop the postulates of determinism and materialism.

I hope that I shall not be misunderstood. I am not advocating a return to an anthropocentric or even a theocentric universe. I am a hardened enough agnostic to think that the cosmos we inhabit is indifferent to our ideals and aspirations. I also think that it is a great mistake to exaggerate the importance of mind; the Idealists who did this by denying or belittling the reality of matter were committing the gravest of philosophical fallacies. But I am entering a plea that our philosophy should allow for the coexistence of mind and matter. If I have not misread the signs, I have the impression, not least from listening to the scientists themselves, that science is at present undergoing another radical revision and that we can soon expect a major transformation in our world view. It is my conviction as well as my hope that parapsychology will have a critical role to play in determining what kind of world view it will be.

Notes

a. No doubt it sounds silly at the present time to give such prominence to the case of Uri Geller but we should not forget the extraordinary impact he made, not just on the public but among scientists, during the early 1970s especially in Britain. I still find myself undecided as to whether he was ever anything other than a charlatan and entertainer or whether he used his knowledge of stage magic to gain the wealth and fame he so ardently desired and which his modest psi ability would not have enabled him to do.

As regards that other psychic superstar, who blazed a trail during the 1960s, Ted Serios, I am much less inclined to dismiss him as a trickster. It is, of course, most unfortunate that he lost his ability just when the controversies surrounding him had reached a peak. Nevertheless, those who worked with him most closely, and were in the best position to judge, have never wavered in their conviction that he was genuine.

b. "Intentionality" may not have been the best term I could have used in this connection. For one thing, the word has been preempted in technical philosophy to stand for that special property of mental events that allows them to refer to something other than themselves (Brentano even took this as the defining property of what it is to be mental as opposed to physical). The phrase "goal-oriented" is popular with parapsychologists and it is the expression favored by Helmut Schmidt in this connection. "Purposeful" or "teleological" might also have been appropriate. The point I was laboring to get across, whatever word we use in this context, is that the end alone is relevant to the exercise of PK; the means follow automatically as if reality were one vast computer programmed to implement the instructions we feed in! For a further discussion of this point see "Teleological Causation" (beginning on page 88).

Backward Causation

Perhaps no other psi phenomenon arouses so much philosophical disquiet as does precognition. Although, in a sense, all our activity is directed towards the future, the idea that it might be possible occasionally to catch a glimpse of that future, as opposed simply to making inferences about it on the basis of past experience, is an idea that many find outrageous, not least because it seems to imply a backward causation. When, therefore, I was invited, again by the Parapsychology Foundation, to participate in a conference on philosophy and parapsychology, in Copenhagen in August 1976, I decided that backward causation would make a suitably controversial topic for such an occasion. Bob Brier (1974) had already set the cat among the pigeons with the publication of his book on this theme. I, for one, had found the book persuasive. Moreover, the recent advent of observational theory was making a bid to interpret all psi phenomena as a retrocausal effect produced at the point of feedback.

The two professional philosophers who took part in the discussion which followed my paper (Parapsychology Foundation 1977), namely Shivesh Thakur and Peter French, seemed amenable to the principle of backward causation, unlike Anthony Flew who at a previous conference (Parapsychology Foundation 1974) had attacked the notion as logically absurd and, with it, the very idea of precognition in a literal sense. I had tried to challenge him at the time but he would not concede anything to my objections; so did Brier, himself, even more forcibly, pointing out that Flew had failed to recognize the elementary distinction between changing the past, which was a logical absurdity, and influencing the past which was not. To this day Flew has clung to his position and refuses to recognize this distinction.

Every paranormal phenomenon must, in the nature of the case, arouse suspicion and skepticism, but the claim to be able to foretell events which have not yet occurred, which is what we mean by *precognition*, is apt to raise doubts as to whether this concept is even coherent. A number of eminent philosophers, including some like the late C.D. Broad (1967) or C.W.K. Mundle (1964) who were known for their interest in and involvement with parapsychology, came reluctantly to the conclusion that precognition, taken in its literal sense as a knowledge of the future, was not just impossible in point of fact but was logically impossible.[a]

I want to start by considering some of these logical objections that have been brought against the concept of precognition. It has been pointed out, for example, that if an event has not yet occurred, then it cannot have any effects and, in particular, it cannot be an object of knowledge. Something which does not exist may be imagined, but it cannot literally be known. Moreover, even if we disregard this obvious point, in order for a future event to become the cause of my present precognition of it, it would have to exert a backward effect in time and this, it has been said, is inadmissible on at least three counts. First, because it is part of the meaning of the word *cause* that a cause should precede its effect, hence a cause which followed its effect would be a contradiction in terms. Secondly, and more seriously, if, forgetting about the semantics of the case, we do posit a backward causation, this would be tantamount to asserting that we could alter the past. But what has been, has been and nothing that anyone can do after the event can change it in any way. Hence, the very idea of backward causation is a radical absurdity. And, thirdly, even if we could somehow overlook the two previous objections and persist with the idea of backward causation, we should find ourselves committed to the following paradox: If it were possible to intervene in the past then, in principle, we could intervene in order to prevent our own birth. But, in that case, who was it that intervened in the first place? We would thereby have negated our own existence!

These are not by any means the only objections that have been raised with respect to precognition and I shall have more to say on the point towards the end of my talk but, in the meanwhile, I want to look very closely at the concept of backward causation which I believe is the real root of the trouble. I hope to show that, contrary to what many philosophers have maintained, there is nothing radically wrong with this concept and hence it cannot be invoked as a reason for rejecting precognition on *a priori* grounds. Furthermore, I shall try to show that, once we have come to terms with this seemingly paradoxical idea, we shall be ready to appreciate an exciting new development in experimental parapsychology, namely the study of backward or retroactive PK. In what follows, I would like to acknowledge my debt to a young American philosopher, Bob Brier, who alerted me to this problem and convinced me that the *a priori* case against precognition could be met. Bob Brier propounded his views in a brief but important monograph entitled *Precognition and the Philosophy of Science* (Brier 1974), with the subtitle "An Essay on Backward Causation." Brier, in turn, was following the lead of the English philosopher

Michael Dummett (1964), whose "Bringing About the Past" first appeared in the *Philosophical Review*. But, having acknowledged my intellectual debts, I consider myself free to develop my theme in my own way and draw my own conclusions. Let us return, therefore, to the objections which I have already listed and see whether they are really as cogent as they may at first appear.

The idea that future events do not exist and can, therefore, have no conceivable influence upon the present is a case of begging the question. For, in fact, many if not most contemporary philosophers of science who have written on the problem of time take a realist or objectivist view of the temporal order. I mean by this that they deny that the expressions *past, present, future* have anything more than a subjective or, at least, mind-dependent basis, indicating the relationship between the observer and the event in question, like the expressions *here* and *there*. In a mindless universe, they argue, no particular instant of the time series would have a preferential status over any other instant. Each event would still stand to any other event in the relationship *earlier than* or *later than* but none would stand out from the rest as representing a unique *now*, that is, the instant which the universe had attained on the time series. All events would simply coexist in the timeless sense in which we talk of facts as existing or *being the case*. Now, I am not saying that the realist view of time is necessarily the correct one or that the concept of *now-ness* or *becoming*, as something extra which an event attains when it actually takes place, is a concept with no clear meaning. I mention this view simply to show that one cannot just assume, without further argument, that future events are any less real than past or present events. And, certainly, those cosmologies which treat the universe as a single four-dimensional continuum, in which every object is represented by a certain determinate world-line, recognize no division of the universe into a past, present and future.

Let us agree, then, that there are no *a priori* objections to our treating future events as sufficiently real to have causal consequences. The question we must then consider is whether the direction of such causation must always extend from earlier to later, never from later to earlier. Let us look again at the reasons that are offered for refusing to admit any sort of backward causation. First, I do not think that the purely verbal objection need to detain us for long. It may well be the case that, in ordinary language, a cause is always understood as preceding its effect, since this, after all, is what happens in ordinary experience. But, given new circumstances, linguistic usage tends to become reasonably pliable and if we can show that there are paranormal cases where the cause comes after its effect, I am quite sure we would not be deterred from acknowledging them by the constraints of language. At worst we might have to write the word "cause" in adverted commas, to signal that this was a rather special kind of cause that we are dealing with.

What is much more problematic is whether the admission of backward causation would lead us into a logical impasse. It seems at first that this would indeed commit us to asserting that the past could be altered and this, I would agree, is nonsense. But, although we cannot alter the past in the sense of making something to have happened which did *not* in fact happen or, conversely, preventing something from having happened which *did* in fact happen, it does *not* follow that what *did* happen might never have happened, or might have happened differently, *but for* certain later events. We may find this supposition strange, but it is certainly not illogical. In fact, the case is no different logically when we are considering the future. If what has been, has been, then, equally, what will be, will be and in this sense one can no more alter the future than one can alter the past. But, of course, we quite rightly believe that what will be may depend on what we now do and, in this sense, we can *influence* the future even if it makes no sense to talk of altering it. The fallacy which previous philosophers have fallen into arises from the fact that they failed to observe Brier's distinction between altering the past and influencing the past. The point to grasp is that the past might not have been what it was, had it not been for some action in the present.

We are now in a position to deal with the other paradox of the man who by dint of backward causation cancelled his own birth. Given the fact that a person was born on such and such a date, it follows that nothing thereafter can *alter* this fact. But it does not follow logically that his having been born might not have been due to some subsequent action that was taken. For example, a pious Christian mother might well believe that her child would never have been born, but for the fact that, at the appointed time, she had it baptized. Now, we may mock her for her credulity as much as we please, but we cannot fault her logic. The fact that we cannot use backward causation to cancel our birth is no more problematic than the fact that we cannot cancel any event once it has occurred.

Critics of backward causation point out that causation is an essentially pragmatic concept. Thus, we say that A is the cause of B when we are satisfied that we can bring about B by taking action involving A. However, if we know that B has already occurred, then any action we take involving A would be superfluous, since we have now obtained B whether or not we do A. Conversely, if B has *failed* to materialize at a given time t_1. Hence, from the pragmatic point of view, every instance we take involving A is then futile insofar as it was designed to make B occur at time t_1. Hence, from the pragmatic point of view, every instance of backward causation must be either superfluous or else futile.

Brier offers an amusing example to show, nevertheless, that backward causation need not be devoid of pragmatic import. Suppose a man were to discover, by sheer trial and error, that whenever he received a letter through the post he had only to clap his hands and, when he then opened the envelope, he would invariably find there a check made out in his favor, while, conversely, if he forgot or failed to clap his hands there would be no check. In this situation,

Brier asks, would any of us, whatever our philosophical prejudices, refrain from clapping our hands? And, if so, could any of us honestly deny that clapping our hands at the right moment was a necessary condition or cause of the check having been inserted into the envelope at an earlier time? Now, you may say at this point: well, supposing the envelope were transparent, what then? The man would then know as soon as he caught sight of the letter either that there was a check inside, in which case he would not bother to clap his hands, or that there was no check, in which case no amount of hand-clapping would help him! And yet, surely, a causal connection which depended for its validity on the knowledge or ignorance of the agent would be a very queer sort of cause.

But consider, any causal connection whatsoever is circumscribed by certain boundary conditions. Indeed, as Ducasse (1969) and other philosophers have stressed, causation actually involves a triadic relationship, A causes B under conditions C. Striking a match will cause a flame but not if the match is damp or the surface is too smooth. It is not, therefore, surprising if what we might call the epistemic aspects of the situation should constitute the boundary conditions where human actions are involved. Here, again, a comparison with actions directed towards the future may help to clarify this point. Thus, if I *know* that tomorrow I shall be killed, it follows logically that nothing I can do today can prevent it, since knowing something logically implies that it is the case, but, granted that I do *not* know whether I shall be killed, it is entirely rational for me to take steps to avoid getting killed.

Similarly, if the letter I receive arrives in a transparent envelope, so that I know that there is no check inside, no magic on my part can conjure one into having been inserted, but, granted that the envelope is opaque and that I do *not* know, it is entirely rational for me to clap my hands. What makes these two cases appear different is that normally we do *not* know what lies in the future, whereas normally we *do* know, or at least we can very easily find out, what has happened in the past. But this is an empirical difference as between past and future and, of course, there are many such empirical differences. The logic of the two situations, however, is entirely symmetrical and it is the logical aspect that now concerns us. From the foregoing we are, I submit, entitled to conclude that there are no logical objections to saying that A is the cause of B, so long as we believe that B would not have happened but for A, regardless of whether A is earlier than B or B is earlier than A.

Up to this point we have discussed the question of backward causation in purely hypothetical terms, using examples drawn from the realm of fantasy or superstition. I now want to turn to the actualities of parapsychological research and consider its relevance in that context. It has been widely held by parapsychologists that ESP is essentially independent of space, time and matter, so that when we use our extrasensory powers, instead of relying on our sensory channels and their associated brain-mechanisms, there is no inherent reason why we should not become aware of events occurring in the past or the future as much as events occurring contemporaneously, just as there is no inherent reason why we should not become aware of events occurring in remote places or events shielded from us by intervening matter. In the case of PK, however, it has been the practice to use target-systems located in the subject's immediate vicinity and much less has been made of the potential time and space transcendence of the phenomenon. And yet it would be very odd if PK behaved any differently in this respect from ESP, considering that the two are so closely linked that it is customary to subsume both phenomena under the generic term *psi*. The trouble is, however, that it would, in the nature of the case, be very difficult, if not impossible, to demonstrate unequivocally the existence of a PK effect directed towards the future that would be the analog of precognitive ESP. For, whereas in a precognition experiment the subject has simply to record his guess at time t_1, and then wait for the target event to occur at time t_2, against which he can compare it, in the case of PK there is no objective way of registering mental effort at time t_1 that might be responsible for the target even at time t_2. The point is that PK is known only through its effects. It cannot be identified with any sort of conscious effort on the part of the subject. Moreover, even if one went to the extreme of killing the subject between the time t_1 when he is given the instruction to try exerting a PK effect on the future and the time t_2 when the effect is observed, one could still not rule out the possibility that the effect was due to a delayed-action PK or, even, that the deceased subject was exerting a PK effect from the life beyond, as it were.

We may note in passing that the problem of demonstrating forward PK is exactly matched by the problem of demonstrating backward ESP, otherwise known as retrocognition. In the latter case, although the subject's response can be recorded prior to verification, the verification would not be possible but for the existence of certain records in the present. Hence, there can be no unequivocal test of retrocognition. Fortunately, there is no such logical barrier in the way of demonstrating unequivocally the existence of a backward or retroactive PK, which is what I want to talk about now. The way it can be done is as follows: Some physical effect can be automatically recorded at time t_1, but kept secret until later. At time t_2, the subject is instructed to try producing this particular physical effect or outcome on this particular target-system and then, but only then, is the result checked against the original record at time t_1. This, basically, is the method used by Helmut Schmidt in his recent experiments on PK with time displacement, but others, too, have been working independently along similar lines elsewhere (Janin 1974). For a straightforward test of PK, Schmidt uses as his target system a device known as a "random number generator." This usually has a binary output such that, when it is operating in isolation, the two possible outcomes will occur with approximately equal frequency. The PK task is to upset the randomicity of the machine by getting it to generate an excess of the one digit or the other, depending on the arbitrary instruction that is laid down. A prominent feature of the Schmidt set-up is the feedback system. This may take a variety of forms, visual or auditory, for example, a recording pen that shifts from side to side or a fluctuating tone etc. The principle, in every case, is that the feedback is controlled by the random number generator in such a way that an excess of hits or successful trials will produce a shift in one direction, while an excess of misses or unsuccessful trials will produce a shift in the opposite direction. This feedback is not just an amenity designed to engage or sustain the interest of the subject; it is, according to Schmidt's (1975) mathematical model of psi, a crucial part of the whole process. It is, indeed, the feedback which is said to activate the psi source. However that may be, the subject is encouraged to concentrate his attention on the feedback and to try getting it to move in the desired direction, and not to bother about the random number generator which actually governs it.

This, as I say, is what happens in the straightforward or contemporaneous type of PK test. To convert this into an experiment on retroactive PK, only one modification is necessary. The output of the randomizer is now determined by a solid state memory on which a sequence of digits has been recorded, based on a previous output from the machine. Hence, instead of generating a fresh sequence of random digits by being triggered from a source of quantum indeterminacy or of electronic noise, it now merely repeats the series recorded at this earlier time. So far as the subject is concerned, however, nothing has changed; he does not need to know that the situation is any different from what it is in the standard case. Nevertheless, if the subject is to succeed in making a significant score under these new conditions, it is necessary for him to influence the behavior of the machine, not as it *is* currently, since it is now strictly determined, but as it *was* when the target sequence was originally recorded. His PK, in other words, is now operating retroactively. Although, so far, very few such experiments have been reported, it is beginning to look as if PK with time displacement may be a fact (Schmidt 1976).

In our department at Edinburgh, Richard Broughton, one of my postgraduate students, has already started work on a project which depends on the retroactive properties of PK. His point of departure is the notorious *experimenter effect,* that is, the idea that the experimenter himself, rather than the ostensible subject, is the real psi source which is responsible for the positive results which are observed. Without some such hypothesis, it is hard to explain why certain parapsychologists obtain positive results time and time again while others hardly ever do so. Indeed, Broughton had begun to wonder whether his own positive results, which he had himself obtained earlier, while working on his thesis project designed to demonstrate a hemispheric lateralization effect in ESP, might not have been the product of such a psi experimenter effect. In this new project, what he does is to generate a certain expectation in his subjects regarding the kind of scores which they may expect, more specifically, that they may expect to do better under one condition in which they perform their

ESP task than they will under another condition, on account of certain unspecified artifacts. Actually, there is no objective difference between the two conditions under which they perform, and it is only when they go to the computer to receive a printout of their scores at the termination of the experiment, that they are told which was the high-scoring condition and which the low-scoring condition, the assignment being arbitrarily determined by the computer. This means that the expectation is generated in the subject, not at the start of the experiment, but only when it is all over. The idea, if you follow me, is that any significant difference that is then found as between these two arbitrary categories must be due to the subject's retroactive PK. In other words, what he expects to find at time t_2 must influence the scoring level recorded at time t_1. A pilot experiment along these lines has already been run which did in fact produce some significant differences and Richard Broughton has been reporting on them to the Parapsychological Association Convention at Utrecht (Broughton 1976). There are further refinements in his experiment which I have not bothered to mention and a much larger experiment is planned for next year, which the Parapsychology Foundation has generously agreed to support, but I have taken it as an illustration of the fact that backward causation is beginning to enter into the current thinking of experimental parapsychologists.

Nor is it only PK that operates retroactively. If we adopt the Schmidt axiom, that all psi interactions depend critically on feedback, then ESP, too, involves backward causation, proceeding from the moment at which feedback is received to the earlier moment in time at which the response was given. Even precognition, on the Schmidt model, is elicited not, in the first instance, by the future event that is precognized, but rather by the subsequent confirmation, whether by the subject himself or the experimenter, that the event in question has come to pass.

Armed with the concept of backward causation let us finally turn back to the problem of precognition which I introduced at the outset of this paper. Undoubtedly, one reason why precognition has engendered so much resistance is that to many people it seems to cut at the root of the belief in free-will. If our future actions could be known, it is feared, this would make a mockery of our claim to be able to determine our actions by a spontaneous act of will. Applying the concept of backward causation, however, this fear would seem to be unfounded. For, when I spontaneously choose or decide upon some course of action, then my choice or decision could just as well have caused you to have had a precognition of it the week before, as it could be the cause of your remembering it a week later. Whether this entirely disposes of the uneasiness we all feel at the thought of the future being already in some sense laid down and knowable, I do not know. Certainly, we like to feel that the future lies open before us waiting to be created, but whether this intuition is philosophically justifiable, I must leave you to judge. I will say, however, that there is one restriction we must impose on the scope of precognition if we are to retain the idea of free-will. We clearly cannot both precognize our own future actions and, at the same time, freely decide upon them when the time comes. For, deciding implies being in a state of uncertainty which is terminated only when the decision is made. But, if we already *know* what we are going to do, it would be absurd to talk of our then *deciding* what to do. Having perfect precognition, which would include knowing all one's future actions, would indeed be incompatible with living one's life in the sort of way that characterizes human existence.

I am not claiming that the concept of backward causation can solve all the problems connected with the idea of precognition — there is, for example, the notorious *intervention paradox* which raises quite different questions — but what I have tried to do in this paper is to show that precognition cannot be dismissed on logical grounds alone, and that the idea of backward causation, so far from being nonsensical, is now being taken seriously by more and more experimentalists as a basis for testing psi in the laboratory.[b]

Notes

a. To be fair to Broad, he does attempt to rescue the concept of precognition in the literal sense by toying with the idea of an additional dimension of time (Broad 1967, pp. 199–204).

b. Despite this confident conclusion, resistance to the idea of backward causation and, hence, literal precognition, is still far from having subsided. Both Jule Eisenbud (1982) and Stephen Braude (1986, chap. 5) repudiate it as an incoherent idea. Braude, a professional philosopher, unlike Flew, does not fall into the same trap, that of failing to distinguish between altering the past and affecting the past. His argument is much more subtle, namely that "Any causal connection we identify will always be part of a larger causal nexus spreading indefinitely into the past and future" whereas the putative counterclockwise causes are never part of any such wider network. My own response to this objection is to challenge the premises of Braude's argument. I do not agree that normal causes are necessarily part of any wider network. The obvious model for precognition is memory, indeed one is tempted to regard precognition as simply memory operating in reverse. Now the relationship between the events remembered and the present memory need be no different from the relationship between the events precognized and the present precognitive experience. It is true that, in the case of memory, one can fill in the time gap by invoking memory traces in the brain; indeed this is what enables us to regard memory as a normal rather than paranormal phenomenon (see my paper on pages 110–122). But, clearly, this is not part of that causal nexus to which Braude alludes and, in any case, Braude has elsewhere (1979) repudiated the trace theory of memory. The point is that when we are dealing with an epistemic relationship there is simply no need for Braude's causal nexus, rather it is a case of the percipient's mind being directed either onto its past experiences or, in the paranormal case, onto its future experiences.

It is curious that, as a consequence of what I regard as their faulty logic, both Eisenbud and Braude (who acknowledges his indebtedness to Eisenbud) adopt what they themselves call an "active" interpretation of precognition. This means that the events said to have been precognized were actually brought about, psychokinetically, by the precognizer! This has long been a favorite fall-back position for those parapsychologists who, for whatever reason, cannot come to terms with literal precognition. Alternatively, when the active interpretation becomes too far-fetched even for its proponents, recourse can be had to superinferential powers of extrapolation from contemporaneous clairvoyant knowledge. Such antics, it would seem, are the price one has to pay for rejecting backward causation.

Teleological Causation

This paper was originally presented to the Second International Conference of the Society for Psychical Research at Cambridge in March 1978. I am indebted to my friend, Richard Broughton, whose helpful comments and suggestions on an earlier draft led me to rewrite the paper in its present form. Even so, I never sought to publish it, hoping always to develop it further. Hence it now appears for the first time in print although it was occasionally cited in the literature.

One of the peculiarities of psi phenomena, it would seem, is that not only do they defy an explanation in conventional terms, but they appear to involve a kind of causation different from that which we associate with familiar physical processes. We have already discussed the problem of backward causation and we have alluded to the concept of acausal correspondence or synchronicity. Here we go on to consider the case of "teleological" or, as some would prefer to call it, "goal-oriented" causation.

At last year's S.P.R. Conference (Beloff 1977), I discussed the question of whether a causal or an acausal analysis of psi phenomena was the more appropriate. The conclusion I reached on that occasion was that, while we could not *prove* that the causal interpretation was correct, as experimentalists we must *hope* that this was so, for there would be little sense in carrying out an experiment if we could not assume that our experimental conditions afforded some prospect at least of bringing about the relevant results, and to talk of bringing something about is just another way of talking about *causing* it to happen. I did not want to deny that there might be coincidences of a meaningful kind, as Jung supposed, although how one was to distinguish these from sheer coincidences remained unclear. Similarly, I did not wish to deny that there might be an inherent nonrandomness in nature such that certain kinds of events tend to occur in clusters, as Kammerer believed, although, here again, we are not told how we could ever know that we were not dealing with a freak run. But, to admit the possibility of synchronistic phenomena, as I am quite willing to do, does not mean that psi phenomena must be subsumed under this category. Jung's mistake was that he too hastily assumed that causation could only mean physical causation and so he invented synchronicity to account for psychic causation.

Let us take a homely example of mechanical cause and effect, namely turning on the electric light. What in this instance connects event A, pressing down the switch, with event B, the light coming on, is, of course, the flow of the current along the wires. Generalizing from this to all cases of mechanical causation, we may identify the cause with some disturbance introduced into some physical system and the effect with some subsequent change in that system. We may then say that the two are connected by the continuous propagation of energy through the intervening spatiotemporal interval. Now Jung was, I believe, perfectly correct in thinking that the psi process did not work in this way. And I do not believe that we can get round this discrepancy by inventing some kind of psychic field of force to deputize for the missing physical field of force. Where, I think, Jung and his present day successors have gone astray is in supposing that, without this continuous transmission of energy, there can be no causation. For, to say that A is the cause of B, implies only that B would not have occurred *but for* A, the actual nature of the connection between them is another matter; so long as I am satisfied that my light comes on when, and only when, I press the switch it would not matter, so far as the logic of the situation goes, whether there *were* any wires involved, the system could just as well work by magic!

But, if psychic causation is not like mechanical causation, what other options are open to us? Believing with Thouless and Wiesner (1947) that the prototype both of ESP and of PK is to be found in the interactions between mind and brain, I shall digress at this point to say something about what philosophers call the mind-body problem and then return later to the problem of psi which I hope may then appear as a special case of mind-matter interaction. In a new book, *The Self and Its Brain,* which is written partly by Sir Karl Popper and partly by Sir John Eccles, Popper makes the following point which provides a clue to our problem when he says: "The great difficulty of the Cartesian theory of mind-body interaction lies in the Cartesian theory of physical causality according to which all physical action must be by mechanical push" (Popper/Eccles 1977, p. 180). Push and pull, attraction and repulsion, is, indeed, the hallmark of *mechanical* causality but it has always seemed to those who have thought about the mind-body relationship exceedingly implausible that mind should operate the machinery of the brain and nervous system by any conceivable set of appropriate pushes and pulls. At the same time Popper, like me, is an interactionist who believes in the self as an active agent and not just a byproduct of brain processes; how, then, does he attempt to depict the action of mind on brain? He does not answer this question directly but he does talk at some length about what he calls "downward causation." Ordinarily in science we like to think reductively and to think of the properties of macroscopic bodies being determined by the behavior of the microscopic particles of which they are composed. We say, for example, that the pressure and temperature of the gas in a container is determined by the motions of the gas molecules. But we could, if we wish, look at the situation the other way round and say that the kinetic energy of the gas molecules and the frequency of their collisions are determined by the size and shape of the container. As I understand the concept, downward causation refers to the influence of an organized system on the components of that system whether that system be a manmade machine or a living organism. Since the hierarchical principle in nature is ubiquitous, as Koestler (1978) is never tired of reminding us, there is everywhere considerable scope for the operation of downward causation. Popper's own ontology comprises three distinct worlds: "World 1," the world of matter, "World 2," the world of mind, and "World 3," that peculiarly Popperian world of culture and objective knowledge that man has created. Within this ontology there is both upward and downward causation but Popper argues forcibly that we cannot understand human behavior without acknowledging the downward causation on the mechanisms of the brain of both World 2 and World 3.[a]

Since such downward causation is common alike to psychophysical beings like ourselves as well as to inanimate machines like automobiles, we may have to look further afield for a type of causation that characterizes the activities of mind. Fortunately, it may not be necessary to invent a type of causation that has never previously been considered. Instead, we may have to reconsider an idea which science discarded some centuries ago but which, before then, under the influence of Plato and Aristotle, was not merely familiar but was regarded as the supreme expression of causal law, namely teleological or final causation. In the world view which prevailed before the scientific revolution of the 17th century, the behavior of objects, organisms and all natural systems had to be explained primarily in terms of those ends or purposes which represented their natural goal and only secondarily in terms of whatever mechanical forces were acting on them, the extent of whose effect was to make them deviate temporarily from their natural goal.

As we now know, teleological causation was swept away by the scientific revolution along with all the other discredited remnants of Aristotelian science. One obvious objection to the concept from a scientific point of view was that one could never be sure, in advance, what *was* the natural goal which a given system was set to pursue; except, that is, by waiting to see what happened and then it was too late to explain anything except retrospectively, which was of no use to an experimental science. Mechanistic explanation, on the other hand, was soon to prove itself an immensely powerful tool for predicting and controlling the forces of nature. Later a further blow was dealt to teleological causation during the 19th century with the advent of Darwinism.

The ostensible design and purposefulness that is evident in plants and animals could thereafter be viewed as no more than the incidental consequences of a mechanistic process of selection which had eliminated all but those organisms which displayed these adaptive features. Eventually, what appeared to be the coup-de-grâce for teleology was delivered during the present century as a result of the combined assault of behaviorism and cybernetics. Behaviorism is best understood as the attempt to explain the behavior of conscious, intelligent beings using the same sort of terms that would be appropriate to an explanation of the behavior of simple organisms, inanimate systems or machines. Cybernetics furnished behaviorism with its most powerful conceptual tool with its concept of "feedback." What, hitherto, had been taken as indisputable evidence of purpose or intention in human behavior could be reinterpreted in mechanistic terms using the idea of feedback loops and of self-correcting servo-mechanisms. The voluntary behavior of man, though doubtless more subtle and complex, was no different in kind from the behavior of a self-propelled missile or rocket or any other self-steering robot. Since these latter could be understood without recourse to any metaphysical notion such as free will, so ultimately could the former. Thus did the scientific revolution, which began by destroying the anthropomorphic conception of nature, end with the creation of a mechanomorphic conception of man.

But, while the behaviorist and mechanist program makes good enough sense if you believe that having a mind is just an incidental consequence of having a brain and nervous system like ours, if you believe, as I do, that mind has at least *some* degree of autonomy and performs *some* function in the determination of behavior, then you cannot escape such questions as how does, and where does, the mind influence the brain? Eccles, for his part, in this same volume on which he collaborated with Popper, does not flinch from this question and is, indeed, exceedingly bold in speculating both on the locus of the mind-brain interface and on its mode of interaction. Thus, he speaks at one point of the mind acting upon certain critically poised "modules" of cortical cells and of its "modifying the dynamic spatiotemporal patterns of the neural events" (Popper/Eccles 1977, p. 495). But, beyond implying that this is some kind of holistic process, typical of downward causation, he does not, any more than Popper, commit himself to the view that some radically different kind of causal process is involved to anything we find in the rest of nature. It is at this point, I suggest, that we need the concept of teleological causation.

A teleological process may be defined as one that cannot be explained or understood except by reference to the end state of that process. Perhaps the most familiar example that we could take of an ostensibly teleological process in behavior is that of simply raising one's arm. What appears to happen in such a case is that the physiological machinery of the body is set in motion in obedience to a volitional command in order to bring about the state of affairs envisaged by the agent. Now we can, of course, adopt a materialistic interpretation of the case and regard the raising of one's arm as no different from any other physical process except, note, that, for some inexplicable reason, the earliest identifiable stage of the process is accompanied by the subjective experience we call a volition which gives us our illusion of being free agents. We can also adopt what I would call a paramechanical interpretation of the events, that is we could suppose that the mind has complete knowledge of the anatomy and physiology of the body and is able to activate the appropriate neurones at the appropriate moments in order to execute its intentions. But, what I am suggesting as a much more parsimonious and plausible interpretation, is to suppose that it is the volition itself that sets in train the sequence of events and constrains them to produce the intended result by whatever means may be available; in other words, that we are dealing with an irreducibly teleological process. A volition may be ineffective if the means are *not* available; I may intend to raise my arm only to discover that I am in fact paralysed so that nothing ensues. What makes volition teleological in this sense is only that, given the appropriate conditions, it produces an effect which would not otherwise have come about through any purely mechanical causes. To take an analogy from the physical realm, we could, perhaps, think of a volition as like a mold. A mold does not produce anything unless some suitable substance is injected into it but, given these circumstances, the substance is then constrained to take on the form of the mold.

There is much to be said, in my opinion, for the view advocated by William James, a psychologist who thought long and hard about the problem of the will in the days before behaviorism has excised words like "will" from the psychologist's vocabulary as indecent. In James' "ideo-motor theory" of action the main function of the will was to sustain one idea or image in the focus of attention against any countervailing idea or image that might come before the mind. Given this situation, this idea *per se,* James thought, would automatically translate itself into action without requiring any additional fiat of the will (James 1890, chapter 26, section 518). The Jamesian "idea" was thus a pure teleological cause. Curiously, there is a remarkable parallel to this conception in the recent parapsychological literature where Haakon Forwald, perhaps the most successful PK subject on record in tests with dice, offers his own view of the PK process based on his own experience as a subject. He worked specifically on placement tests where the aim is to make the die deviate, to whichever side is designated as target for that trial, when it reaches the bottom of the chute down which it falls. This is what he has to say:

> In order to obtain positive results in a PK experiment, the subject must put himself in a special psychological situation, generally characterized as "willing" or "desiring." According to the author's experiences, however, results can be obtained in other psychological situations. A person with the ability to produce strong mental images of physical events may well succeed in obtaining PK results without relying on the mental capacities *will* and *desire.* This would mean that the mental image

is projected to the physical world outside the subject and produces there a real, meaningful effect. A mental picture which the author has successfully used on many occasions in the actual placement experiments is an imagined wall at the foot of the incline where the cubes roll out on the horizontal plane. The wall is imagined as forming an angle with the moving direction of the cubes so that, when hitting the imagined wall, the cubes would be deflected to the target side of their movement [Forwald 1969, p. 71; italics in original].

I do not think Forwald is asking us to believe, here, that an imaginary wall can take on the mechanical properties of an actual wall; the way I interpret this passage is that the idea of the cubes being deflected to the right, as represented by Forwald's image of the wall, acted as the teleological cause of their swerving to the right.

We are now ready to look again at psi phenomena generally. However, to simplify my task I shall deal only with the case of PK because, although I believe that teleological causation is relevant to an understanding of ESP, it is not usually clear in the case of ESP just what constitutes the cause. Now a typical PK phenomenon may be conceptualized in a number of different possible ways. One of these is what I would call the "paracybernetic model." Suppose that the task in question is to make a die fall with a given face uppermost. We could, if we wished, imagine that we kept track of the orientation of the die as it tumbled down the chute by means of a clairvoyant feedback and that, at the appropriate moments, we put forth ghostly fingers, as it were, so as to impart the requisite PK impulse in order to make it land finally in the right position. However, this model is, in my opinion, grotesquely extravagant in assumptions. Thus, for one thing, unless we had clairvoyant ability far beyond anything we could demonstrate independently this mode of operation would be useless, there would be too much scope for error to allow even for the modest success rate of a good PK scorer. But the model becomes even more grotesque if we move from the macroscopic to the microscopic level and consider what is involved in the electronic type of PK test. Thus, in Schmidt's experiments, where the subject has to influence the output of a random number generator in order to score a hit, it would be necessary to assume that the subject could somehow arrange for the electron, emitted from the radioactive source, to arrive at the Geiger counter at the precise moment when the high-frequency oscillator was in the right phase. No wonder that Schmidt, for one, has abandoned the paracybernetic model in favor of his own teleological theory of PK. As he puts it: "it may be more appropriate to see PK as a goal-oriented principle in the sense that it aims successfully at a final outcome, no matter how intricate the intermediate steps are" (Schmidt 1974, p. 272).

Schmidt prefers to talk of a "goal-oriented principle" rather than of a "teleological cause," as I have been doing, perhaps because, being a physicist, he tends to think of causality as equivalent to physical causality and hence wrongly assumes that a goal-oriented principle must be noncausal, but I do not think that anything more here is involved than a question of semantics. What *is* important is that Schmidt has designed and carried out a successful experiment specifically to throw light on the nature of teleological causation (Schmidt 1974a). Briefly, what happened in this experiment is that two different types of RNG were involved, the one based on a relatively simple circuit diagram, the other a more complex design. However, the subject knew nothing about the electronic equipment used which was even housed in a separate room. All that the subject had to go by was the feedback display which, in this instance, consisted simply of two lamps of different color, the one representing a hit, the other a miss. His instructions were just to increase the frequency of the hit-lamp coming on relative to the frequency of the miss-lamp. PK was implied inasmuch as there were no normal ways by which this could be done. Now, trials on which the feedback display was controlled by the simple RNG were randomly and automatically alternated with trials on which the complex RNG was operative. Some 35 subjects participated in the confirmatory test and the results were as follows. Although scoring on those trials on which the simpler RNG was operative was slightly higher than the scoring on those trials on which the more complex RNG was operative, there was no significant difference between the two, both conditions yielding highly significant deviations from chance with scoring rates of around 54 percent as against a 50 percent baseline.

This crucial experiment was carried out in 1973 and, unfortunately, I know of no subsequent work that has been done to confirm it. But Schmidt's findings are very much in accord with the earlier research with dice where it transpired that using a multiplicity of dice or similar target objects did not depress the rate of scoring. All such evidence supports the teleological model which assumes that, so long as the means are available, the same end will be attained no matter how complex those means, but it contradicts the para-cybernetic model which would predict that an increase in the information load should lower the rate of success.

Schmidt has attempted to formulate his model in terms of what he calls his "mathematical theory of psi" (Schmidt 1975). What is critical in this conceptualization of PK is the feedback received by a motivated subject or "psi source" as Schmidt would have it. It is only at the point where the subject obtains confirmation of success that the psi process is activated and, tracing back events to the start of the experiment, these can then be shown to follow a teleological course to produce in the end the very results whose observation constitutes the feedback. Schmidt goes further and extends his theory to all instances of psi, all of which now become a species of PK. Precognition, for example, is no longer a case of the future fulfilling event causing a present precognitive response in the subject, rather it is now a question of the observation of that event, when this eventually comes to pass, retroactively and psychokinetically eliciting the precognitive response from the subject's brain which, in Schmidt's model, here corresponds to a random number generator.

Schmidt has repeatedly insisted that his theory is a mathematical or formal one and he is understandably cagey about allowing any concrete interpretation of that theory, he has even expressed reluctance to acknowledge the expression "retro–PK" (1975, p. 227). However, if we are to take what he is saying as anything more than a pure formalism and try to give it intuitive meaning, there is no escaping the conclusion that what is being implied here is that psi is not just teleological in its operation but also retroactive. For, since the process cannot get started until the outcome is known, the only effect it can produce is a retroactive one. Thus, when Schmidt uses a set of prerecorded digits as the PK target sequence, a successful run *means* that when the subject, or psi source, becomes aware of his score he thereupon influences retroactively the random number generator which originally recorded those digits!

However well shrouded in mathematical symbols, this is, without doubt, a fantastic theory. Why, we may well wonder, should anyone wish to hold it? The reason, it turns out, is both empirical and theoretical. The chief empirical grounds, apart from Schmidt's own experiments, is the discovery of the so-called "psi experimenter effect." It has become increasingly clear that, when all normal explanations have been eliminated, certain individual experimenters tend consistently to get positive results, no matter what hypothesis they test, while others no less consistently obtain only chance results. Now, if we posit a retroactive effect at the point where the experimenter inspects his data and if, further, we assume that some experimenters are natural psi sources, then this psi experimenter effect becomes intelligible. For now it is the experimenter or "checker," not the ostensible subjects, who is responsible for the success of the experiment by retroactively and teleologically getting his subjects to produce whatever scoring pattern his hypothesis has predicted.

The main theoretical reason for introducing this kind of retroactive theory of psi has to do with quantum physics and, more particularly, with the so-called Copenhagen interpretation of quantum theory. While this aspect of the problem clearly weighed with Schmidt when he came to formulate his mathematical model, it is made much more explicit in the work of Walker (1975) and his followers. Leaving aside the equations and technicalities, the point of departure for these theorists was the quantum-theoretical assumption that a given physical event or state acquires a determinate value only when it has been observed. So long as the object in question is *not* being observed, all that quantum theory can say about it is that it obeys the Schrödinger equations and exists simultaneously in a range of possible states, each associated with its respective probability, the totality representing what is known as the "state vector." Only when the critical measurement or observation is eventually made do we get a collapse of the state vector giving us the one determinate outcome or result of the experiment. So long as we are dealing with neutral observers everything proceeds as in conventional physics. If, however, we introduce an observer who happens also to be a psi source and is motivated to obtain one rather than another outcome of the experiment, then we get the systematic bias which we interpret as a significant psi score. Thus, theoretically, a paranormal event is no more than a highly improbable event brought about by the psi source who can modify the distribution of probabilities defining the state vector. On this showing, PK does not act like a physical force, rather it is, as Schmidt points out (1975a, p. 226), a stochastic phenomenon that "violates the second law of thermodynamics without violating the conservation laws for energy etc." Since virtually every physical object in nature exhibits at the microscopic level a certain fuzziness or noisiness, there is always ample scope for PK providing that object is coupled with a motivated psi source which feeds information into the system.

Following Schouten (1977), I shall use the expression "observational theory of psi" indifferently for all such theories as those of Schmidt and Walker in which feedback is critical for the psi process. It represents an entirely new theoretical approach to parapsychology and whatever it portends there can be no doubt of the strong attraction it has already had for such experimentalists of the new generation as Richard Mattuck, Brian Millar or Richard Broughton. The reasons for this appeal are not hard to seek. In the first place this approach holds out the promise of linking parapsychology with advances in quantum physics and thereby ending its long isolation as an unattached and anomalous field of inquiry. In the second place it offers, perhaps for the very first time in parapsychological history, the possibility of precise, deductive, quantitative predictions. For example, we could deduce that the noisier the target system the more sensitive it should be to a PK effect. Admittedly there are still some awkward implications that need sorting out, for example the so-called "divergence problem" raises the question of who is to count as the ultimate observer? Until this question is settled we cannot even know when an experiment is concluded. But the theorists are actively struggling with such questions and we must give them time.

As a mere layman, I can, of course, offer no opinion as to the soundness of such theories, whether, for example, they represent a legitimate extension of quantum theory, whether Walker (1974) is justified in identifying consciousness and will as hidden variables of the quantum process, and so on. But, even as a layman, there are certain logical aspects of the observational theory that I find disconcerting and to which I feel justified in drawing attention. Now, as I have argued elsewhere (see the preceding paper in this volume) there is no fundamental objection, that I can see, despite what some philosophers have said, to the idea of backward causation *per se*, hence I have no *a priori* objection to its apparent circularity. Such circularity exists already in connection with the so-called intervention paradox in precognition. Thus, if an accident about which I have dreamt should occur because of certain steps which I took in consequence of my dream, we would have a typical self-fulfilling prophecy while, equally, if the accident is avoided only because of certain steps

I took in consequence of my dream, we would have a typical self-defeating prophecy. In either case we become involved in what I would call a causal loop, in this instance an event A (the accident) retroactively causes an earlier event B (the precognitive dream) which, in turn, becomes a causal ancestor of the original event A; of, even more paradoxically, in the negative example, becomes the causal ancestor of an event not-A. What, on the face of it, we appear here to be saying is that an event may be indirectly the cause of itself or even the cause of its own nonexistence! Various more or less far-fetched theories have been advanced in order to deal with the paradox of intervention including the idea of multiple universes and potential futures. But while we may have to resign ourselves to living with paradoxes in the case of precognition, the price we are being asked to pay by the protagonists of observational theory is to have to tolerate such paradoxes in every case where psi is involved since, whether it be an instance of ESP or PK that we are considering, we are confronted with an event A, the feedback event, influencing an earlier event B, the psi response, which in turn, eventually produces the event A. The theorists themselves do not appear to be specially worried by these consequences of their theories; Schmidt (1975), for example, claims that his mathematical formalism can take care of the intervention paradox, but whether we, their customers, ought to be so unconcerned, I am less sure. Even if, from the formal point of view, there are no inconsistencies in their theories, we still have a duty to try and make sense of it all intuitively. Hence, while I would hesitate to proclaim that what I have been calling causal loops are logically inadmissible, in the way, for example, that self-referring statements are logically improper, they are, to say the least, troublesome.[b]

Finally, on the assumption that a psi effect is involved in normal voluntary action, can the observational theory be extended to cover this situation as well? This would mean that my capacity to raise my arm when I will to do so depends not only on the intention, volition or Jamesian "idea" which can translate itself into motor responses, plus a muscular system that is in working order, but also on my subsequent perception of my arm as having risen. At first it struck me that such an interpretation of what was involved in every voluntary action was altogether too far-fetched and implausible to be worth defending. However, when I came to try and formulate specific objections to it, I found that none of them stood up to examination. Hence, rather than sacrifice the symmetry between normal and paranormal action, or PK, I am inclined to think that if the observational interpretation is valid in the latter case, it must be valid in the former case also. What complicates the issue, where ordinary voluntary behavior is concerned, is that it is a continuous process involving a continual feedback cycle between output and input. When we perform some skilled action, such as writing a word, for example, there is a constant visual and kinesthetic monitoring of the action from start to finish. Certain skilled actions, it is true, are executed so swiftly that such continuous feedback is not theoretically possible and accordingly they are presumably simply run off from a preprogrammed sequence—piano playing would come into this category—but the point is that all our perceptuo-motor skills *can* be understood in terms of the accepted principles of cybernetic control. At what point, then, would the intervention of mind, in the form of a volitional act, take effect?

It is here, above all, that we have to distinguish between ends and means. Behavior consists very largely of automatizing our habitual skills so that our conscious attention can be directed towards the novel contingencies in life that call for special decision-making. Raising an arm is a case in point, so is walking towards a chosen destination. We have schooled our body in the past to execute such performances like a well-programmed cybernetic robot. All that we then require is to initiate, or, in the case of a repetitive or extended sequence of movements, to sustain the relevant process which then automatically unfolds in a self-regulating way. The teleological element in all this would enter only at the higher level of control which supervenes to make the whole performance an intentional action as opposed to a mechanical routine.

To sum up what I have been saying in this paper, I would make the following points:

(1) Psi phenomena, properly so called, are causal phenomena although this fact neither asserts nor denies the possibility that there may also be acausal or "synchronistic" phenomena such as meaningful coincidences.

(2) Causality may be either mechanical or teleological. Psychic causation is teleological in its mode of operation, that is to say psychic phenomena can be understood *only* in terms of the ends which they are designed to bring about.

(3) The observational theory of psi, which has only recently been propounded, implies that psychic causation is both teleological *and* retroactive in its effect. It is too soon to say whether this new theory of psi will be vindicated by further experimental work but, if it is, then for the first time since the demise of Aristotelian science, we would have an acceptable scientific theory which uses the notion of an irreducibly teleological cause for explanatory purposes.

(4) I have suggested that the explanation of PK cannot be divorced from an understanding of normal voluntary action. Both involve teleological causation at the point where mind intervenes in an otherwise physical process.

Notes

a. I have elsewhere discussed this work in a review article I wrote for The British Journal for the Philosophy of Science *under the title "Is Mind Autonomous?" (Beloff 1977).*

b. The debate continues: Stephen Braude (1979), in his article in J.A.S.P.R.,

"The Observational Theories in Parapsychology: A Critique," presents a rigorous formal analysis of the causal loop paradox. Recently, however, he has been challenged by Brian Millar, a well known exponent of observational theory. See Millar (1988) "Cutting the Braudian Loop: In Defense of the Observational Theories" and Braude's (1988) rejoinder, "Death by Observation: A Reply to Millar."

Voluntary Movement, Biofeedback Control and PK

The focus of my interest in the paranormal has always been its implications for the mind-body problem. According to the conventional standpoint, the only physical effects we can produce are those we exert on our own bodies as mediated through the voluntary nervous system. An exception might have to be made to allow for the ancient technique of yoga whereby an adept could acquire control over various physiological processes normally regarded as outside voluntary effort. Recently the technique of biofeedback has demonstrated that anyone can gain control over their autonomic nervous system by this means without resorting to the arduous discipline of yoga. Whether a psi factor is or is not involved in such biofeedback control is open to question but at least it offers an intermediate category between normal motor activity and a genuine PK *performance.*

Once again it was the Parapsychology Foundation that provided me with a forum when they invited me to participate in a conference on "Brain/Mind and Parapsychology" (Parapsychology Foundation 1979) in Montreal in August 1978. As was customary at their conferences, the occasion brought together leading figures of the parapsychology community with eminent scientists and scholars who had made their names in other fields. The former category here include such familiar names as Charles Honorton, Charles Tart and Edward Kelly, the latter include Thomas Budzynski (an authority on biofeedback), Norman Dixon (the authority on subliminal perception), Jan Ehrenwald and Karl Pribram.

The question I want to raise in this paper is the following: Is the power which enables us to influence the target system in a PK experiment the same power, basically, as that which we deploy every time we voluntarily move our limbs (using the word "power" in its most general and noncommittal sense)?

100

Or, in other words, can PK be regarded as the extrasomatic (and hence paranormal) extension of what, in ordinary volitional activity, is endosomatic (and hence normal)? The question was first explicitly raised, I believe, by Thouless and Wiesner (1947) in their classic paper, where they also put forward the idea that ESP is the extrasomatic extension of what occurs in normal perception and cognition where the mind extracts information from the brain to create a meaningful conscious percept or thought. Here, however, we shall be concerned exclusively with the problem of PK. If the answer to this question is no, if the Thouless-Wiesner thesis is mistaken, then, presumably, PK represents some special power or faculty that is *sui generis* and radically different from anything else that forms part of our ordinary mental life. The question is, I consider, worth raising again both because of the light it may throw on the nature of PK and because of its implications for the mind-body problem.

At first it may seem that there is little to commend the analogy. In the first place, whereas voluntary movement is a universal fact of life, PK is an exceedingly rare and dubious phenomenon, at any rate insofar as it can be demonstrated experimentally. Secondly, the amount of conscious control that can be exerted in the case of PK is almost nil.[a] This is so even in those exceptional cases of directly observable or macro–PK effects, where objects move or metals bend. Indeed, it may be doubted whether we can rightly speak of "willing" in connection with PK. At most the subject can *wish* for a certain result to come about, but there is not much he can then specifically do to *make* it come about. In the case of RSPK phenomena even the conscious wish may be absent, so that it is only by a process of elimination and inference that we identify a particular individual as the subject or "poltergeist focus." In view of these obvious differences between voluntary movement and PK many would wish to argue that there was nothing to be gained by pressing the analogy and subsuming both under the same rubric.

Nevertheless, in spite of such asymmetries, there are important respects in which the two processes resemble one another. In the first place, they are both goal-oriented or teleological-type processes, in the sense that a given state of affairs is achieved without there being any awareness on anyone's part as to the precise means necessary for such an achievement to be possible. Thus, when I stretch out my hand to pick up an object off the table, I know nothing at all about the sequence of physiological events starting in the motor cortex of my brain and leading up to the contraction of muscle groups in my arm and fingers that must precede any action on my part. But, even with regard to the overt movements which I then proceed to execute, I am largely dependent on a stock of tacit knowledge which never enters my focal awareness. In much the same way, the successful PK subject becomes aware of the results which he produces while remaining totally ignorant of the microprocesses, mechanical or electronic, which must take place in the target system for such results to be possible. In the second place, voluntary movement and PK are intimately bound up with the provision of feedback. Our muscles are not just effectors but also receptors, so that with every contraction of the muscles there is some proprioceptive feedback and, at least in the case of the manipulatory skills we perform with our fingers, there is usually some visual feedback as well, although touch typing would be an exception. To what extent PK is dependent on the visual or auditory feedback that is usually provided by the experimental set-up is still a matter for speculation, but, for one school of thought, at any rate, that represented by the influential "observational theories" of PK associated with such theorists as Helmut Schmidt and Evans Walker, it is critical. According to these theories, it is not until feedback is received that the train of events leading up to the observed outcome is determined. This implies, paradoxically, a causal loop in time between aiming at a given result and observing its realization. Whether a similar "observational theory" of voluntary movement is conceivable is not a question I shall pursue here, as it would take me too far afield. In the present context I want only to stress that feedback enters into both voluntary movement and PK in this integral way in virtually every instance that we can cite.

I am going to suggest that we may be able to arrive at a better understanding of the connection between voluntary movement and PK if we look at an intermediate class of phenomena which partakes of some of the characteristics of each. It is here I wish to introduce the topic of biofeedback control. We can now demonstrate that people can acquire control over certain physiological functions which, in the ordinary way, are beyond conscious control by adopting certain special techniques. The functions in question are mainly those associated with the autonomic nervous system, heart-rate, vasodilation, glandular secretion etc. but may include functions of the central nervous system such as brain rhythms and measures of arousal. There is one function, rate of breathing, which ordinarily operates automatically, but which can be consciously controlled without using any special technique, but here I shall be concerned only with those where a special training is required. There are a variety of such special techniques, the oldest of which are the systems of yoga, but the one with which I shall be concerned is that known as biofeedback, which is based on allowing the subject to monitor his own physiological output through appropriate visual or auditory displays.

Biofeedback is a normal phenomenon, in the sense that it does not, as far as is known, transcend any limits of what is considered within the natural capacity of the nervous system. Moreover, anyone can acquire a moderate degree of proficiency in biofeedback control; no special ability is presupposed. At the same time, from the psychological point of view, there are important respects in which the phenomenon resembles PK. I am thinking especially of its dependence on what Elmer Green (1976) has called "passive volition." One cannot produce a biofeedback effect, as one might the raising of one's arm, by a simple fiat of the will. Rather, one has to want the effect to come about and wait hopefully, in a half expectant yet relaxed frame of mind, for it to appear spontaneously. This is notoriously the case with the control of alpha rhythm, for it is one of the paradoxes of the biofeedback technique that alpha rhythm will vanish if the subject makes a conscious effort to produce it! There is a parallel here with the finding that the best scores in a PK test are often obtained when the subject is least trying to produce them. Rex Stanford coined the expression "release of effort" to cover cases in which significant scores are obtained by the subject after the termination of the official run when, unknown to the subject, the target generator is kept going. But others too, have noted that a state of relaxation is conducive to success. Thouless and Wiesner suggested that this might be due to the fact that active volition would have the effect of channeling the influence directed onto the target system back into the subject's own motor system.

Certainly, at a purely formal level, there is a striking similarity between the typical biofeedback set-up and the PK set-up as this has been developed especially by Helmut Schmidt and has since become standard laboratory practice. Of course, objectively, there is a world of difference, depending on whether the feedback display is coupled with the subject's own body, as with biofeedback, or with an electronic random event generator, as with PK, but this does not preclude the possibility that the same basic phenomenon underlies both. And this possibility begins to loom larger when we venture beyond biofeedback studies of the routine kind to consider certain virtuoso performances by those who, in one way or another, have learned to control their own organism. Take, for example, such performers as Swami Rama or Jack Schwarz, to name but two who have both been tested in some depth at the Menninger Institute. Swami Rama has demonstrated differential control over the arteries of his right hand to the extent of producing changes of temperature in opposite directions on two spots of his right palm only a few inches apart amounting to a differential of about 10°F. He has also demonstrated control of his heart beat to the extent of completely arresting the circulation of his blood for as much as 17 seconds, having been dissuaded from prolonging the effect (Green et al., 1976). Jack Schwarz, a Dutch-American who belongs by rights to the Indian fakir tradition, has, for his part, demonstrated feats of self-wounding which not only fail to elicit any pain reaction or even any bleeding but, more surprisingly still, the wound never becomes infected no matter how severe or how soiled the implement used (Rorvik 1976). It is, further, of interest to learn that both Swami Rama and Jack Schwarz are credited with special powers of self-healing of a kind that psychic healers are supposed to be able to exert on an alien body.

But, to return to biofeedback proper, I want next to discuss one particular study which is linked with the problem of voluntary movement and to which Honorton (1976) drew our attention in his presidential address to the Parapsychological Association in 1975. I refer to the electromyographic experiments of John Basmajian (1972) as reported in *Science*. His experiments consisted of training his subjects to activate specific motor units within certain selected skeletal muscles; he used mainly the forearm, shoulder and neck muscles. His subjects were given both visual and auditory feedback of the varying myoelectric potential in the specific motor unit in question as recorded by means of microelectrodes planted in the muscle fiber. It transpired that any normal volunteer subject could, within a few minutes, learn to control the appropriate unit. From then on he could be taught increasingly difficult discriminations, for example activating one given unit rather than another neighboring unit, varying at will the rate at which it was firing and, finally, being able to control it even in the absence of any exteroceptive feedback. To quote the author: "Some persons can be trained to gain control of isolated motor units to such a degree that, with both visual and aural cues shut off, they can recall any one of three favorite units on command and in any sequence. They can keep such units firing without any conscious awareness other than the assurance (after the fact) that they have succeeded. In spite of considerable introspection they cannot explain their success except to state they thought about a motor unit as though they had seen and heard it personally."

This is an unusual application of the biofeedback technique, inasmuch as the effect involved is not some involuntary autonomic function, but rather a highly specific component of our ordinary voluntary motor activity. Ordinarily, all that we are able to do, voluntarily, is to control the gross movements of our limbs, but, after a Basmajian type training, we can, it seems, turn on or off at will the firing of a single motor unit. We have no idea how we do this any more than we know how we succeed in wagging a given finger. All we know, in both instances, is that, by taking thought, we can bring about the desired effect. The relevance of the Basmajian work for our present purposes is that it shows how, at the microscopic level of analysis, voluntary movement and biofeedback control converge.

I want next to discuss a very different experiment which attempts, rather, to bring together biofeedback control and PK. This is an experiment of William Braud's which he reported at the 1977 P.A. Convention where he introduced his intriguing concept of "allobiofeedback." It is evident that any biofeedback set-up could be converted into a PK set-up by the simple expedient of coupling the feedback display to another person's body in place of the subject's own body. In Braud's experiment he himself acted as subject and his task was alternatively to increase or decrease, according to a random schedule of instructions, the GSR amplitude of a target-person whose GSR tracing he was meanwhile monitoring. The design of the experiment was a very complicated one, inasmuch as the target-persons were themselves acting as subjects with respect to a test involving clairvoyance and relaxation, but these complications need not detain us here. Suffice it to say that the allobiofeedback test was successful in that, out of the ten target-persons involved in the confirmation experiment, eight produced higher GSR amplitudes during those runs in which Braud was aiming to increase them and that a t-test of the difference between the two conditions was significant at the one percent level of confidence. Discussing his findings, Braud claims that the concept of allobiofeedback is the simplest way of conceptualizing the situation; in other words that what we have here is a feedback loop that is closed by a PK influence directed onto a live target system. As is always the case, however, in a parapsychological experiment, there is enough ambiguity in the situation to permit other interpretations. As he points out, the results could have been due to a telepathic influence that he might have been exerting on the target-person's mind rather than on his body and even more devious interpretations are possible that we need not pursue here.

At all events, before the concept of allobiofeedback becomes established, several pertinent factors call for clarification. First, how critical was the provision of feedback in this instance? Could the subject have influenced the activity of the target-persons had he *not* been monitoring their output? It is noteworthy that, in another experiment by Braud and Braud reported at the same Convention, PK effects on a random event generator were obtained in the absence of feedback. Secondly, is a live target-system such as this a more sensitive detector of PK than an inanimate random event generator? On the Thouless-Wiesner hypothesis that PK is essentially the power we normally use to control our own brain, we should expect this to be the case, since one brain is more like another than it is like an electronic machine.[b] However, since the great majority of PK experiments have been done with artificial target-systems we have little basis for comparison. There may even be a flaw in the argument which would lead us to expect better results from a live target-system since, if we adopt an observational theory of psi, it would make no difference in the last resort what processes were involved in the production of a given PK effect; all that counts is the final awareness of the effect that has been produced. Whatever the outcome may be, we must hope that many more allobiofeedback experiments will be forthcoming in the years ahead. It would be of particular interest to take a subject who had first mastered autobiofeedback control and switch him without warning to the allobiofeedback condition. Would there be a carry-over from the normal to the paranormal condition? Would he proceed to control both his own and the target-person's output in unison? Or would conflicting exteroceptive and interoceptive feedback make such a deception impossible, so that the experiment would founder with the subject in a state of total confusion?

Leaving such questions unanswered, let us revert to the familiar case of normal volitional activity. We must start by recognizing that, according to the orthodox view that still prevails alike in science and philosophy, there is, strictly speaking, no such thing as a volition. The distinction between voluntary behavior on the one hand and involuntary, automatic or reflex behavior on the other, depends on the kind of brain processing that goes on, not on whether such behavior is, or is not, preceded by, or accompanied by, an "act of will," whatever we are to understand by that phrase. For, ultimately, in the orthodox view, it is the brain alone which governs the activity of the limbs. The organism as a whole may be conceived of as a self-regulating cybernetic machine and the interaction of the organism and its environment constitutes a closed physical loop which admits of no extraneous influences and interventions of a nonphysical kind. As for the familiar experience of free will on which we humans set such store, the experience of acting freely according to conscious decisions for which we as persons or selves take sole responsibility, that is no more than a subjective or epiphenomenal reflection of whatever physical brain states are the real causes of our behavior.

One notable brain physiologist of recent times who has never accepted this orthodox view of voluntary movement is Sir John Eccles, who gave the invited address to the P.A. Convention in Utrecht in 1976 (Eccles 1977). Already in his Waynflete lectures in Oxford in 1952 (Eccles 1953), that were later published as *The Neurophysiological Basis of Mind,* he shocked the scientific and philosophical establishment, which were particularly well entrenched at Oxford, by putting forward what he has called his "neurophysiological hypothesis of will." This is based on the observation that the situation at the synapse through which the neural impulse must pass is so delicately poised that factors at the level of quantum uncertainty may decide whether the impulse is discharged or not. In such a situation, a psychic influence might tilt the balance one way or the other since, whether or not there is a ghost in the machine, the brain appears to be just the kind of machine that a ghost might be expected to operate! Furthermore, given the prodigious interconnectedness of our brain cells, even one such intervention might produce an appreciable effect on the overall output of the brain or, as he puts it (Eccles 1970): "within 20 milliseconds the pattern of discharge of even hundreds of thousands of neurones would be modified as the result of an 'influence' that initially caused the discharge of merely one neurone." But there is no need to stop there. The same mind influence could conceivably operate holistically by exerting spatio-temporal "fields of influence" on the cortex, which would be uniquely fitted to respond. It is of some interest to note, in passing, that, more than a century before, the great physiologist, Johannes Müller, had proposed a very similar conception of the will when he declared that: "the fibers of all the motor, cerebral and spinal nerves may be imagined spread out in the medulla oblongata and exposed to the influence of the will like the keys of the pianoforte."

Recently Eccles joined forces with the philosopher Karl Popper and last year the two of them published a large volume entitled *The Self and Its Brain* which bore the subtitle *An Argument for Interactionism* (Popper & Eccles 1977). In his section of this book, Eccles further elaborates, with plentiful anatomical detail, his ideas about the interaction between what it pleases him to call "the self-conscious mind" and the "liaison brain." The latter, he speculates, consists of complex modules of neurones in columnar formation, each module comprising some 10,000 neurons including many hundreds of pyramidal cells. In his chapter on "Voluntary Movement," Eccles draws attention to the work of H.H. Kornhuber, a German neurophysiologist, which, he claims, illustrates in its purest form the action of mind on brain. Essentially, what Kornhuber did was to get his subject, who had first been carefully trained to maintain a relaxed posture, to wag his right index finger at irregular intervals, entirely of his own volition, when care had been taken to exclude any possible triggering stimulus from the environment. While he was doing this, certain electrical potentials were recorded from various sites on the subject's scalp and these were then averaged over some 250 recordings. The resultant curve revealed a concentration of neuronal activity in the pyramidal cells of the motor cortex occurring at about 1/20th sec. before the muscular response, an interval which, as Eccles points out, is just about adequate for transmission of the impulse from the pyramidal cells down to the muscle fibers in the finger. This, then, provides at least a partial answer to the question of what goes on in the brain when a willed action is in process of being carried out. The more searching question is whether it provides evidence of the action of mind on brain.

Eccles repeatedly insists that it does, although he realizes that the upholders of the orthodox view will be reluctant to admit it. They will argue that, when the subject receives his instructions, the brain, like a computer, stores the information and duly programs the subject to emit the required response at irregular intervals. But Eccles will have none of this. "The stringent conditions of the Kornhuber experiment," he insists, "preclude or negate such explanatory claims. The trained subjects literally do make the movements in the absence of any determining influences from the environment and any random potentials generated by the relaxed brain would be virtually eliminated by the averaging of 250 traces." He concludes, therefore, that: "we can regard these experiments as providing a convincing demonstration that voluntary movements can be freely initiated independently of any determining influences that are entirely within the neuronal machinery of the brain" (1977, p. 294).

I think I need hardly say that not even the authority of an Eccles, nor yet the argumentative skill of a Popper, is likely to make much impact on the committed materialist. It is significant, however, that neither Eccles nor Popper is prepared to avail himself of the parapsychological evidence and bring it to bear on the issue, indeed neither is yet willing to acknowledge the existence of PK. Eccles, at one point, expresses some surprise that the activity of the "self-conscious mind" should be limited to a single individual brain, but he never pauses to consider whether this is indeed always, and necessarily, the case.

Thus, much as I admire these two great men for doing battle on behalf of the autonomy of mind, I consider that their case is weaker than it might be for lack of this crucial prop and that, if, for our part, we can place the evidence for PK on a footing where it can no longer be ignored by official science, we shall succeed in clinching the argument in favor of treating voluntary movement as an expression of free will.

I have tried, in this paper, to show that the assumption that PK is a form of volitional activity directed onto the outside world has implications for the philosophy of mind and, conversely, the dualistic view of the mind-body relationship has implications for the study of PK. However, as I am always being reminded by my more experimentally minded associates, a theory is no use unless its implications are testable and so, in what remains of my time, I want to say a few words about the sort of lines along which such tests might hopefully be conducted, even if I cannot as yet be very explicit. If I am correct in thinking that in PK we use the same basic means to influence the target-system as normally we use to control the brain, then two possibilities suggest themselves. Either we might try preventing the subject from exercising normal voluntary movement hoping that, in desperation, he will be driven to exteriorize his powers in the form of PK or, alternatively, we could arouse the subject's normal volitional activities in such a way that the powers involved will spill over onto the target system. As it happens, support can be found in favor of each of these possibilities in the existing literature. With respect to PK of the microscopic or statistical kind, I have already mentioned the importance of adopting an attitude of passive volition suggesting, perhaps, that PK might here function as a substitute for normal voluntary effort. In that case, it may be worth testing those who either happen to be paralyzed or could be experimentally made so and would thus be physically debarred from control of their limbs, but it might also be worth seeing what happens to a random event generator during the REM stage of sleep when we are all of us paralyzed. However, with respect to PK of the macroscopic or directly observable kind, the evidence suggests that the successful subjects are usually in a state of high arousal. This was specially the case with Nina Kulagina, but even with a physical medium like Rudi Schneider, who was in a complete trance when he produced his phenomena, it was observed that both his breathing and heart rate underwent an astonishing acceleration. If this "spill-over" model of PK should prove more appropriate in certain circumstances we would have to find ways of arousing the subject.

While I was still engaged in speculating on these possibilities for research, I was happy to learn that Charles Honorton had been thinking along rather similar lines and had, indeed, already carried out some pioneering work in this connection which had yielded positive results. His particular strategy (as described in a paper he is presenting at this conference; Parapsychology Foundation 1979) was to use biofeedback in order to train his subjects to control their alpha rhythm. A random event generator is then brought into play and the experimenter finds out whether its output is significantly biased from the random baseline during the critical phases when control of the alpha rhythm is achieved. Honorton's experiments, which have already provided some promising data, are based on a rationale that is somewhat different from either the substitution model or the spill-over model that I discussed earlier. Presumably, like me, Honorton was impressed with the similarities he had observed as between the biofeedback situation and the PK situation and took this as his point of departure. But, be that as it may, he has added a further impetus towards searching for a common thread uniting the phenomena of voluntary movement, biofeedback control and PK.

Notes

a. In the course of the subsequent discussion, Tart pointed out that one of the reasons for this difference is that normal voluntary movement has obvious survival value and is practiced intensively from the cradle onwards whereas, in the case of PK, *the whole ethos of our culture is against trying to foster it. Tart may well be right but, to clinch the argument, we would need the example of at least one society where* PK *was successfully inculcated.*

b. William Braud has coined the expression "bio–PK" for the case where PK *is exerted on living organisms. One can say that most of the research he has carried out since he moved to the Mind Science Foundation in San Antonio, Texas, has been concerned with the bio–*PK *effect (see Braud and Schlitz 1983). The allobiofeedback experiment can be seen as a special instance of bio-*PK *and it has obvious implications for the question of paranormal healing. As an example of their latest work, see "A Methodology for the Objective Study of Transpersonal Imagery" by William Braud and Marilyn Schlitz,* Journal of Scientific Exploration 3, 1989, 43–63.

Is Normal Memory
a "Paranormal" Phenomenon?

It is not only parapsychologists who challenge the mechanistic explana-
tion of mental activity. There exists an influential school of thought, of which
Wittgenstein was the most renowned exponent, which does so likewise though
for quite different reasons. While I recognize the importance of Ludwig Witt-
genstein in the history of 20th century philosophy and his outstanding
originality as a thinker, I have never been attracted by his style of philoso-
phizing and have found unenlightening the work of his disciples and ex-
positors.

In this paper I consider the nature of memory and I go into action on two
fronts: against those neuroscientists who claim that memory can be fully and
satisfactorily explained with reference to brain processes and against those
linguistic philosophers who claim that memory is not the sort of thing that re-
quires an explanation in the first place. I argue here that, while memory
depends on a suitably functioning brain, the process of recall suggests that the
brain is being activated teleologically by a mind or self for its own ends. The
paper is based on a talk I gave at the Fourth International Conference of the
S.P.R. at Brighton, in April 1980.

The paradox of my title arises as follows. We use the word "normal" in
two different ways. We say of some fact or occurrence that it was normal meaning that there was nothing strange or unusual about it, it was just what we
would have expected. In this usage it is more or less synonymous with "ordinary" or the opposite of "extraordinary" or "abnormal." In parapsychology,
however, "normal" is used in opposition to "paranormal." Now I do not think
"paranormal" can be defined at all precisely but it carries with it the implication that the event in question cannot, even in principle, be explained in
mechanistic terms so that there exists, as it were, an explanatory gap between

cause and effect. Thus, ESP is said to be a paranormal phenomenon precisely because, when a given object is apprehended by ESP, there appears to be a hiatus in the causal chain of events connecting the object and the percipient unlike the situation in normal perception.

Now there can surely be no fact of life more familiar, more commonplace, more normal in one sense, than memory. Hence, in asking whether normal memory mght be a *para*normal phenomenon, I am asking, in effect, whether it is possible in principle to give a mechanistic explanation for the facts of memory. Well, what is to stop us? We may not be able as yet to supply the details but why should we doubt what everyone already takes for granted that what happens when something is said to be remembered is roughly along the following lines. An individual undergoes a certain experience in consequence of which his brain or nervous system is modified in some more or less specific way. This modification or "trace," to give it its technical name, then persists indefinitely until, in due course, it is reactivated by some appropriate stimulus with which it is linked. When this occurs some appropriate response is elicited which we describe as a manifestation of memory.

Of course the word "memory" covers a wide variety of diverse cases. In the simplest case we have some learned response which, though caused by some earlier experience, conveys no reference to that earlier occasion. With every word we utter we manifest memory in this sense though we may never actually remember when we learned the word originally. Very different is the case we naturally think of as typifying memory, at least in humans, which implies a certain thinking about or bringing to mind some particular episode of our past life. Memory in the first sense is a universal property of animal life but memory in this second sense is presumably a uniquely human achievement inasmuch as it would seem to necessitate the use of language or at least a capacity for conceptual thinking. In the literature it is sometimes referred to as "personal" or "episodic" memory. Bergson (1911) called it "true memory" and contrasted it with "habit memory" which was simply the residue of our learning. For the moment, however, the distinction is unimportant because the point I want to make is that, according to all but universal assumptions that currently prevail among both scientists and laymen, *no* manifestation of memory of whatever description would be possible unless certain specific traces in the brain were duly reactivated. It is this assumption that I shall be calling the "trace theory of memory" though, in fact, it is usually something we simply take for granted rather than think of as an explicit theory. The question we must now ask is whether we have any good reason to doubt it?

One could, of course, produce a case for skepticism by raising the sort of objections that are so often directed against parapsychology, namely that investigations have been going on for a very long time and yet there is still so little by way of positive proof, the traces remain obdurately hypothetical. In both cases, however, it would be foolish to build too much on the basis of a mere lack of progress. The brain, as we are always being reminded, is the most complex organ in the universe in terms of the sheer multiplicity of its interconnections, is it any wonder that our knowledge of it is still so sketchy? However, recently, an attack on trace theory has been pursued by a group of philosophers who base their case, not on such empirical grounds, but on conceptual and semantic considerations. It is *not,* they argue, that we still lack even the foggiest idea as to how experiences might be encoded and stored in the brain or how they might be decoded and retrieved as the need arises, it *is* that the very notion that memory could be explained in this way rests on an inadequate analysis of what memory involves. Trace theory, they claim, is not just another speculative hypothesis that could conceivably be correct but happens to be mistaken, it is a radical absurdity that just cannot be formulated in any way that makes sense.

I must at once hasten to add that these same philosophers do not conclude that, because there can be no mechanistic explanation of memory, therefore memory must be regarded as a paranormal phenomenon, indeed they would be aghast if anyone were to draw such an inference from their argument. They conclude instead that memory is simply not the sort of phenomenon that calls for a mechanistic explanation. They support this contention by drawing attention to other familiar facts of social life which we would never think of explaining in this way. All we need to do, they insist, if we want to understand what is involved in memory is to pay more attention to the way in which we talk about memory in our everyday discourse.

On the other side, most parapsychologists who have hitherto concerned themselves with memory have done so in the hope that memory might afford a suitable model when it comes to considering ESP (Blackmore 1980). My aim, in this paper, is rather different. I shall be asking *not* whether memory, perception, imagination or whatever might help us to understand better the nature of psi phenomena but, rather, what we might be able to conclude about the nature of these familiar mental processes by viewing them from a parapsychological perspective.

My plan of action will be as follows. I will commence with some comments about the current state of research on the neurophysiological basis of memory with a view to distinguishing what it can and what it cannot yet explain. I will then address myself to the arguments of those philosophers who maintain that the facts of memory do not require a mechanistic explanation. I will try to show that, while neither their premises nor their conclusions need be accepted, nevertheless some of their criticisms of trace theory are both valid and important and, certainly, we cannot afford to ignore them. Finally, I will offer my own interpretation by pointing out what I would retain of trace theory and why I believe it needs to be supplemented with a special sort of psi hypothesis.

Turning, first, to the empirical evidence for the trace hypothesis, there are, I shall suggest, three main approaches which have a direct bearing on the issue. These are (1) the study of brain damage cases, (2) direct brain stimulation using electrodes applied to specific loci in the brain and (3) the construction of abstract, information-flow models of memory processing and their instantiation in computer programs. Of these, the first has been the most important so far inasmuch as it has successfully identified particular regions of the brain which are necessary for particular manifestations of memory. Basically it involves observing the peculiar and often bizarre defects or memory that occur in brain damaged patients and noting where, in the anatomy of the brain, their lesions are located. Thus a former colleague of mine studied over many years a particular patient who, as a result of head injuries, was no longer capable of reading even the simplest words and yet, if pressed, was usually able to respond to some given test word with another word having a definite semantic connection with the test word, thereby revealing that, at some level at least, his memory was still functioning.[a]

All of this is relatively uncontroversial. Even the philosophical skeptics will grant that an intact brain is necessary if our memory is to function normally. What they contest is that there is, or indeed could be, any kind of one-one relationship between a specific brain state and a specific act of memory. In other words, they acknowledge that we could neither think nor remember unless our brains were working normally but refuse to acknowledge any causal connection between the contents of our thoughts or memories and brain activity that makes it possible for us to have these thoughts or memories. At this point it might be suggested that the technique of direct brain stimulation might provide the positive proof that is lacking and, indeed, at one time the celebrated Canadian neurosurgeon, Wilder Penfield, was claiming that his findings were a demonstration of the existences of traces. Thus he found that, when he stimulated a particular spot on the temporal lobe of his patient (whose brain had been exposed in preparation for surgery), the patient would experience a vivid re-enactment of some long forgotten scene from his past life, so vivid that it was more like an hallucination than an ordinary memory. Before long these demonstrations were being cited in the textbooks of psychology as evidence for the truth of trace theory. However, a more careful reading of Penfield (1958) and of the attempts that have since been made to repeat his observations show that they were no such thing (Valenstein 1973). Thus, Penfield, himself, reveals that, when he again stimulated the same spot only a few minutes later the patient experienced some quite different recollection. Moreover, when other neurosurgeons attempted to apply his procedures they often failed to obtain anything comparable—a situation all too familiar to parapsychologists. Other investigators found that the reported experience depended at least as much on the patient's thoughts at the moment of stimulation as it did on the locus stimulated. It seems, then, that, whatever was going on in Penfield's situation, whatever trains of thought or feeling he was able to unleash in this way, nothing like a one-one relationship between a specific brain trace and a specific conscious experience was ever established. Nor should this surprise us for normal memory, as all theorists agree, is utterly unlike a simple playback mechanism.

It is, I think, noteworthy that even the basic nature of the memory trace, let alone its function in the total process, is still a matter of controversy. At present at least three quite different and mutually incompatible theories hold the field concerning the nature of the trace. The favorite view is that, in long-term memory at least, actual structural modifications take place at the synapse where the brain cells meet and that the encoding of a particular experience consists essentially of a particular pattern of interconnecting cells which are all activated by the same impulse. However, a biochemical theory of traces still has it supporters who believe that experiences are encoded by means of molecular changes in specific macro-molecules. There is an obvious analogy here with the genetic code which we now know to be encoded in the DNA molecule, a discovery that was, of course, one of the triumphs of 20th century biology. Originally it was thought that the RNA molecule might play a corresponding role with respect to the memory process and some experimenters were bold enough to claim that RNA extracted from the brain of a rat trained in some task would, when injected into the brain of an untrained rat, facilitate the learning of that task. But the chemical theory of memory was another example of research that was notorious for its lack of repeatability so the implications of such findings remained unclear.

Yet another trace theory that rests upon an even more far-out analogy is the so-called holographic theory of memory which has been taken up recently with much enthusiasm by no lesser an authority than Karl Pribram. Here the basic idea is that memory functions like a hologram in holography. The point about a hologram is that the total information it contains is represented in every fragment of it. For memory theorists its attraction was that it was one way round the "Lashley paradox." Karl Lashley used to cut out portions of the brain of rats who had learned specific tasks hoping thereby to locate the trace or engram of that learning. He discovered, instead, to his great surprise, that in fact it made little difference where he made the excision or even, within limits, how much he excised, the animal was still able to run the maze. He could never figure out, therefore, how learning was possible at all unless, conceivably, every item of learning is multiply represented at many different loci. But, while the holographic theory gets over this puzzle, it is very hard to reconcile with what we know about the structure and functioning of the brain or to see how the hologram could be instantiated in terms of brain cells. So far its only known instantiation is in the field of photography.

The third approach I mentioned was by way of model building, artificial intelligence and computer simulation but, while it has certainly been influential in contemporary theorizing, it is too oblique an approach to enable us to decide the issues under discussion. It provides us with analogues of the way in which memory might function in people if people were just special kinds of natural machines but this, of course, is precisely the assumption that the philosophical skeptic is unwilling to concede. Hence to say that trace theory *must* be true, or, at least, possible, because computers use physical traces is to beg the question. Computers are, indeed, machines for storing and retrieving information but they necessarily depend on the information being fed in in a specific way and on the retrieval being outputted in a specific form; what makes human memory so problematic is precisely that there appears to be no such constraints on the way in which a given experience can be encoded or decoded, almost everything may serve as a manifestation of memory in the appropriate circumstances.

This brings us to the philosophical critique of trace theory. Like much else in modern Anglo-American philosophy it stems from the writings of Wittgenstein. Consider the following remark of Wittgenstein's:

> I saw this man ten years ago. Now I have seen him again, I recognize him, I remember his name. And why does there have to be a cause of this remembering in my nervous system? Why must something or other, whatever it may be, be stored up there in *any form?* Why *must* a trace have been left behind? Why should there not be a psychological regularity to which *no* physiological regularity corresponds? If this upsets our concept of causality then it is high time it is overturned [Wittgenstein 1967, section 610, cited by Malcolm 1977, p. 166; italics in original].

On one point, at least, we can surely agree with Wittgenstein: our concept of causality would indeed be overturned. Thus, if my recognition of someone depended solely on the fact that I saw him ten years ago and on nothing else this surely would be every bit as paranormal as if it depended solely on the fact that I would meet him again ten years hence and on nothing else. Indeed, each act of memory would then become a case of retrocognitive autotelepathy (i.e. a direct awareness of some previous experience) as opposed to a case of precognitive autotelepathy (i.e. a direct awareness of some future experience). Not that Wittgenstein was the first philosopher to suggest that memory might work across a gap in time. His teacher, Russell, discussed the possibility that there might be such a thing as "mnemic causation" which would operate in this fashion and, significantly, Russell (1921, p. 78) pointed out that this was, indeed, the only alternative to assuming some "hypothetical modification of brain structure."

Norman Malcolm, however, erstwhile pupil and now authoritative expositor of Wittgenstein, to whom I owe this quotation from the master, does not see the problem in this light at all. His recent book *Memory and Mind* (1977) (which could be regarded as a footnote to this remark of Wittgenstein's, much as an earlier book of his *Dreaming* could be regarded as a footnote to another of Wittgenstein's enigmatic remarks) argues that memory is not, after all, a problematic phenomenon and to try and explain it whether in physicalistic

or in mentalistic terms can only result in absurdity. Mnemic causation, he insists, seems strange only because of the "common assumption of philosophers
and psychologists that the phenomena of memory require a memory *process*
going on continuously between a past experience and a subsequent response
to it" (author's italics) whereas, according to Malcolm, "the *concept* of an accurate memory is not the concept of an effect produced by some properly functioning causal process" (my italics). Now, no one would disagree that what
makes a given memory claim correct or veridical is whether it corresponds with
the events to which it purports to relate, certainly no reference to any
hypothetical intervening causal process is ever involved in validating a case of
memory. But from this it simply does not follow that, as he puts it, "when this
is seen, the notion that a proper understanding of the concept of memory inevitably leads us to accept the requirement of a physiological memory trace
loses all force. The 'causal argument' for memory traces collapses." Trace theory
is, after all, an empirical scientific hypothesis. No trace theorist has ever
claimed that the existence of traces is a necessary or analytic truth about the
concept of memory, only that since, as Russell said, the only alternative to trace
theory is to assume action at a distance in time, it is not an unreasonable
hypothesis.

It seems that Malcolm is much too prone to assume that psychologists and
physiologists are really simple-minded folk who are constantly at risk of falling
into verbal traps unless philosophers continually come to their rescue. Thus,
discussing the relationship between retention and storage he once again correctly points out that to say of something that it has been retained in memory
does not imply that it has been stored in the brain. "To take the storage
metaphor as giving some warrant to the assumption of traces (literal storage)
is" he declares "both humorous and saddening . . . it has the comical aspect
of being deceived by a pun. But when one sees the pun playing a part in the
creation of a mythology of traces, were theories and research are pursued in
dead earnest, one cannot help feeling a kind of grief." But who, one wonders,
is the victim of a confusion, the trace theorist or Malcolm? Logically of course
retention does not imply storage any more than the existence of some disposition logically implies that the disposition is a property of some material
structure, but one would be hard put to think of any other instance in nature
where information of some kind is retained in a dispositional form without it
being encoded in a material sense. Thus, empirically, there is every reason to
connect retention with storage.

The attempt to short-circuit trace theory by these and similar arguments
has, I would maintain, completely misfired. However, Malcolm is on much
firmer ground in his critique of isomorphism and in his contention that trace
theory presupposes an isomorphism between the traces and the act of recall.
Perhaps the most perfect example of isomorphism with which we are all acquainted is the phonograph where the grooves of the record that is being

played are exactly isomorphic with the sounds that issue from the loudspeaker. The Gestalt psychologists, following Köhler, sought to show that an isomorphism obtained between perceptual experience and its concomitant brain processes but it is now generally conceded that the attempt was misconceived. Malcolm has no difficulty showing that it is futile to look for such an isomorphism in the case of memory. The crucial point is that there is always an indefinite number of different ways in which we may demonstrate that we have succeeded in remembering some fact or some incident. It is, for example, by no means the case, as certain psychologists have suggested, that for memory to be possible certain relevant images must come before the mind and, even if they did, they would not of themselves constitute the act of memory, they would still have to be interpreted as memory images just as if they were actual pictures. Nor does it help if we switch to a behavior analysis of memory for there will still be an indefinite number of behavioral responses, be they verbal or non-verbal, that can equally serve to indicate that recall has been achieved. And yet, in default of an isomorphic principle it is difficult to see how the trace theory could ever get started.

A related argument goes even further towards undermining the credibility of trace theory. If we postulate an isomorphism between a given neural representation and the given mental event it purports to explain we would have to assume a formal similarity of structure between the former and the latter. But, who is to say what constitutes the structure of a given mental event or, for that matter, a given item of behavior? Clearly there will always be as many different structures as there are different ways of describing, interpreting or "parsing" the event in question, which is to say an indefinite number of ways. In other words the idea on which isomorphism rests, namely that there must be some one correct or objective structure in lived experience is untenable. This argument, let us call it the contextual argument, has been exploited to good effect recently by Stephen Braude (1979) as a general argument against what he calls the "myth of internal mechanism" in psychology. But it has long been one of the cornerstones of Wittgensteinian philosophy that our actions gain their meaning from the social context in which they occur and it is precisely this context dependent aspect of behavior and experience which, it is argued, no internal mechanism can capture.

Yet, perhaps this argument ends by overreaching itself. It may not be necessary for the internal mechanism to account for every aspect of behavior or experience. It may suffice if the internal mechanism ensures that the appropriate movement is produced at the appropriate instant leaving it open to the social context in which these movements occur to determine how they will be interpreted and described. Moreover, the trace theorist will argue that the individual's whole world, not just specific memories, is somehow represented physically in the brain thereby providing a context which governs each separate item of behavior or experience. However, given that each person's experience of the world will be unique and this uniqueness will reflect itself in the fine structure of his brain, it just cannot possibly be the case that there could be any sort of universal correspondence between a particular *type* of brain state and a particular *type* of mental state or experience. Isomorphism in this sense must be a nonsense. However, despite the views of the philosophers whom I have been discussing, I can see no *a priori* reason why we should rule out the possibility that every unique experience of a given unique individual should be univocally related to, or coordinated with, certain unique brain events. In the current jargon, while we must forego a type-type relationship between brain states and states of mind the possibility of a token-token relationship remains an open question. Whether such a token relationship would be of any use to science, even if it could be established, is, of course, another matter; science concerns itself with general laws not with unique instances.

But the real crunch for any trace theory of memory comes, I believe, not over the question of storage but rather over the question of retrieval. Even Donald Norman, that well known and orthodox authority on memory theory, confesses himself baffled by the problem of retrieval. "Even the very basic question of how one recognizes that the correct answer has been retrieved has not been studied" he writes "This last point is extremely important. If you know the answer for which you are looking, then you would not need to look. But, if you don't know the answer, then how can you recognize it when you find it?" (Deutsch 1973, cited by Malcolm 1977, p. 219). Students of Plato will recognize here a restatement of the famous Meno paradox. Norman, no doubt, is still looking for an answer to the paradox along orthodox lines but Howard Bursen, a young American philosopher writing in the wake of Malcolm, argues forcefully in his new book—*Dismantling the Memory Machine* (1978)—that any attempt to explain retrieval on mechanistic principles inevitably runs into the following trilemma: either (a) we find ourselves caught on an endless regress of mechanisms depending on yet other mechanisms and so on or (b) we need at least one mechanism that requires an homunculus to operate it or (c) we arrive at an explanatory gap in our account which can be filled only by attributing magical powers to our machine.

Bursen invites us to consider the familiar situation where we are trying to remember some tune we wish to hum, the situation which psychologists have called the "tip-of-the-tongue phenomenon." Let us suppose that we can institute a search through all the numerous traces of tunes that we have learned until the right tune is discovered, much as we might search through the shelves of a library until we come across the book we are looking for. The question which then arises is how the search mechanism that we have set going knows where to stop? (It was this that puzzled Norman.) If we say that the mechanism just *knows* when to stop we are clearly begging the question: "It is," says Bursen, "to attribute to the retrieval mechanism the very power that was denied to people at the outset: memory. The idea of a machine which knows, thinks or remembers, is the idea of a little black box with the homunculus inside.... Since the trace theory requires a retrieval device, and since the retrieval device requires a homunculus to operate it, I conclude that trace theory is a fruitless attempt at a scientific or causal theory of memory." For, the only way of avoiding Bursen's homunculus or ghost-in-the-machine is to postulate yet further mechanisms and so embark on an endless regress of mechanisms or else endow some mechanism with magical powers. A machine that could just recognize things in some inexplicable way would be a magical machine. Thus do we find ourselves impaled on Bursen's trilemma.

This is clever stuff but perhaps a shade too clever. Consider an analogous question: how do we recognize when an object is in focus? How do our mechanisms of accommodation, convergence, etc., know when to switch off once the object is in focus? We can say that an object in focus just looks different from an object that is out of focus and we can try to spell this out further in terms of the double imagery that intrudes in the latter case and so on but there seems to be no great difficulty of principle about envisaging a perceptual mechanism that can deal with this particular reflex activity. Is the situation so different when it comes to recognizing a face? A familiar face *looks* different from an unfamiliar face. That, at any rate would be the phenomenological account of the matter but a trace theorist could plausibly argue that when a trace is reactivated it produces a different effect from that which occurred when the trace was originally laid down and this is the basis of the feeling of familiarity. Whether this is a viable explanation or not it would be rash to jump to the conclusion that Bursen and these other philosophers are trying to purvey, namely that an attempt to propose a physiological basis of recognition must be a futile waste of time. For the weakness of an antitrace theory of memory is that it leaves us without any answer to the question as to why brain processes should be necessary to memory in the first place. It cannot be for nothing we carry round with us all that elaborate computing machinery in our head; what is the brain for if it does not play a part in memory, bearing in mind that neither perception nor problem solving would be possible without recourse to memory? The critical question therefore must be: what is the function of the brain with respect to memory?

In the remainder of this paper I want to sketch out a possible theory of memory that combines a trace theory of storage with a psi theory of retrieval. From an interactionist point of view the critical function of the brain in all mental activity is to realize our intentions or translate them into physical fact. This function is most clearly exemplified in a typical voluntary movement. Naturally the organism has to be suitably prepared or primed if the intention is to be put into effect otherwise the result is a fiasco. I cannot go onto an ice rink and just will my limbs to start skating like Robin Cousins! However, once certain learned movements have become part of my repertoire it is sufficient, it would seem for me to *will* a certain action for my brain or motor cortex to initiate that complicated train of events in my nervous system that will result in my performing the act in question. Now I will maintain that the situation is no different in the case where I will to recall some missing item of information. Again willing is never enough. Unless the information had been properly learned in the first instance, which may well involve the laying down of appropriate traces, I shall not be able to recall it when I need to do so. The brain, in other words, imposes severe limitations on what is accessible to us at any given time. Nevertheless, granted that it is accessible, the retrieval of it follows no less automatically the effort at recall than the raising of my arm follows my will to raise it. In both cases, the traces may be physical but their activation is a mental act. The brain processes represent the means whereby the act is accomplished but the mind supplies the ends which they subserve or, in other words, the mind acts upon the brain in a teleological fashion.

The interactionist view of memory has recently been stated in a telling way by Sir Karl Popper who has this to say:

> My suggestion is that when we search our memory, we feel that we are sitting in the driver's seat of our car.... Like a driver we have at best partial knowledge of what we are doing—of the causal chains we are setting in motion. The combination between the feeling that we operate a known mechanism and the other feeling that we do not know how the effects of our actions are actually brought about can be taken as a model of the way in which the self interacts with the brain.... I think the interaction between the self and the memory may not only be similar or analogous to, but may possibly actually be the same as, the interaction between the self and the brain [Popper & Eccles 1977, p. 485–486].

Popper may, of course, be wildly mistaken but the alternative to an interactionist view is not the obscurantist Wittgensteinian view that memory does not *call* for a scientific explanation but, rather, the materialist view that the brain "does it all for us," as it were, that the experience we call remembering something is in fact no more than an epiphenomenon of its underlying brain processes. Now, there is still a good deal to be said for the materialist view whatever these philosophers may say but, as parapsychologists, we cannot allow the materialist to have the last word. Since we already have abundant evidence that the mind can, on occasion, extract information from the external world without the mediation of our sensory apparatus and can equally, on occasion, produce physical effects in the external world without the mediation of our muscular effectors, why need we deny the mind such powers with respect to its own brain?

Bursen, like most of the philosophers of his persuasion (with the honorable exception of Braude) is scared of invoking the paranormal which, for him, would represent a lapse into magical thinking and the abandonment of reason. There is no reason, however, why we need feel similarly inhibited. Magic is a loaded word but we possess what he clearly lacks, a concept of "psi process." It is true we know precious little about this "psi process" but it is enough for our present purpose that it exists and that it functions in a wide variety of contexts.

It might be argued at this point that if we introduce psi we can dispense with physical traces in the brain even for purposes of storage. Thus, if there are genuine cases of memory for previous lives—and the evidence can no longer be ignored (Stevenson 1977)—or if there are genuine cases of postmortem communications as some parapsychologists would maintain (Gauld 1977), then we are dealing with cases of what can only be described as "extracerebral memory" where the information cannot have been stored in any brain cells if only because the original brain no longer exists! If that is so, why do we need to postulate brain storage in the normal case? I think the answer must be that while the brain may not indeed be essential to mental activity in all circumstances, it may still be the natural instrument of mind for as long as we have a body. Because the brain cannot be invoked to explain extrasensory perception it does not follow that the brain plays no part in ordinary perception. Similarly, if there are paranormal cases of extracerebral memory it still would not follow that the brain plays no part in normal memory.[b]

Conclusion

The trace theory of memory is still no more than a theory, in no sense is it an established scientific fact. However, if we reject it, if we take the view that no physical record of experience is necessary for memory to work, then we are committed to the belief in a causal action across a gap in time that would, in the fullest sense, be paranormal. The plea that nothing paranormal is implied in abandoning trace theory, which certain contemporary philosophers in the Wittgenstein tradition have argued on the grounds that memory is not the sort of phenomenon that requires a causal explanation, cannot be allowed. For memory cannot be compared with a social custom, like marriage, as Bursen proposes, each act or manifestation of memory is an event which must either be in principle capable of a physicalistic explanation or else must be deemed paranormal. The particular view of memory that we have proposed is one that combines a trace theory of storage with a paranormal theory of retrieval. Our view is one that accords with the interactionist view of the mind-body relationship which Popper and Eccles have defended but, unlike them, we adopt a parapsychological perspective. It seems to us only natural to regard the brain as, among many other things, a recording instrument whereby we keep a physical record of our experiences. At the same time, the incredible flexibility of memory in the human case makes it difficult to believe that the retrieval process can be due wholly to the automatic action of the brain feeding us, in computer-like fashion, with just the right items of information that we require at just the right instant. For it is not just in cases of deliberate recall that we retrieve information but in every case of learned behavior, when we speak, when we perform a skilled action and so on. Relative to the speed of computer processing, neural transmission is very slow so that the time factor alone would appear to rule out the amount of processing that would be required in these cases. At all events, it is suggested that it is at this point, at the point of recall, it is the mind that takes over from the brain and makes possible the manifestations of memory that we all know.

Notes

a. *The colleague in question was John C. Marshall, a distinguished neuro-psychologist now at Oxford.*

b. *One theory that I omit to mention in this paper is that of Rupert Sheldrake (1981; 1988). This was, of course, the "early days" and it was, in fact, at this conference in Brighton that I first met Sheldrake. Since then I have always taken a keen interest in his bold and original ideas although I have yet to be convinced of their validity. Sheldrake believes that our memories are recorded not in our brains but in certain "morphogenetic fields" to which our brains are attuned. If Sheldrake is right then memory is, indeed, a "paranormal" phenomenon. Unlike so many unorthodox theories, including the one I have here expounded, Sheldrake's is eminently testable even if it requires considerable ingenuity to devise a critical experiment that would exclude all alternative normal explanations.*

Could There Be
a Physical Explanation for Psi?

A question that constantly arises is where parapsychology rightly belongs in the array of the sciences. More particularly, could parapsychology be subsumed under physics, either as it exists or as it may yet become? Some philosophers today would deny that physics occupies any privileged position in our understanding of nature, insisting that such a view is no more than a reductionist fallacy. Nevertheless, physics is surely unique in that it purports to apply to every event that occurs in the objective world of space and time whereas all other sciences take as their domain only some delimited range of phenomena. Psi phenomena are problematic precisely because they involve events in the real world and thus become candidates for a physical explanation, yet at the same time they are critically bound up with certain states of mind. Thus they cross the dividing line between objectivity and subjectivity which normal mental phenomena do not.

Classical physics, from the time of Galileo onwards, took great pains to eliminate the observer as a potential influence on what is observed. Modern physics, however, taking its stand on quantum theory, contrives to bring the observer into an intimate relationship with the objects of observation. It is this that has led many contemporary parapsychologists to try again to reconcile psi and physics in a way that was not open to those operating within the classical framework.[a] Whether this attempt will be successful and whether it can be done without lapsing into an idealist metaphysic that, in effect, gets rid of an independent objective reality, are questions that I have addressed in the paper that follows. It is based on a talk that I gave to the Third International Conference of the S.P.R. when they met in Edinburgh in April 1979.

A characteristic feature of our civilization is our belief in the potential omnipotence of science and technology. And, indeed, they are, perhaps, the one truly progressive enterprise on which humanity has embarked since the beginnings of history. We all have, therefore, a natural inclination to believe that, given time, everything will in due course be explained in an acceptable scientific way and become absorbed into the ever expanding body of scientific knowledge. A typical expression of this belief is the phrase we often hear about the brain being the last great frontier of science, the implication being that once we have really got to grips with the mechanisms of the brain the whole of human behavior and experience will fall into place in the scientific scheme of things.

What, then, are we to say about the so-called paranormal phenomena which are our special concern on this occasion? Are they the exception to the rule? Or are they anomalous in a provisional sense only, so that, after another revolution or so in science, they will cease to qualify as paranormal and instead will take their rightful place in the natural order? Until recently I would have said that a case could be made for either point of view. However, I have come increasingly to the conclusion that the possibility of a physical explanation of psi phenomena is not just doubtful, in the sense that all the existing candidates look so unpromising, but is, from the very nature of the case, an absurdity that can be ruled out on *a priori* considerations. I am not alone, of course, in holding this view; for one thing most scientists who reject the parapsychological evidence do so primarily because they see no way of reconciling it with physical theory. However, my position is, in a sense, the reverse of theirs: they assume that what cannot be explained in physical terms does not exist; I believe that since psi phenomena do exist not everything in nature can be explained in physical terms.

This is of course, a heresy and, in proclaiming it, I am sensible of the possible harm I may be doing to the cause of parapsychology. To begin with, the physicalistic approach to psi, as I shall call it, is a very useful protective camouflage for us to adopt in dealing with the scientific establishment. So long as it is thought that we are engaged in the same game as the physicists and other natural scientists, there is more hope that we shall be given funds and facilities to pursue our researches while, if word got around that really we were in the business of showing up the limits of scientific inquiry, we would be given short shrift. I am sure that Soviet parapsychology, for instance, would never have got off the ground if its proponents had not contrived to make it sound like the science of the future. Moreover, some of the liveliest and most talented individuals who are currently active in parapsychological research have come into the field from a background in the physical sciences and have done so precisely because they see it as the next big challenge to physics. They are all agog to take up this challenge and, hopefully, to make their name by finding a solution. My only defense therefore, for my indiscretion, is the faith on which all academic life is predicated, namely that, in the long run at least, it cannot hurt to tell the truth. Besides, if what I have to say is not true, then the quickest way of getting at the error of my arguments is by proclaiming them for you to criticize.

Even so, some of you may be thinking that it is the height of presumption, after all that has happened, to say about any phenomenon at all that science will never find an explanation. For, how can we possibly know what surprises science still has in store for us? Might not our Victorian forebears have argued, in like vein, that television was a manifest absurdity? That is a good question but I shall try to answer it. The plan I shall adopt is to start by stating what I understand by a physical explanation and then attempt to show that a theory which is physical in this sense cannot possibly cover psi phenomena while, conversely, a theory which could encompass psi phenomena could not be strictly physical.

Briefly, then, what I mean by a physical explanation is one that is expressed exclusively in physical terms, i.e. in terms of space, time, mass, energy, etc. plus whatever logicomathematical expressions may be necessary to frame the particular law or equation involved in such an explanation. If there are any terms left over in our explanation which cannot be expressed in these basic physical parameters, which can be understood only in intuitive or subjective terms or whose connotation is irreducibly qualitative, then we know at once that we have not got a truly physical explanation. It is also preferable, though not essential, that the relevant laws and equations be formulated in quantitative terms for it is conceivable that there may be phenomena that cannot be measured on any scale or metric but could be described only with the aid of some logical or topological calculus.

There is also a somewhat weaker type of explanation which may qualify as physical even though it dispenses with any explicit laws or equations. This is the type of explanation which relies on a working model of the underlying mechanisms involved. Here we must be careful, however, because there are some kinds of explanatory models of a purely abstract kind which are, in fact, no more than diagrammatic redescriptions of the phenomena in question. To qualify as physical such a model must be capable of being embodied in concrete physical form. This type of explanation is of particular importance when it comes to explaining how our cognitive functions might operate. Thus, if we can program a computer so that it is capable of performing certain tasks of, say, pattern recognition, problem solving or information retrieval then it would seem sheer dogmatism to deny that this affords a physical explanation of, at any rate, *one* way in which such tasks could be performed. On the other hand, the mere fact that human mental functions can readily be discussed in information processing terms, does not necessarily imply that we have a physical explanation of such processes. Information theory is, after all, just a branch of applied mathematics and, as such, tells us nothing about whatever mechanisms may be involved.

Having, I hope, made clear what I understand by a physical explanation

I would like next to turn to the attempts that have actually been made to explain some instance of ESP or PK and consider why they fail to meet the case.
If anyone were to compile a catalogue of all the various theories that have been
put forward in this connection it would make curious reading, for parapsychologists have not been lacking in imagination and ingenuity. Fortunately, for our purposes, there is no need to survey each of these proposals since
they can conveniently be classified into two main categories. These I shall call
respectively "communicational theories" and "observational theories." The
former are very obviously based on the analogy with radio, radar or other
known forms of telecommunication; the latter, which are of very recent vintage, are either based on, or inspired by, a special interpretation of quantum
theory. It is, of course, arguable that there are physical theories of psi which
belong to neither of these two main categories—one must never be dogmatic
in such cases—but, if so, I do not know what they are. I have, for example,
deliberately excluded from consideration synchronicity theories of psi, despite
the fact that they have gained so much in popularity in recent years, because
they are not, in my opinion, physical theories; they belong, rather, to the occult world view. Accordingly, if, for the sake of argument, we take these two
categories as exhaustive, my task will be concluded if I can show that neither
of them answers our requirements. To anticipate, I shall seek to prove that the
former, the communicational theories, are all necessarily nonstarters inasmuch
as they contrive to gloss over what is the key problem, namely how the information is encoded, while the latter, the observational theories, succeed only by
dint of the fact that they surreptitiously import mentalistic concepts; which
disqualifies them as physical theories.

Let us start, then, with the communicational theories which go back to
the earliest days of psychical research and still have their supporters at the present time. To simplify the discussion let us concentrate on the phenomenon
that, on the face of it, appears most amenable to a physicalistic interpretation,
namely the classic telepathic paradigm, what was originally called "thought
transference." Now there are two aspects of the target material which may
figure in a typical telepathic situation: there are, first, the thoughts and ideas
that may be going on in the agent's mind as he contemplates a given target
and there are, secondly, the percepts or images that enter into his consciousness. And the question is: how might the agent make the percipient
aware of the one or the other?

Now, if this were a question of normal sensory communication we know,
in general, what the answer must be: to communicate his thoughts or ideas the
agent must use language or, in other words, he must express them in proposi-
tional form and then convey them in speech, writing, or by means of any other
set of conventional signals with which the receiver is familiar. In the case of
the percepts and images a pictorial mode of communication is possible that
does not depend on a conventional coding system. But what can we say in the

case of extrasensory communication? What now corresponds to the linguistic, pictorial or symbolic content of normal communication? Let us grant, for the sake of argument, that my thoughts and ideas can be unambiguously represented by certain traces in my brain whatever these traces may be, and let us further grant that there exists some hypothetical radiation, field of force or whatever, which could transmit signals from my brain to your brain. The question then arises as to how these traces could modulate this hypothetical radiation in such a way that they could be decoded by your brain to yield a coherent message? It has never been suggested that we can communicate telepathically only with other members of the same linguistic community, because what appears to be conveyed in a telepathic exchange is some meaning rather than some particular form of words. But how could a meaning, as such, be communicated physically unless there were some agreed code between the parties involved? To suppose that we might be born knowing how telepathic messages are encoded is as nonsensical as to suppose that we might be born with a knowledge of the English language. It would therefore clearly have to be something that was learned, but how and when could this learning take place?

It is only necessary to ask these questions to see that they admit of no answer. Moreover, even if we confine the argument to the simplest case, that of transmitting a given pictorial symbol such as a star or circle, we would still have to suppose that the trace which represented that symbol in my brain could modulate the hypothetical radiation in such a way that when it reached your brain it could be duly converted into a corresponding trace which would unambiguously represent a star, circle or whatever. And, even if we ignore all the other complications which confront us, such as how the signal would be discriminated against the background noise, this is utterly implausible.

In order to present the communicational model of psi in the most favorable light possible, as I am obliged to do if I am going to attack it, I have spoken so far as if there were no problem about representing thoughts or images by brain traces in some unequivocal way. In fact there are two insuperable problems. First, no two brains are identical, each reflects the individual's particular life history. Hence, the way in which my brain traces will represent the fact that I am thinking about Arthur's Seat, or even looking at Arthur's Seat, will be specific to my brain so that even if, *per impossible,* my brain processes *could* somehow duplicate themselves in your brain this would still mean nothing to you. But there is an even more radical objection to this conception of telepathy and it is this. The whole idea that every mental event must correspond to some specific brain state will not bear examination. Thus the idea that, when I am thinking about Arthur's Seat, my brain is in state A while, when I am thinking about the Scott Monument, it is in state B and when I am just thinking about Edinburgh in general it is in state C, etc. cannot be right if only because the way in which we partition our mental life into such segments is so clearly arbitrary, nature could not have provided for a specific brain state which unambiguously represented a particular thought of mine on a particular occasion. I am not denying that brain activity of some sort is necessary if we are to have any thoughts at all but to suppose that the semantic content of our thought must correspond in a one-to-one fashion to discrete brain states is, as Stephen Braude (1978) has recently been at pains to emphasize, a complete fallacy. Thus the popular science-fiction notion that, if we had a machine that could scan a person's brain with sufficient thoroughness we would be able to read his thoughts is based on a misunderstanding. And yet, once we have exposed this fallacy the whole broadcasting analogy of psi collapses.

It is ironical that, although philosophers have been pointing out the logical shortcomings of the communicational model at least since H.H. Price wrote his classic paper of 1940, parapsychologists have discussed the problem as if the question at issue were what properties the hypothetical radiation would have to have if it were to explain the evidence for ESP, whether such radiation could span the appropriate distances without too much attenuation, whether it could penetrate a Faraday cage, whether it could jump an interval of time and so forth. Yet such discussions are a complete irrelevancy if one cannot suggest at least in principle how this energy could carry the relevant information. A striking example of such misapplied ingenuity is the recent article by John Taylor and Eduardo Balanovski in *Nature* (1978) which is entitled: "Can Electromagnetism Account for Extra-Sensory Phenomena?" After several years of experimental research they came to the conclusion that it could not. We could surely have saved them much time and effort. Furthermore, it is not just electromagnetism which cannot account for ESP, the quest would be just as futile if, for EM radiation we were to substitute "thermodynamic radiation" (whatever that may mean), or beams of neutrinos, gravitons, tachyons, psitrons or any other of these entities drawn from science or science fiction. If we are barking up the wrong tree then we shall not find what we are looking for no matter what kind of ladders we use.

The time has come, surely, to bury the communicational theories of psi and to give them a decent funeral. Certainly the vanguard of what I am calling the physicalist school of parapsychology realize that there is no future in this approach and that is why they have transferred their allegiance *en bloc* to the observational theories to which we must now turn. This is no easy task because such theories have been devised by physicists, they presuppose a certain familiarity with the basic concepts of modern quantum physics and are presented using mathematical equations. Fortunately, there is an excellent introduction to such theories written for the layman by Brian Millar to which I can refer you in the *European Journal of Parapsychology* (Millar 1978). For such theories there is no question of energy being transmitted from a given source to a given receiver; instead the psi effect is produced at the instant where an observer enters the situation. Their point of departure is the assumption, in line with the so-called "Copenhagen interpretation" of quantum theory, that any system comprising any degree of quantum indeterminacy remains strictly indeterminate until an observation or measurement is performed on it. Where they go beyond conventional quantum theory is in the assumption that there exist certain observers, usually called psi sources, who not only determine the state of the system but can bias it in a prescribed direction. The paradigm situation with reference to which these theories have been developed is the PK test using a random number generator or RNG. Depending only on the strength of the psi source the output of the RNG can be made to deviate by a given ratio from its chance baseline. However, the application of these theories is not limited to PK, ESP can be similarly explained if we assume that the brain functions somewhat like an RNG with quantum indeterminacy. In a telepathic experiment, for example, we might suppose that the agent was able to bias the output of the subject's brain so as to make his guessing score exceed chance expectation. What is critical in all such theories is the provision of feedback, the moment of truth is the moment when we become aware of the results.

Now, whether these theories are sound physics is obviously something on which only other physicists are competent to express an opinion, I can merely mention, for what it is worth, that a colleague of mine at this university who is a quantum physicist and whom I have tried to interest in this approach is very dubious on this point. What worries me much more, however, is whether these theories are logically tenable. The trouble is that, however you dress them up using whatever mathematical formalism, they imply the existence of a casual loop in time, since observation and feedback must necessarily come *after* whatever effects are registered and observed. Hence we seem committed in the end to saying that the cause of my *scoring* above chance in a given test of PK or ESP is the fact that I subsequently observed that I *had* scored above chance and, equally, of course, the cause of my *observing* that I had attained such a score was the fact that these events had already taken place! Cause and effect here chase each other in a temporal loop rather like a dog chasing its own tail. Now I have, in the past, defended the idea that there is nothing logically vicious in the idea of backward causation (Beloff 1977), but I am not at all sure that I would be prepared to defend the logical propriety of a causal loop. There must, one feels, be a more convicing answer to the question why a given subject guesses correctly on a given trial than the mere fact that he was subsequently *found* to have guessed correctly![b]

However, for my present purposes, I am perfectly willing to suppress all the philosophical misgivings I may feel about the observational theories and proceed on the assumption that there is nothing logically or theoretically objectionable about them. The question I now want to raise is whether they are, indeed, genuine physical theories? Let us therefore examine two concepts that are fundamental to all such theories, the concept of an observer and the concept of information. Let us begin with the observer. It is necessary to the theory that some *person* become consciously aware of the results displayed in feedback or is it sufficient if that person be replaced by some piece of apparatus? If the latter, then the theories must specify the properties of such an apparatus so that we could construct one which could then duly produce psi phenomena. However, my reading of observational theory is that the former is implied; certainly Walker explicitly identified the hidden variables of the quantum equations with what traditionally we would call consciousness and will. But, granted that it is a person that is involved, is it his mind or his brain that is critical? We are told by observational theorists that such factors as the observer's attitude, expectations, beliefs, hopes, even his mood and his prevailing needs may all be critical for the outcome of the experiment. Indeed, one of the selling points of the observational theory is that it alone appears able to account for the so-called psi experimenter effect. But the question is, can these psychological factors be identified with the states of the brains? And when we ask this question we find that we are back again in the same impasse as we encountered when we were discussing the communicational model of psi. Thus, the possibility of specifying in physical terms the state of the brain when subject O is expecting good results must always elude us if only because such a state would never be the same for any two individuals or on any two occasions. We hear much talk about quantum events in the brain but these seem to be as irrelevant as the hypothetical radiation of the communication theorists. The stark fact of the matter is that the observational theories are, when you start to probe them, really dualistic theories in disguise.

Once again, in order to present these theories in their most favorable light I have so far tried to discuss them in their own terms, that is to say as explanations of the quantitative effects such as are found in laboratory experiments in ESP or PK as typified by the RNG set-up. Indeed, a moderate observational theorist, like Schmidt (1978), does not claim that his theory has much relevance outside this context. But, as parapsychologists, not to say philosophers, we cannot confine our attention to these wholly artificial situations. How, we want to know, are we to interpret qualitative psi effects? For the difference between one target and another in a free response test is never a matter of information or entropy, nor is the difference between one thought and another or one image and another. And this holds equally of PK if we consider its wider manifestation which would include cases of psychic photography, psychic healing, teleportations, materializations etc. Each of these cases exemplifies the fulfillment, by paranormal means, of some intention (whether that intention be conscious or unconscious). But such intentions can no more be differentiated in quantitative terms than can any other item of experience. Accordingly, the observational theorist is faced with a dilemma. Either he must give up the theory or he must ignore all the qualitative aspects of psi phenomena, which is to say everything that gives them relevance to real life. And, even then, one of the key assumptions of observational theory, namely that the brain can be regarded as a quasi RNG seems wrong to the point of perversity when it is well known that the one task no subject can ever do is to generate any sort of a random series—patterns and meanings invariably intrude.

I regret having to speak so critically of observational theory because there is no doubt that it has been one of the more exciting developments of recent years, which has infused new life into experimental parapsychology and has attracted to the field valuable talent from outside. Indeed, thanks to it parapsychology has once again become a topic of concern to physicists as it was in the early days of psychical research. Nevertheless, whatever may be its incidental merits, I cannot but agree with Thakur (1979) in his critique of Walker that the theory, for all its mathematical trappings, cannot be expressed in purely physical terms. This, then, concludes my argument. I have argued that, if we are to seek a physical explanation for psi our choice lies between a communicational theory or an observational theory. However, the former comes unstuck over the logical impossibility of encoding the necessary information, while the latter, even if it could survive all the logical or theoretical objections it has to face, would not constitute a physical theory, not at any rate by the criterion which I proposed. Before I finish, however, I would like to add a few words to avoid possible misunderstandings.

I have *not* been arguing that physics is irrelevant to parapsychology. On the contrary, inasmuch as I see parapsychology as concerned with mind-matter interactions I welcome any light which physics can throw on the physical aspects of the mind-matter interface. What I *have* sought to challenge is the assumption that these so-called mind-matter interactions can all ultimately be reduced to matter-matter interactions.[c] Further, in arguing that there can be no physical explanation for psi, I have not been claiming that I know of a better, non-physical, explanation whether mentalistic, mystical or occultist. Rather, I would take leave to doubt whether there could be any explanation of psi in any sense of explanation that would be recognized as such in the exact sciences. Consequently, if I were a materialist I would remain a skeptic, that is to say I would deny for as long as possible that there were any genuine psi phenomena; and that, let us not forget, is still the position that most scientists take at the present time.

Notes

a. *One of the first clear indications of this new trend was the conference which the Parapsychology Foundation held in Geneva in August 1974 on "Quantum Physics and Parapsychology" (Parapsychology Foundation 1975). The theme was suggested to Eileen Coly by Arthur Koestler, who attended as an observer although he, himself, never went beyond suggesting that there were analogies to be drawn. An interesting attempt to bring together ideas from quantum theory and the hard data of the parapsychology laboratory is the new book by Robert Jahn and Brenda Dunne (1988),* Margins of Reality.

b. The paradox of the causal loop was discussed in my paper "Teleological Causation" (see pages 88–99). It is still an issue. See Millar, B. (1988) versus Braude, S.E. (1988).

c. This is still my position. I revert to this topic in a later paper, "Parapsychology and Physics: Can They Be Reconciled?" for the new journal Theoretical Parapsychology *Vol. 6, 1988, 23–29.*

Science, Religion and the Paranormal

In the spring of 1984, I was approached by Dr. James A. Hall, M.D., a Jungian psychiatrist and a friend of parapsychology. He explained that in Dallas, where he lived, he was associated with a lay organization calling itself the "Isthmus Institute" which was dedicated to studying the connections between science and religion. I mentioned that I was not, myself, religious but he seemed to think that that would be no impediment so I accepted the invitation. There is no question that any study of the paranormal must impinge on religion and this seemed a good opportunity to consider where I stood on this issue. Was parapsychology, perhaps, a substitute religion? I could not agree with the well known critic of parapsychology, James E. Alcock, that parapsychology was, in effect, a backdoor attempt to vindicate religion under the guise of science (Alcock 1981, chapter 2). The upshot of my ruminations is the paper which follows. It is based on the talk I gave to the Isthmus Institute in Dallas in November 1984. It was later published in a humanist journal Free Inquiry *at the invitation of its editor, Paul Kurtz, where it was paired with an article by Alcock entitled: "Parapsychology: The 'Spiritual' Science."*

Psychical research was one of the byproducts of the conflict which came to a head in Victorian England in the aftermath of the Darwinian revolution. Its leaders, Frederic Myers, Edmund Gurney, the Sidgwicks, were among those who had lost their faith in revealed religion but were not ready to embrace the new creed of scientific materialism which was then in the ascendent. In some cases, and this was true both of Myers and Gurney, personal bereavements gave them additional incentive to examine, for what it might be worth, the evidence for survival that was being put forward by the spiritualists. Their aim in founding the Society for Psychical Research was to bring to bear on the problem of the paranormal the methods and standards of evidence that we associate with science. For they shared the optimistic Victorian faith in science as the universal key to true knowledge. At the same time they believed that, when the scientific approach was applied to these traditional mysteries, it would vindicate a conception of man and of the cosmos that had more in common with the teachings of religion than it did with the contemporary scientific outlook. Even J.B. Rhine, whose name is usually associated with the transition from psychical research to parapsychology, that is to say from a preoccupation with mediumship and with survival to research of the strict laboratory kind, went on record as saying that parapsychology stood to religion as biology stands to medicine or physics to engineering.* And, although it would be unwise to press Rhine's analogy too far, I think we can agree that the findings of parapsychology are not irrelevant to religion. Indeed, I would like to add that the events associated with certain religious figures, saints, mystics and the like, cannot be irrelevant to parapsychology.

Let us look, first, at the implications of parapsychology for religious belief. I would maintain that the parapsychological evidence legitimates religion in the same sense and to the same extent that physicalism invalidates it. By "physicalism" I understand the doctrine that everything that happens in the universe, happens strictly in accordance with the laws of physics. Rhine held, correctly in my opinion, that if psi phenomena (ESP or PK) were real then we have instances of phenomena which cannot be explained in terms of the impersonal laws and equations such as physics seeks to establish. Insofar, therefore, as religion is incompatible with physicalism, it cannot be indifferent to the kind of evidence which undermines the physicalist position.

But, is it true that religion is incompatible with physicalism? Many modern theologians, of whom Don Cupitt (1984), dean of Emanuel College, Cambridge, is the best known representative in Britain, would emphatically deny this. His arguments, however, strike me as specious. For example, I cannot see how the concept of moral accountability, that is so central not only to every religious creed but to any system of morality, could be reconciled with the view that all our thoughts and actions are, in the last resort, determined by processes in the brain operating in strict accordance with the impersonal laws of electrochemistry. Likewise, I cannot see how divine intervention in nature would be possible if we accept that the world is a closed physical system. And even if, as a concession to modernism, we forego divine intervention, what sense can we make of petitionary prayer? Or, again, consider the question of survival. The different religions differ markedly among themselves with regard to what they teach about a life after death but, setting aside, for the moment, the views of some sophisticated liberal theologians who contend that belief in survival is a positive hindrance to the religious life, one can safely say that there

---

* See J.B. Rhine (1954) New World of Mind, chapter 7, "The Importance to the World of Religion," p. 189. For a recent discussion of Rhine's views on religion, see James A. Hall "The Implications of Rhine's Work for Religion" in K. Ramakrishna Rao (1982), ed., J.B. Rhine: On the Frontiers of Science.

is no known religion which does not affirm an afterlife of some shape or form. Certainly, in Christianity, it has been absolutely central and indispensable to the whole concept of salvation. It is true that the Church has preferred to keep the nature of our postmortem existence shrouded in mystery, to discourage speculation on the topic and to forbid, as an anathema, all attempts to communicate with the deceased. Now, from the physicalist standpoint, there is, of course, nothing to survive once the brain is defunct. For all these reasons, therefore, I cannot see what would remain of religion under a physicalist dispensation other than some kind of special attitude towards life dressed up in religious language. It is hard to imagine that such a diluted and minimalist religion could for long satisfy the spiritual needs of ordinary people.*

The relevance of parapsychology to religion can, perhaps, be best summed up by saying that, in the absence of any paranormal phenomena, the physicalist interpretation of science would be difficult to challenge and, hence, the religious option would be difficult to defend. Obviously parapsychology cannot prove the supposed truths of religion if only because no mere empirical evidence can ever establish a religious or metaphysical doctrine, it is only scientific hypotheses that can be established in this way.[a] Even if parapsychology could prove the truth of survival, in itself a problematical enterprise, this would still not vindicate the Christian conception of heaven or of the life everlasting. At best it would prove that the mind was independent of the brain; it would not imply that our souls are created by God. On the other hand, those who, unlike me, already have their faith to sustain them, could then reasonably invoke such evidence to strengthen that faith and could reasonably draw comfort from the thought that this life, with all its miseries and tribulations, did not represent the sum total of our existence.

Let us now turn to the other side of the question, the implications of religion for psychical research. The most striking fact here is that some of the most remarkable paranormal events on record are those that occurred in a religious context. I refer to those events which, in religious terms, would be described as miracles or manifestations of supernatural or spiritual powers. That this should be so presents a problem for the secular parapsychologist who cannot assume divine intervention in nature. From the sociological angle, the prime function of a miracle is to serve as propaganda. A miracle is to the pious what a victorious battle is to the patriot. In both cases, however, the efficacy of the propaganda will depend to some extent on the credibility of the claims and it is here that the expertise of the parapsychologist can be brought to bear. It is somewhat ironical, I find, that, on the question of the historicity of

* *Cupitt's broadcast series sparked off a lively controversy but his view of God was repudiated both by professing Christians, like Hugh Montefiore, Bishop of Birmingham, and Gerald Priestland, the religious affairs broadcaster, and by the philosopher, Sir Alfred Ayer who protested that Cupitt's view was no different in substance from the atheism which he, Ayer, professed.*

particular miracles, the religious community displays much the same broad spectrum of belief as one finds within the parapsychological community with respect to the authenticity of particular parapsychological evidence. This was brought home to me recently as a result of the appointment of David Jenkins, a professor of theology at the University of Leeds, as Bishop of Durham. Consternation erupted among his Church of England flock when it became known that he did not believe, in the literal sense, either in the Virgin Birth or, more shocking still, in the Resurrection. Indeed, he considered that all the miracles of the New Testament required a symbolic rather than a literal interpretation.[b]

As a rationalist, I had some sympathy with the good Bishop in his struggles with his own backwoodsmen and I would agree with him entirely that, if the case for Christianity had to rest on the miracles attributed to Jesus, it would rest on shaky ground indeed. For considered as accurate reportage it would now generally be conceded that the Gospels leave much to be desired.* I have sometimes teased my Christian friends by pointing out that, had the Gospels been submitted to me, in my capacity as editor of the *Journal of the Society for Psychical Research,* they would never have got beyond my referees! This is not to deny their value as symbolic or mythic truths but simply to stress that they do not meet the criteria which we would now automatically apply to claims of this kind. On the other hand, there are a great many historical, postbiblical miracles which no parapsychologist could afford to ignore on pain of being charged with inconsistency because they can stand comparison with some of the best spontaneous cases in the literature of psychical research.

The variety of miracles is endless but, for the sake of this exposition, I shall confine myself to two types of miracle — bodily levitations of the kind that have been attributed to certain saintly or enlightened individuals, usually in an advanced stage of meditation or in the throes of ecstasy, and miracles of healing. These latter may occur at the hands of some divinely inspired healer, or at some sacred spot such as a shrine, or they may be taken as the answer to a prayer, or as a token of divine mercy. Both types of miracle are to be found in a wide range of different cultural settings, in tribal as well as in civilized societies, so that to acknowledge them is not to take sides with one faith or Church as against another. All in all, the Catholic Church has, I suppose, the edge over all its rivals in this regard but it certainly has no monopoly.

One advantage which the Catholic Church can offer in this context is that, before an individual could qualify for canonization, he or she was expected to produce at least one properly authenticated miracle. The so-called Congregation

* *After writing this I was pleased to find support from an impeccable Catholic source. Thus, the editor of* The Month *(a religious periodical with an all-Jesuit editorial board), discussing the problem of miracles in contemporary Catholic thought, apropos of the recent miraculous case in Glasgow (see pp. 142–143), wrote (Oct. 1976): "It should also be noted that our Lord's miracles would probably not have passed the tests of the Sacred Congregation for the Cause of Saints."*

of Rites was assigned the specific duty of authenticating the miracle or miracles in question. Scholars who have studied the deliberations of this august body in the Vatican archives have been impressed with their thoroughness and with their judiciousness and I have no reason to doubt their word. They brought to their sacred task a degree of critical intelligence that makes them worthy forerunners of the Society for Psychical Research. Unhappily they labored under two disadvantages that did not apply to the psychical researchers. First they could conduct their inquires only *after* the death of the individual concerned. Secondly many individuals with quite as strong a claim to have produced miracles were never candidates for canonization and so did not benefit from their attention. Thus, to quote Father Herbert Thurston S.J., the great authority on the physical phenomena of saints and mystics, "not a few of the most interesting cases of alleged levitation are to be found in the lives of mystics who have never actually been beatified."* And he cites as an example the great Spanish mystic Father Francis Suarez. However, there are two individuals who did ultimately achieve both beatification and canonization for whom there is strong evidence for levitation.

The first of these whom I shall discuss is St. Teresa of Avila. If one is willing to recognize anything as miraculous, it would be hard to doubt the testimony given under oath, before the authorities of the Holy Office, by her subordinate, Sister Anne. She testified to the levitations she had witnessed while Teresa was engaged in her devotions. It is true that her deposition was given some thirteen years after Teresa's death and some thirty years after the events they describe. However, they correspond so closely to the account given by Teresa herself who kept a diary (her autobiography was published in 1566) that the two accounts can be regarded as corroborating one another. Thus, if we only had Teresa's own word for it, we might well conclude that she was suffering from some kind of illusion despite her reputation as a woman of sound sense and good intellect. But this combination of eyewitness report and the subject's self-report rules this out. Another aspect of the case is worth mentioning here. Teresa's attitude towards this unsolicited gift was remarkably negative. Deeming herself unworthy of such a special grace she prayed to God that her "raptures" as she called them might forthwith cease (as they eventually did) and, meanwhile, her nuns were under strict orders to say nothing to anyone about them. I have sometimes wondered whether, as head of her convent, it might have offended her sense of decorum to be found thus by her acolytes with her feet off the ground. In any case it is hard for someone like

---

* *See H. Thurston (1952)* The Physical Phenomena of Mysticism, *chapter 1, "Levitation," p. 28. Thurston writes (p. 26): "In the imperfect and limited inquiry which I have had time to make, I have taken note of the name of something over two hundred persons alleged to have been physically lifted from the ground in ecstasy. In about one third of these cases there seem to me to be evidence which, if not conclusive, is, to say the least, respectable." For the case of St. Teresa I have relied almost wholly here on Thurston.*

me to appreciate her attitude. As a jobbing parapsychologist I have suffered
all my life from the exact opposite, a dearth of miracles! The point is, however,
that her negative attitude does, at least, scotch the suspicion that the whole
affair might just have been a pious put-up job.

Our next levitator was a person of a very different sort, Joseph of Copertino.* He was a kind of holy fool or simpleton whose only qualifications for
sainthood, apart from his miracles, was his piety, his childlike enthusiasms and
his extreme asceticism. With regard to his levitations, however, it can be said
without much fear of contradiction that they have never been surpassed both
from the point of view of their magnitude, duration and frequency and as
regards the amount of evidence that can be mustered for their authenticity.
For it must be understood that we are talking here of prolonged suspensions
in midair and of aerial flights to tree-top heights so that there can be no question of sudden leaps into the air being misperceived by the pious as genuine
levitations. Moreover witnesses to these events include three cardinals, Joseph's
personal physician who attended him during his final illness when levitations
were still occurring, and other persons of repute.

Within three years of his death in 1663, the authorities began to collect
sworn depositions and an official biography was duly published in 1678. It was
not, however, until 1751 that Joseph became a candidate for beatification and
the Congregation of Rites met to adjudicate his case. The *promotor fidei* (better known as "Devil's advocate") on this occasion was none other than Prosper
Lambertini, a formidable scholar later to become Pope Benedict XIV (see
Renée Haynes [1970], *Philosopher King,* chapter 2, "The Devil's Advocate").
It says something, I feel, for the enlightened outlook of this man that, as Pope,
he won even the admiration of Voltaire, an admiration that was apparently
reciprocated (Haynes 1970, pp. 178–81). If anyone could be expected to see
through a mere pious imposture it was surely he, the more especially when cast
in the role of Devil's advocate. Yet, succumbing to the sheer weight of the
evidence, he duly acknowledged the "celebrated levitations and remarkable
flights of this servant of God." Joseph was canonized in 1767.ᶜ

What is so frustrating from the point of view of a parapsychologist is that
nothing on this scale has ever been seen again. Sporadic reports of isolated cases
of levitation have continued down to the present, sometimes in connection
with pious mystics like Joseph, sometimes in connection with cases of alleged
demonic possession in children† but perhaps the only individual of a later age

---

* *For the case of Joseph of Copertino, I have relied mainly on the account provided by E.J.
Dingwall (1947) in his* Human Oddities, *with its extensive annotated bibliographical appendix, but Thurston also discusses this case.*

† *Some of these latter-day cases are mentioned by D. Scott Rogo (1982) in his* Miracles—
*see chapter 2, "Levitation." He discusses, in particular, the case of "Roland Roe," a
13-year-old boy of Washington, D.C., who was treated by exorcists for demonic possession. An authoritative account of this case is given by a Catholic priest, John Nicola (1974)
in his* Demonic Possession and Exorcism. *According to Fr. E. Gallagher of Georgetown*

who can stand comparison with Joseph is the celebrated Victorian medium, D.D. Home. According to William Crookes, one of the foremost British scientists of the time who has given us a graphic description of one such levitation in his own home, there were "at least a hundred recorded instances of Mr. Home's rising from the ground in the presence of as many separate persons" and he goes on to say: "to reject the recorded evidence on this subject is to reject all human testimony whatever: for no fact in sacred or profane history is supported by a stronger array of proofs."* Yet, with due respect to Crookes, conditions in the case of Home were far from ideal. The levitations took place in semidarkness often at the tail end of a lengthy séance when excitement and expectation were high. Joseph's levitations, on the other hand, usually took place in the open air or in a large church and were not preceded by any psychological build-up apart from the occasional shrill cry that Joseph would utter when he was about to take off. In his case we even have accounts of onlookers who endeavored to restrain him and then found themselves hoisted up with him! Nevertheless, the comparison with Home may remind us that divine grace does not seem to be a prerequisite of levitation. Far from being a saint, Daniel Home was a rather vain and worldly man and an ambitious social climber. However, he does seem to have taken seriously his life mission to propagate the new gospel of spiritualism in Europe so perhaps we should not regard his phenomena as having a purely secular character.†

Levitation, in the West at any rate, seems to have reached a climax in the Church of the Counter-Reformation. It is almost as if it were a necessary adjunct of Baroque art and architecture. St. Joseph was, after all, a contemporary of Bernini whose sculpture and buildings likewise appear to defy gravity. As propaganda, moreover, an important consideration in the Counter-Reformation, Joseph's miracles were very effective. Thus, when Johann Friedrich, Duke of Brunswick, a Lutheran now best remembered as the patron of Leibniz, visited Italy, he happened to attend a Church service[d] at Assisi where, to his astonishment, he saw Joseph floating just above the altar steps for about quarter of an hour. The Duke returned to Germany a Catholic convert!

University, the boy would sometimes, in the course of these rituals, break loose from his attendants and soar through the air! William Blatty, who was a student of Fr. Gallagher at Georgetown University, wrote a novel based on this case which then became the basis for the much publicized film The Exorcist.

* From an article that first appeared in the Quarterly Journal of Science (of which he was then editor) for Jan. 1874. It is reprinted in R.G. Medhurst, K.M. Goldney & M.R. Barrington (eds.), Crookes and the Spirit World, p. 116.

† Perhaps the last notable medium to be credited with levitation was Carlos Mirabelli, who flourished in Brazil in the 1920s and '30s; see G.L. Playfair (1975), The Flying Cow, chapter 3, or Brian Inglis (1984) Science and Parascience, pp. 221–7. Levitation was, however, only one of the numerous marvels attributed to this extraordinary individual who, unfortunately, has, for whatever reason, remained a somewhat shadowy figure.

In the East, levitation has always been associated with the practice of yoga. Levitation, or *laghima*, is listed by Patanjali in his classic treatise as one of the eight recognized *siddhis* or supernormal powers which an enlightened yogi may hope to attain. One modern British authority, Professor Ernest Wood, in his book, *Yoga*, which Penguin issued in 1959, speaks of levitation as a "universally accepted fact in India" and somewhat casually goes on to recall one instance, for which he could personally vouch, when "an elderly yogi was levitated in a recumbent posture about six feet off the ground in an open field for about half an hour while visitors were permitted to pass sticks to and fro in the space between"!(p. 104). The late Arthur Koestler, who had an abiding interest in the phenomenon of levitation, takes Wood to task for failing to give the precise date and place for such an astounding event as this. During his tour of India in 1958, Koestler tried hard but in vain to obtain some objective evidence of such yogic levitations. (See Koestler [1960], *The Lotus and the Robot*, especially chapter 3, "Yoga Research.") Already a number of institutes in India were beginning to study yoga from a scientific standpoint but no data on levitation were available.

Let us pass on now to a different type of miracle, which involves healing. This is obviously a far more complex phenomenon than levitation and it is also much harder in these cases to draw the line between what is merely very exceptional and what is truly paranormal. Short of the acquisition of a new limb it is very hard to be sure, given the uncertainties of medical science, that a cure defies explanation in natural terms. When all is said and done, however, there are some cases in the religious literature when the recovery was so sudden, so complete and so unexpected that it would be disingenuous to deny it the epithet of miraculous. I suppose the name of Lourdes springs to mind for most people in this connection but, whatever else it may be that Lourdes can offer its pilgrims, as a powerhouse of healing its record is not impressive, especially when one considers the large number of those who annually undertake the pilgrimage. Indeed, the Vatican itself has been very reticent about claiming miracles.*

At all events, in search of a shrine where miracles occurred in abundance, I had to go back to the 18th century, to the cemetery of St. Médard, then on the outskirts of Paris. There, at the tomb of the Abbé François de Pâris, a saintly priest belonging to the sect known as the Jansenists, there occurred

---

* *By 1957, when Dr. D.J. West published his* Eleven Lourdes Miracles, *he had only these 11 cases to go by that had passed all the stages of an official Vatican endorsement. West is highly critical of the Lourdes Medical Bureau and cool, to say the least, about the cases under review. Thus he writes (p. 122): "Close examination of the eleven modern miracle cases yields scant indication of any absolutely inexplicable recovery. Some are in fact readily explained in ordinary terms and only appear as evidence of the supernatural by virtue of over-enthusiastic interpretation and much special pleading on the part of the authorities responsible for putting them forward."*

within the space of about five years, from 1727, the year he died, to 1732 when the civic authorities had the place closed down, an unprecedented profusion of healing miracles. In making this bold assertion one is not relying on hearsay. The relevant documents and depositions were painstakingly collected by one who, though initially a skeptic in matters of religion, became the faithful chronicler of these events. This man was Carré de Montgeron, a nobleman, a magistrate and a member of the royal parliament.* He had the good sense to dedicate his book to the King (Louis XV) but was promptly sent to the Bastille for his audacity! Presumably he had not reckoned with the power of the Jesuits who were determined to stop at nothing to stamp out the Jansenist heresy. Anyone rash enough to testify to the authenticity of a St. Médard miracle incurred their wrath and suffered harassment and persecution at their hands. Montgeron, however, was not easily cowed and even succeeded in bringing out two more volumes of case studies while still in prison.

I have space to discuss just one of the many cures that Montgeron records. This was the case of Mlle. Louise Coirin.† This unfortunate woman had suffered for twelve years from a cancer of the left breast which had destroyed the flesh and the nipple of that breast and was said to have produced an odor which made her unapproachable. Since her father and two of her brothers were officers in the royal household, we can presume that she had access to the best medical opinion of the day but all her physicians agreed that her condition was incurable. Eventually, in desperation, in 1731, she made the pilgrimage to the tomb at St. Médard.ᵉ She was then 45 years old. There, we are told, in the best miraculous fashion, she duly recovered, instantaneously, completely and permanently. Montgeron produced depositions from no less than five eminent physicians or surgeons in addition to those from lay persons of repute testifying to the fact that both her breasts and the nipples were perfect and free from any trace or scar. One of these witnesses, a M. Souchay, listed as surgeon to the Prince de Conti, had previously pronounced her to be incurable but now went of his own accord to a notary public to make his deposition.

Such, it would appear, are the facts so far as these can now be ascertained. What we make of them is our affair. Was François de Pâris exerting posthumous powers of healing from beyond the grave? Was God active on his behalf? Or were the pilgrims imbued with such faith that they brought about their own healing? One who put his own construction on these bizarre events was the great Scottish skeptic, David Hume. In his well known essay on

---

* *According to E.J. Dingwall, Montgeron's original work is now inaccessible. I have relied for an account of this episode mainly on Dingwall himself as given in his* Human Oddities *(1947); see chapter 4 which, again, has a copious annotated bibliography.*

† *Her case is further discussed by two 19th century writers: William Howitt, in his* The History of the Supernatural *(London: Longman & Green, 1863, 2 vols.), Vol. 2 pp. 145–6; and P.F. Matthieu,* Histoire des Miracules et des Convulsionnairs de Saint-Médard *(Paris: Didier et Cⁱᵉ, 1864), pp. 169–73.*

miracles, he goes out of his way to draw the reader's attention to these events at St. Médard. (See *An Inquiry into Human Understanding*, 1748, section 10, "Of Miracles.") But not, as one might suppose, in order to heap ridicule on them but, on the contrary, to make the point that, even in a case like this, where, he agrees, the evidence is overwhelming, a reasonable person must still reject the miraculous. These events, he admits, were of recent vintage; they were not culled like so many miracles from the dim and distant past. They had taken place in the most civilized city of Europe, not in some remote spot. They had been enacted in the full glare of publicity and in the teeth of the implacable opposition from the authorities who sought every means to discredit them but whose own doctors insisted on testifying in their favor. The claims were "proved upon the spot before judges of unquestioned integrity attested by witnesses of credit and distinction."

"Where," asks Hume, "shall we find such a number of circumstances agreeing to the corroboration of one fact?" Hume might well ask, but the answer he gave to his own rhetorical question is one to which we must pay careful attention because it has resurfaced in every discussion of the paranormal ever since. What Hume tells us, in effect, is that we must take our stand on the absolute *a priori* impossibility of miracles. The point is that a miracle is, by definition, a singular event which runs counter to the universal experience of mankind as to the way nature works. Hence, no mere human testimony can ever outweigh the reasons we have to doubt it in such cases. This, Hume contends, "in the eyes of all reasonable people will alone be regarded as sufficient refutation." But will it? To me, at least, what Hume, all unwittingly, has succeeded here in doing is to provde us with the *reductio ad absurdum* of all *a priori* arguments against the paranormal.*f

In discussing levitation it looked as if the age of miracles was, indeed, past. Healing miracles, on the other hand, however infrequent, continue to crop up from time to time. The most recent case known to me that attracted worldwide attention occurred in Glasgow on March 5, 1967.† The protagonist was a 53-year-old retired Glaswegian dockworker, John Connolly Fagan, a Catholic. He had been taken ill two years before, when he was found to have a cancer of the stomach for which he was duly operated on May 26, 1965. The surgeon was not able to remove all traces of the malignant tumor but he was nevertheless discharged in July. Then, in November 1966, he again developed

---

* *Hume's position is forcefully attacked by the great naturalist, Alfred R. Wallace, who was, of course, a firm believer in miracles; see "An Answer to the Arguments of Hume, Lecky and Others Against Miracles," in* On Miracles and Modern Spiritualism: Three Essays *(London: James Burns, 1875).*

† *My main source for this episode is a book by two journalists, Des Hickey and Gus Smith (1978),* Miracle. *There is also a concise account of Fagan's medical case history by one of his doctors, A.P. Curran, in his article "Cure and Canonization,"* The Month, *2d n.s. Vol. 9, No. 10 (Oct. 1976), pp. 333–5.*

pains and vomiting which the surgeon assumed to be due to the original cancer but there was nothing further that the hospital could do for him and, although his condition steadily deteriorated, he was thereafter cared for at home. At the end of January 1967 he was given the last rites and by March 5 he was not expected to live another day, having by then taken virtually no food for seven weeks. That day a group of religious friends and well wishers gathered at his bedside and held a prayer meeting. They beseeched the Blessed John Ogilvie, the Catholic martyr who was hanged for treason in Glasgow in 1614, to intercede on behalf of the dying man. The following morning when his wife entered the bedroom expecting to find her husband dead he was sitting up, free from pain, and demanding a meal. There were no further relapses and he was alive and well some ten years later.

Did he owe his life to the Blessed John Ogilvie? His parish priest, Father Thomas Reilly of the Church of the Blessed John Ogilvie, certainly thought so and, together with a group of Glaswegian priests, brought the matter to the attention of the Vatican. In 1971 the Vatican sent their own medical expert to Scotland to look into the affair and a medical commission was duly appointed. The experts, however, were not unanimous. Dr. Gerard Crean, an authority on gastrointestinal disorders at the University of Edinburgh, though himself a Catholic, offered a nonmiraculous explanation. He suggested that the surgeon may have been mistaken in thinking that the operation was not a complete success and hence the relapse may have been due, not to a metastasis of the original carcinoma, but to a stomach ulcer. Hence the recovery may have been due to a spontaneous discharge of that ulcer. On this hypothesis it was, of course, no more than a coincidence that the ulcer should have discharged itself during the night following the prayer meeting.

This illustrates a common feature in the assessment of nearly all alleged miraculous cures, namely the possibility of misdiagnosis in the first place. However, in this instance, Dr. Crean was overridden by the other authorities, especially after Fagan underwent further extensive medical examinations in 1971 and 1972 both at the Western General Hospital in Edinburgh and at the Royal Infirmary in Glasgow. At all events, the Vatican was eventually satisfied that the case could *not* be explained by medical science and must be attributed to the intercession of the Blessed John Ogilvie. Accordingly, in February 1976, Pope Paul VI issued a decree officially declaring the case a miracle and the following October the famous Scottish martyr was duly canonized at a service in St. Peters at which Mr. and Mrs. Fagan were present.

I shall mention one more such case from this century. This one concerns a woman who was, by all accounts, herself a natural saint and the miracle in question took place in London on February 18, 1912. Dorothy Kerin was born in 1889 and died in 1963. She was of Irish extraction but belonged to the Anglican Communion though she was, in her career, very much in the

Catholic mold. The medical facts are briefly as follows.* Her health began to deteriorate when she was 13. At 15 she contracted diphtheria and spent nine weeks in hospital. On her return home she developed pneumonia and pleurisy and hovered on the brink of death. She was thereafter bedridden for many years after a bacterial examination revealed that she was infected with general tuberculosis. In 1911, at the age of 22, a diagnosis of tubercular peritonitis was recorded that was complicated by a tubercular meningitis that eventually rendered her blind and unconscious. She was kept alive for six weeks on a diet of brandy, opium and starch but by February 18 her doctor declared that she was unlikely to last another day. Her friends duly gathered at her bedside to pay their last respects and by 9:30 p.m. it looked as if she had breathed her last and as if her heart had stopped beating. It was then that she sat up, called for her dressing-gown and, to the consternation of those present, calmly announced that she wanted her supper. Her doctor arrived the next morning, expecting to sign the death certificate but was amazed to find her well and healthy. She had weighed a mere 63 pounds when he had last weighed her and he reckoned that she must have put on about 28 pounds overnight! A subsequent X-ray showed that her lungs, which had wasted away, were as if new and blood tests revealed no sign of the former infection.

How had it happened? According to the patient herself it was simplicity itself. She had had a vision of an angel surrounded by bright light who spoke to her saying: "Dorothy, your sufferings are over, get up and walk"! In any case, medical science has no better explanation to offer in its stead. She lived to a ripe age and the rest of her life was devoted to good works and, more especially, to the practice and promotion of healing through the power of Christ, as she conceived it to be.

---

* *I was unable to locate an account of her case in the medical literature despite an inquiry I made with the Dorothy Kerin Trust. The warden, in her reply, writes: "The records of Dr. Norman who attended her are not likely, in any way, to be available after two World Wars and, to my knowledge, there is no record in medical journals of her case, though research would discover this." I have had to rely, therefore, on a biography by Dorothy Musgrave Arnold,* Dorothy Kerin: Called by Christ to Heal *(Tunbridge Wells: K & SC Printers, 1965), a work of devotional literature, not a scientific treatise. The author quotes at some length from a contemporary booklet that was issued by the Rev. J.L. Thompson, who had ministered to Dorothy's spiritual needs during her five years of illness with the signed testimony of seven witnesses who were present at the critical event. According to the author, "The stir made in the medical and journalistic worlds by the miraculous healing of Dorothy Kerin was widespread" (p. 18). It is of some interest in the assessment of this case to note that, in December 1915, Dorothy developed the stigmata which remained visible for the remainder of her life and I have been shown copies of the testimony of priests and others who were permitted to examine her. In 1929, Dorothy founded her first nursing home at Ealing, London, under the patronage of the Archbishop of Canterbury and, in 1948, this was moved to Burrswood in Kent, where it still flourishes under the auspices of the Churches Council for Health and Healing as, in the words of the Trust: "a centre for divine healing and medical care, a partnership between orthodox medicine and Christian ministry in the healing of the whole person."*

I have dwelt on two spectacular cases but, of course, the practice of psychic or spiritual healing has become widespread and a great many remarkable cures are to be found in the relevant literature. It is, however, worth noting in this context, that, although most healers in the West operate under the auspices of a church or religious body and regard themselves as no more than a channel for the divine power, psychic healing of a very similar kind, with the laying on of hands, etc., is now quite common in the Soviet Union and there have been some outstandingly successful exponents there. But they do not, to my knowledge, claim divine inspiration.

So much for miracles. But, if we acknowledge them as genuine paranormal events, they pose a problem alike for the theologian and for the parapsycholgoist. For the theologian they pose again what I like to call the central paradox of theism — or should we call it Job's unanswered question — namely why is God so sparing with his miracles? If He can intervene at all, why so seldom? Is it possible that He does not care? An uncaring God would seem to be a contradiction in terms and such an entity would scarcely deserve our worship. Is it possible that He is powerless to prevent suffering as we so often are? This is, I suppose, conceivable but, quite apart from the fact that an impotent God lacks credibility, the implications of the miracles we have been considering is that God does *not* lack the power provided he chooses to use it. Even more perplexing is the question as to why He should see fit to afflict his creatures with all manner of dreadful diseases so that once in a while He can arbitrarily single out one of their number for a spectacular reprieve? For reasons such as these, I, for one, cannot accept the idea of God as a person, however mysterious or otherworldly, as is clearly implied when we use such traditional epithets as "creator," "ruler," "law-giver," "judge," or "father."

On the other hand, miracles cannot be easily assimilated to a purely secular science either. When confronted with some paranormal manifestation, parapsychologists have tended to attribute it to certain unconscious powers residing in the living person. J.B. Rhine always held fast to that interpretation (see my article, "J.B. Rhine and the Nature of Psi," in K.R. Rao [1982]). Yet one reaches a point where one hesitates to go on stretching indefinitely even such an elastic concept as that of the unconscious. When that point is reached, the parapsychologist may have to consider the possibility of there being some kind of a suprapersonal dimension to psi.* Jung, who had a better nose for the paranormal than Freud, was driven to extend the personal unconscious and introduce a collective unconscious. But even the collective unconscious may be inadequate. The parapsychologist may need to come to terms with something in the nature of a cosmic mind conceived as being at once a universal data bank and a reservoir of power which suitably endowed individuals can occasionally

* *Thus, Robert Morris (1975) suggests the term "superordinate psi source" in his paper "Tacit Communication and Experimental Theology."*

draw upon in order to achieve some paranormal goal. Perhaps it is just such a cosmic mind that the great mystics, from all ages and from all faiths, have been alluding to when they claim to be in direct communion with the godhead.

Notes

a. Most thoughtful Christians would, I am sure, agree with me. Thus, Michael Perry (1984, p. 49) writes: "It all boils down to the fact that, when we talk of the "transcendent" or of "God," this world is a world of faith and not of proof," or, again, "Christianity insists that, in this life we walk by faith and not by sight and the Christian who comes across the paranormal can help people see where knowledge ends and faith takes over." Where I, as a rationalist, part company with a devout Christian, like Perry, is precisely my refusal to accept any proposition on the basis of faith and without adequate reason.

b. Ironically, his view contrasts sharply with that of his archdeacon, the Venerable Michael Perry whom we have just cited in a above. In his essay "Resurrection" (Perry 1984, pp. 151–66) and, in his earlier book, The Easter Enigma *(1959), he has defended a paranormal interpretation of the events surrounding the death of Jesus.*

c. I revert to this case in somewhat more detail in my paper "Extreme Phenomena . . ." (see pages 175–90).

d. This is not quite correct; the event described took place in a private chapel where the Duke and his two companions were permitted to watch unobserved while Joseph was saying mass (see note c above).

e. This is incorrect. She was far too ill to make the pilgrimage herself but sent a friendly neighbor in her stead. The case is discussed in greater detail in my paper "Extreme Phenomena . . ." (pages 175–90) after I had access to the account given in Montgeron (1745).

f. Flew (1986) objects to the use of the expression "a priori" in connection with Hume's argument even though Hume himself used this phrase. "[I]t is simply grotesque to complain," Flew writes, "in the absence of any falsifying evidence that these appeals to the BLPs [Basic Limiting Principles] and the named laws of established physics are exercises in a priori *dogmatism. For what "apriori" means is: prior to and independent of experience." In the light of Flew's stricture, I am willing to withdraw the term "a priori" and substitute a phrase such as "blanket rejection." The point is that Hume's position, taken to its logical conclusion, which would mean in the last resort denying the evidence of one's own senses, leads to a* reductio ad absurdum.

What Is Your Counter-Explanation?
A Plea to Skeptics to Think Again

I was one of the contributors to the Handbook of Parapsychology *(Wolman 1977). It came as a surprise, nevertheless, when almost ten years later I was invited by Paul Kurtz to contribute to his* A Skeptic's Handbook of Parapsychology. *I had been told that Piet Hein Hoebens had persuaded Kurtz that his handbook would be improved if he included contributions from "believers" as well as skeptics in contrast to the Wolman handbook, which had no contributions from skeptics. The paper which follows represents my response to Kurtz' welcome invitation. I was fortunate that Hoebens himself offered to read my original draft and it was his valuable comments that led me to rewrite it drastically in the form in which it was published. This gifted Dutch journalist, though an avowed skeptic whose investigative journalism had been put to good skeptical use, was also a highly respected figure in the parapsychological community. His suicide in October 1984, at the early age of 36, was a devastating blow to all who knew him (see the obituary by Brian Millar [1985] in the June issue of J.S.P.R.). He thus did not survive to see the* Skeptic's Handbook *to which he had himself contributed (Hoebens 1986) but I duly dedicated my own contribution to his memory.*

Belief is not a matter of choice. In the end, either one is convinced by the evidence or the arguments or one is not. Long before that stage is reached, however, there is ample room for dialogue. Perhaps the evidence on which we based our belief was inadequate. Perhaps the arguments on which we relied were unsound. At all events, I think it is important that the dialogue between parapsychologists and their critics should continue. There will always be those who will say that controversy is a waste of time, that the two sides will never see eye to eye, that time spent in this way would be better spent on research. But, while I have some sympathy with this view, I regard it as short-sighted.

So long as incredulity remains the typical response of the scientific community to parapsychological claims, parapsychology will be accorded a low level of priority in the competition for funding and resources, and this, in turn, will retard its progress, thereby reinforcing the initial incredulity. Is there any way out of this impasse?

There are, I suggest, two assumptions skeptics habitually make that should not go unchallenged. The first is that only the strict experimental evidence needs to be taken seriously, that any other kind of evidence can be dismissed as anecdotal and unscientific. The second assumption is that, given the antecedent improbability of the phenomena, nothing short of their becoming commonplace—which means, in effect, finding a way of producing them on demand, could ever justify our accepting them at face value. The two assumptions go hand in hand. Thus, if there were, at the present time, some unequivocally repeatable psi effect, there would be every reason to emphasize the experimental evidence because it alone would allow us to satisfy ourselves as to its validity without having to take anyone else's word for it. But, of course, if such were the case, parapsychology would no longer be the controversial science that it now is. The present controversy takes as its point of departure the fact that the disputed phenomena are too unstable and elusive to permit such an outcome. We cannot even say at the present time whether such an outcome is even theoretically possible. In these circumstances the experimental evidence takes on a very different complexion. For an unrepeatable experiment is just another unique historical event; it no longer represents a recipe for obtaining similar results as experiments ordinarily purport to do.

Hence, to rely exclusively on the experimental evidence to settle the question of the basic existence of psi is to betray a profound misunderstanding of the role of experimentation in science. Scientists do not carry out experiments with the aim, primarily, of making converts, though every successful experiment strengthens the credibility of the phenomenon under investigation. They carry out experiments in order to test hypotheses and thereby advance our understanding of the phenomena. And, if a truly repeatable experiment should prove possible, it is precisely by increasing our knowledge of the phenomena that we shall arrive at it. That is why most parapsychological researchers at the present time are avowedly "process oriented" rather than "proof oriented" in their work, even when their original belief in the reality of psi may have sprung from some personal experience and not from their work in the laboratory. But, however important such process-oriented research may be in the long run, I do not think we have yet reached the stage where it can be made to bear the weight of the controversy directed at the proof issue.

Meanwhile, there is a danger that exclusive preoccupation with the experimental evidence may lead us to overlook the fact that what we may be getting in the laboratory is no more than a weak, fitful, or degenerate manifestation of psi. After all, no one would ever have had recourse to the laboratory in the first instance had there not been a strong presumption that psi occurs in the outside world and has done so in every age and in every society of which we have knowledge. Obviously the laboratory affords a degree of security, rigor, and control in a way that is hardly possible in the field, but such advantages must be set against the disadvantages of dealing with psi effects whose very presence can only be detected by means of statistical analysis. Should the skeptic's attention, then, be redirected to the spontaneous evidence?

The snag is that it is then that the second assumption comes into its own. The argument is essentially that which David Hume first propounded in his famous essay on miracles.* A miracle, he pointed out, is, by definition, a singular exception to some law of nature. But, since the laws of nature are daily confirmed in our experience, no mere human testimony, however imposing, could ever suffice to outweigh the reason we have for doubting it. The fatal weakness of this argument, as I see it, is that it is bound to fail when put to the test. Thus we would have no difficulty envisaging a *hypothetical* situation where we would be left in no doubt whatsoever that a paranormal event had occurred. To take a concrete, if jocular, example, we could imagine a press conference in the White House at which the president of the United States, in full view of audience, security officers, and television cameras, were suddenly to vanish and, as suddenly, reappear elsewhere. Whether any *actual* event similarly rules out the element of doubt is, of course, quite another matter, although Hume, to his credit, does try to make his argument proof against such a contingency. Thus he goes out of his way to remind the reader that, only shortly before the time he was writing, a whole series of miraculous cures had been reported from the cemetery of St. Médard in Paris. (For an account of these events, which puzzled not only Hume but even Voltaire, see Dingwall 1947, chapter 4.) He then concedes that, other things being equal, the evidence for their authenticity must be acknowledged as overwhelming. But, precisely because they are miraculous, a rational person has no option but to reject them as spurious. But, in saying this, Hume is surely mistaken. A point may be reached, as our hypothetical example showed, where no one, rational or otherwise, has any option but to believe. What, in fact, Hume has done, all unwittingly, is to furnish a *reductio ad absurdum* of his own argument. If the evidence he cites for the events in question were indeed so overwhelming, we would have to accept it, miracles or no miracles. Actually, few skeptics are content these days to base their case on the *a priori* impossibility of psi phenomena. We have witnessed so many upheavals in science that we are much less prone than were Hume's contemporaries to suppose that either science or common sense can tell us in advance what can or cannot be the case.[a] Perhaps we are more ready these days to agree with St. Augustine when

* *David Hume,* An Enquiry Concerning Human Understanding, *1748, section 10, "Of Miracles."*

he pointed out that a miracle was not so much contrary to nature as contrary to what we know of nature (*The City of God*, 21:8).

Let us assume, anyhow, that we are not all Humean skeptics and that we are willing to consider the possible existence of phenomena that do not meet the strongest criterion of validation production on demand. How then are we to set about deciding rationally between belief and doubt? The main aim of this paper is to suggest an appropriate strategy. It is the following. Whenever one is confronted with a claim, from whatever source, that has certain paranormal implications, one should ask oneself what normal explanation there could be that would obviate the necessity of invoking anything of a paranormal nature. The question, then, is whether this alternative explanation is more or less plausible than the original paranormal claim. This strategy will not solve the controversy, if only because what to one person may seem a perfectly reasonable scenario may strike another as wildly implausible and far-fetched. Nevertheless, such a strategy can, I maintain, serve to sharpen a controversy that is always likely to get out of focus.

The Problem of the Counter-Explanation

The significance of the counter-explanation was brought home to me some years ago when, in answer to a challenge, I wrote a paper for the *Zetetic Scholar* in which I discussed seven classic experiments in the parapsychological literature that I regarded as strong evidence for the existence of psi (Beloff 1980). Of the four well-known skeptics whose commentaries were also published, only one, Christopher Scott (1980), offered a specific counter-explanation for any of my seven experiments. The other critics were all content to disagree with me on general grounds. The particular experiment that Scott elected to probe was the so-called "Brugmans Experiment," which took place at the University of Groningen in Holland in 1921 (perhaps the earliest parapsychological experiment to be conducted under university auspices). Only a single special subject was involved in this experiment, and the task on each trial was to point to a square on a checkerboard of 48 squares that corresponded with the square designated as a target for that trial. Scott's suggestion was that the instructions might have allowed a certain ambiguity as to when a trial was concluded and so which square had been chosen. In that case, an overzealous observer might consistently misread the signals, and this could have accounted for the highly significant scores obtained. I am not by any means convinced that this is what *did* happen. On the contrary I would have thought it inconceivable that any experimenter (and here there were three) could be so foolish as to carry on a lengthy experiment that ran to many sessions when, all the time, there was some doubt about what response the subject was actually making — which is, after all, the one critical item of any experiment.

Nevertheless, I had to concede that Scott's counter-explanation was compatible with the account we have of the experiment, and I gladly acknowledge its ingenuity and the spirit in which it was offered.*

Some readers may suspect that, by insisting on a counter-explanation, I am attempting to shift the burden of proof from the claimant, where it rightly belongs, onto the critic who contests the claim. I must therefore point out that, once he has published his claim, the claimant has already done everything that is initially required of him. If someone then wishes to query it, it is up to that person to state his objections. Of course no one needs to set up as a critic. There are many situations in life when the wisest course of action is simply to admit ignorance or bafflement and leave it at that. But anyone who enters the arena of controversy cannot shirk the consequences. Too often critics of parapsychology are content to use mockery and ridicule in their efforts to bring the field into disrepute. And, since the literature of psychical research is full of fraudulent and farcical incidents, they are assured of an easy time. But in the interests of truth this temptation should be resisted. My demand for counter-explanations is a plea to forego rhetoric and examine the facts. Even so, is it reasonable to expect a critic to be able to come forward with a counter-explanation in all cases? How can we be sure, for example, that the case we are being asked to consider has been fully and accurately reported? How do we know that there might not be somewhere a fragment of evidence that, if it were available, would cast a different light on the case as a whole? Perhaps there are telltale clues buried in the data that, if we could but interpret them, would invalidate the claim. It took, after all, some thirty years and recourse to computers before definite evidence of data manipulation was finally discovered in the famous Soal-Shackleton series (Markwick 1978; 1985). Certainly, if the demand for a counter-explanation meant putting one's finger on exactly what was amiss in a given case, we could well be accused of trying to force the issue. But it is not unreasonable to expect a critic to indicate the weak points in the evidence and state where we should look for the most promising counter-explanation.

This much, at least, is presumably now common ground between parapsychologists and their critics. Where they still cannot agree is whether a given counter-explanation is more or less credible than the alleged facts that it purports to dispose of. Understandably, most critics concentrate on the latest experiments to attract attention, where information about methods and conditions are still open to inspection. But, although the task of finding a counter-explanation in this area is becoming increasingly more difficult because, with the advent of computers and automation, so many of the pitfalls that were relevant in the days of J.B. Rhine now no longer apply, for the reasons I have

---

* *Prompted by Scott, Piet Hein Hoebens of Amsterdam was able to obtain from Groningen an earlier version of the report, where, sure enough, this ambiguity was more apparent.*

discussed, I do not think this is the ground where we can yet expect a showdown. If asked what it is that makes me side with the believers rather than the skeptics, I would have to say, I suppose, that it is less this or that particular case than the global impression I derive from my survey of the literature that something real is going on that defies conventional explanations. However, one cannot argue about global impressions, so it is necessary for me to pick out a concrete example that can serve as the basis of discussion. What should that example be? People differ with regard to what they find persuasive so I can only say that, for my part, the most convincing evidence I know in the literature of psychical research is to be found in the careers of those exceptional individuals who (a) appeared to possess psi ability to a very high degree and (b) were willing to allow themselves to be used in the interests of research. This combination has, unfortunately, become increasingly rare over the years, but there still remains a galaxy of such star subjects from whose well-documented case studies one can choose. The one I have chosen to illustrate my theme is Eusapia Palladino.

The Case of Eusapia Palladino (1854–1918)

The case of Palladino will no doubt strike some of my readers as little short of perverse. Was she not long ago discredited, I can hear them ask, when she was caught cheating and all her so-called phenomena were shown to be mere tricks? But, as so often in this treacherous field, a closer look shows how superficial such a judgment would be. There are undoubtedly a great many blemishes in her case but, equally, there are many valuable lessons we can learn from studying it. It was true enough that she preferred to operate under cover of darkness, as was the wont among mediums of that epoch, and reserved the right to veto any condition that she did not fancy. It is true enough that she cheated repeatedly, shamelessly, and outrageously. Nor can we take too seriously her own standard excuse that she could not be held responsible for anything she might do in her trances. Too many of her tricks were too contrived and rehearsed for that. And it is true, finally, that her phenomena were notoriously ludicrous, inconsequential, and repetitious even by the standards of the familiar mediumistic repertoire of the time. But, having said all that, one then has to add that all these facts were well known to her investigators from the very outset. And yet, in spite of this, they were undaunted, and their curiosity to observe ever more remained insatiable. Moreover, these same investigators were not obscure individuals or simple-minded spiritualists; they included some of the outstanding names in European science, who had everything to lose if it could be shown that they were being duped. For the fact is that Eusapia was investigated more frequently, more intensively, and by more different qualified investigators than any other individual in the annals of psychical research. Consequently, whatever construction we care to put on this fact, we cannot evade the question of how this uneducated peasant woman from Naples who could barely write her own name succeeded for nearly 20 years in enthralling the scientific elite of Europe. For, with very few exceptions, nearly all those who studied her at first hand, however incredulous they might be to start with, came to the conclusion that her phenomena were genuine—that is to say, whatever else they might portend, they were not due to trickery—and they adhered to this conclusion to the end.

So what were these strange phenomena that she purveyed?* They can be divided for convenience into the following main categories: (1) Acoustic phenomena, mainly loud raps. This was a very common accompaniment of sittings with physical mediums. (2) Kinetic phenomena, e.g., the movement of small objects, the playing of musical instruments, and—a prominent feature of her mediumship—the total levitation of the séance table; or very occasionally, of the medium herself. (3) A sudden loss of weight during a séance when the medium was seated on a weighing machine. (4) Cool breezes of sufficient force to cause the window curtains to billow out into the room or the medium's skirts to billow outwards. (5) Luminous phenomena, e.g., transient light effects, luminous apparitions, etc. And, perhaps the queerest item of the whole repertoire, (6) Materializations. These were much cruder than those associated with some of the famous materializing mediums and usually took the form of rudimentary heads or hands that would emerge from behind the curtains. Sometimes, however, it looked as if the medium herself had sprouted additional limbs, or "pseudopods," as they came to be known. Sitters would also sometimes feel themselves gripped or pinched as if by a living hand that they did not see. All the foregoing phenomena were familiar to psychical researchers of that era; indeed, Palladino's phenomena were much less spectacular than those of some other mediums. One phenomenon that does appear to be unique to her case was the jet of cool air that would sometimes be observed to emanate from a scar in her forehead, usually at the end of a séance.*

Her phenomena always occurred within the vicinity of her body, although not necessarily within her reach. I know of no instance where she was able to exert an effect on a remote object or on one inside a sealed container. The arrangement at her séances, which eventually became standard, was to have at least two controllers, one on each side, to keep hold of her hands and feet, although sometimes another person would lie on the floor to hold her legs. She was seated in front of a curtained recess that diagonally cut off a corner of the room. This was known as the "cabinet" and was regarded by spiritualists as a

---

* *The most comprehensive account known to me is Carrington (1909), but see also entry under "Paladino" in Fodor (1966 [1934]) and Dingwall (1950, chapter 5). Dingwall's essay is still the best general introduction that I know and has an invaluable bibliography.*

sort of powerhouse for generating physical phenomena. Illumination varied a great deal even within a single séance, depending mainly on her whim. Sometimes the only illumination came from a bare window; but, as the sittings were always held in the late evening or at night, this was somewhat residual. Sometimes, however, artificial light was permitted, and toward the end of her career electric light was regularly used, but always shaded to give a red glow. In the more important investigations a stenographer would be employed, whose sole duty was to write down an account of every incident as it occurred, dictated by one or another of the sitters. In this way, nothing would be left to memory.

The list of those who sat with her is an imposing one. I do not think there is any doubt, however, that her most assiduous investigator, who could boast of having sat through more than a hundred of her séances, was Charles Richet of the University of Paris, a Nobel Laureate physiologist, a psychologist, and a psychical researcher. Richet has been portrayed as a rather credulous man,* so it is only fair to point out that, when he began his career in psychical research, he was just as skeptical as most of the other scientists of that time and even joined in the chorus of derision that greeted William Crookes, though he later had the good grace to retract his words.† His "credulity" seems to have consisted of an inability to doubt the evidence of his senses! But, in any case, he was by no means alone in his endorsement of Eusapia, and I must now try rapidly to cover the principal investigations of her that were undertaken between 1891 and 1907 (much of this is taken from Carrington 1909, part 3).

The first person of international standing to be converted to a belief in Eusapia's abilities was the psychiatrist Cesare Lombroso of the University of Turin, now best remembered as the founder of criminology. He and a group of scientists held sittings with her in Naples in 1891 and duly issued a positive report. The following year a second investigation, in which Richet himself participated, was carried out in Milan, under the direction of G. Schiaparelli, the head of the Milan observatory. The report that issued from this investigation included photographs of complete table levitations obtained in good light. But it is of interest, in view of what I was saying about Richet's reputation for credulity, that he was not satisfied that every possibility of deception had yet been eliminated and refused to sign the report. Richet again participated in the series of sittings held in Rome from 1893 to 1894, but it was not until after he had held sittings under his own direction and at his own residence, in the summer of 1894, that he was ready to relinquish further doubts about the

---

* Most recently by Ruth Brandon, who in her caustic book (Brandon 1983, p. 135) speaks of "his will to believe and his disinclination to accept any unpalatable contrary indications."

† See Richet (1922, p. 35). His long treatise is dedicated to William Crookes and Frederic Myers. An account of Richet's involvement in psychical research is given in Fodor (1966 [1934]) under "Richet."

phenomena. *"C'est absolument absurde mais c'est vrai,"* he used to say. These investigations took place partly at his château at Carqueiranne (near Toulon) and partly on the Ile Roubaud, a small Mediterranean island (near Hyères), where his cottage was the only dwelling and where, apart from the lighthouse-keeper and his wife, Richet, his family, and his servants were the only inhabitants, a fact that made him feel all the more confident that there could be no accomplices lurking in the vicinity.

The sittings with Eusapia on the Ile Roubaud were particularly productive of phenomena, including some of the most impressive that are attributed to her, although it must be admitted that artificial light was excluded so that the only illumination came from the windows and the night sky. The sitters, however, were all seasoned psychical researchers. Oliver Lodge and Frederic Myers of the Society for Psychical Research (SPR) were Richet's guests from England, and they were joined later by Henry and Eleanor Sidgwick. Julian Ochorowicz, the Polish psychologist and psychical researcher, who completed the team, had already directed 40 sittings with Eusapia in Warsaw, which had impressed him. Otherwise there was just the professional stenographer to keep the minute-by-minute record of the proceedings. A very positive report on these sittings duly appeared in the *Journal of the SPR* in November 1894, written by Lodge but endorsed by Myers and by the Sidgwicks.* One detail is worth quoting. Lodge mentions that "raps on the table, which were frequent, were so strong as to feel dangerous: they sounded like blows delivered by a heavy mallet."

One outcome of the Ile Roubaud experience was that the SPR decided to investigate Eusapia for themselves. A series of sittings were held with her in the late summer of 1895 in Cambridge, at the house of Myers, where she stayed. They were a severe disappointment. The phenomena were sparse, and time and again she was caught cheating. Her ruse was to free one of her hands by first bringing her two hands together and then, after a certain amount of wriggling, contrive to make the controllers on either side think that each was still holding a different hand when in fact they were grasping different parts of the same hand. Why the Cambridge sittings were such a flop is still a matter of controversy and speculation. Eusapia's supporters protest that she was uncomfortable in the stuffy atmosphere of Cambridge academic society, although Eleanor Sidgwick denies that this was so and insists that they all did everything they could do to make her stay a cheerful one.† Others lay the

---

* *Lodge (1894) writes: "Any person without invincible prejudice who had the same experience would have come to the same conclusion, viz: that things hitherto held impossible do occur." Lodge never saw any reason to retract this conclusion and, in his autobiography (Lodge 1931), he amplifies his account of his experiences on the Ile Roubaud.*

† *In a footnote to her review of Morselli's* Psicologia e Spiritismo *in the* Proceedings of the SPR, *21 (1909): 522. She was even then not yet satisfied as to the authenticity of the phenomena.*

blame on Richard Hodgson (this is certainly the view taken by Cassirer 1983a). Hodgson had come over from Boston especially for the occasion and soon took command of the situation. Ten years previously his report on Mme. Blavatsky had been issued by the SPR. He had openly accused her of fraud on an exten- sive scale.[b] Probably he was now hoping to add Eusapia to his trophies. At all events, he had heard about her mode of cheating and decided that the best way to find out more about it was deliberately to let go of a hand at certain critical moments to see what she would then do. The result deeply shocked both Myers and the Sidgwicks, who felt that they had been betrayed and even doubted whether they could any longer assume that the events they had witnessed on the Ile Roubaud were all that they seemed to be. Lodge, on the other hand, took it more philosophically. But the upshot was that henceforth it became official SPR policy not to continue working with a medium who had once been caught cheating.

The policy was curiously illogical on the part of a philosopher of Sidgwick's caliber, since it was the medium's ability not her morals that were on trial. The question, after all, was never whether Eusapia *would* cheat if the opportunity arose but rather whether she *could* cheat in the circumstances and, if the answer is that she *could* cheat, then the test was invalid in the first place.* Fortunately, the Continental researchers were not so easily put off, so the Cam- bridge fiasco did not bring her career to an abrupt end. Thus, in 1898, in Paris, a large committee under the direction of Camille Flammarion, the astronomer, went into action in Flammarion's own house. One of the incidents described by Flammarion himself involved an accordion that apparently played of its own accord while he held the end opposite the keyboard and Eusapia's hands were tightly restrained. Richet participated in these sittings but then held some fur- ther sittings for her in the library of his own house in Paris. One of those invited was the distinguished Swiss psychologist Theodore Flournoy of the University of Geneva, who has given us his own account of these sittings, which fully con- vinced him of the authenticity of the phenomena.†

The next big investigation took place in Genoa under the direction of Enrico Morselli, head of a clinic for nervous and mental diseases, who held 20 sittings with Eusapia from 1901 to 1902 and then 6 further sittings there in the winter of 1906–1907. The latter attracted widespread publicity in the Italian press and Carrington describes them as "among the most remarkable and

---

* *It is curious how often this point has been misunderstood. Thus Ruth Brandon (1983) writes: "In all other scientific fields to be caught out just once in fraud is to be instantly discredited." But this confuses the experimenter and the subject. An experimenter who cheats is instantly discredited in parapsychology as in all other sciences and all his results discounted as suspect. But, if a subject cheats, this shows only that the experimenter has been careless and should try harder.*

† *See Flournoy (1911, chapter 7). He mentions there that "Myers was this time—as were all the others—absolutely convinced of the reality of the phenomena" (p. 246).*

convincing that have ever been held," but Morselli himself thought that her powers already appeared to be waning when compared with her performance during the earlier sittings. One of the sitters at the Genoa investigation was Philippe Botazzi, head of the physiological institute of the University of Naples, who in 1907 had an opportunity to test Eusapia in his own laboratory and, as did so many others, underwent the process of having his initial incredulity converted into complete conviction.

In the same year, Lombroso came back into the picture. He organized a series of sittings in the department of psychiatry at the University of Turin that was attended by a number of medical men. It was followed by a fresh series of sittings in Turin under the direction of Pio Foà, professor of pathological anatomy and general secretary of the Academy of Sciences. His committee stated in their report: "Without the objective irrefutable documents which remained, we should have doubted our sense and intelligence." It is worth citing one incident that involved a strong white-wood table (2' 9" high, 3' long, and 22" wide, weighing 17 lbs.), which, instead of just receiving the loud raps like those Lodge had described, actually broke into pieces before their astonished gaze and in what is described as "very good red light" (Carrington 1909, p. 106). This incident followed an announcement by the medium herself that she intended to break the table for them. (It was characteristic of her to say in advance what was going to happen.) It must, one supposes, require an extra-strong dose of skepticism to doubt evidence of that magnitude!

There were still other investigations that need not detain us, but some mention should be made of the lengthy series of sittings with Eusapia in Paris, organized by the Institut Général Psychologique between 1905 and 1908. A report on these sittings was issued under the name of Jules Courtier, secretary of the Institute. The importance of this series is twofold: Photography and instrumentation, including electrical security devices for monitoring the medium's feet, were used more extensively than in any of the previous series. Secondly, the list of sitters included such luminaries as Pierre and Marie Curie and Henri Bergson. Eusapia was also subjected to a battery of psychological tests, although nothing notable emerged from this. Many of the special tests devised for her failed, and on several occasions she was caught cheating, but the report is far from being dismissive of the phenomena in general.*

Yet, in spite of this load of testimony and the huge number of professional man-hours it represents, in 1908 it could still be said (quite unfairly in my opinion) that scientists are the last people who can be trusted to see through

---

* *A lengthy review of this report by Count Perovsky-Petrovo-Solovovo appeared as a supplement to the issue of* SPR Proceedings *that contains the Feilding Report (Feilding et al. 1909). Flournoy is rather more brusque with the Courtier Report, which he accused of prevarication. Since they appeared incapable of saying either* oui *or* non *when it came to the authenticity of the phenomena, Flournoy (1911, p. 272) suggested that they ought to reply in chorus:* Nouin!

a wily imposter, that only a trained illusionist can appreciate the manifold possibilities of deception and sleight-of-hand.* This objection, however, does not apply to the investigation to which we must now turn, where all three investigators not only were themselves highly proficient in the art of conjuring but were, indeed, the acknowledged experts on the special techniques of fraudulent mediumship.

The Feilding Report

At the beginning of the year 1908, the American psychical researcher Hereward Carrington went to see Everard Feilding, then honorary secretary of the SPR. Some 22 official reports on Palladino had already appeared, but Carrington persuaded Feilding that, despite its earlier ban, it was time for the SPR to have another go before it was too late, and the consent of the Council was duly obtained. The two men took themselves off to Naples, where they were later joined by W.W. Baggally, a Council member and an expert on trickery, who had sat with Palladino but without becoming convinced that she was genuine. It was this trio who made up the "Naples Committee" and, as a testimonial to their competence for the task at hand, I cannot do better than quote the words of that distinguished scholar and erstwhile fellow of the Committee for the Scientific Investigation of Claims of the Paranormal (CSICOP), Eric Dingwall (1950):

> I was intimately acquainted with all three investigators. Mr. Carrington was one of the keenest investigators in the United States. He had unrivalled opportunities to examine the host of frauds and fakers who flourished there, and his results led him to suppose that of the alleged physical phenomena the vast bulk was certainly produced by fraudulent means and devices, as he himself asserts in his book (*The Physical Phenomena of Spiritualism*, New York, 1907; London, 1908). Mr. Feilding was also a man of vast experience and one of the keenest and most acute critics that this country has ever produced. ... Moreover his scepticism was extreme, although it was modified by an attitude of open-mindedness and an unwillingness to accept critical comments when these were not accompanied by properly adduced evidence. Mr. Baggally almost equalled Mr. Feilding in his scepticism

---

* *This view was first, I believe, put about by the celebrated illusionist, J.N. Maskelyne. He and his son had been invited to participate in the Cambridge sittings of 1895 and he soon formed a very poor opinion of Eusapia and perhaps an even poorer one of her investigators. "No class of men can be so readily deceived by trickery as scientists," he asserted. "Try as they may they cannot bring their minds down to the level of the subject and are as much at fault as if it were immeasurably above them" (cited in Brandon 1983, p. 138). Feilding, on the other hand insisted that scientists, as a class, are far more reluctant than conjurers to acknowledge any sort of supernormal force (see Feilding et al. 1909, Final Note). In fact, Maskelyne himself once stated to a journalist who interviewed him that, as a result of personal experiences with friends, he had to admit that there was something we could not explain about "table-turning" phenomena, though he felt sure it was not the action of spirits (Brandon 1983, p. 166).*

and desire for investigation. He knew more about trick methods than his illustrious colleague and thus he was better able to concentrate on essentials. For over thirty years he had attended seances, but had come to the conclusion that rarely, if ever, had he encountered one genuine physical medium. This, then, was the committee which Eusapia consented to face.

The three men booked into the Hotel Victoria in Naples and there, in their rooms on the fifth floor, between November 21 and December 19, 1908, 11 sittings were held, the minutes of which go to make up what I am here calling "The Feilding Report" (though all three put their name to it). It was published the following year in the *Proceedings of the SPR* with a gracious foreword by Eleanor Sidgwick (Feilding et al. 1909). It is a document that is still worth reading, not just as an account of certain extraordinary phenomena but also as a record of the moral struggle of each man with himself as he wrestled with his doubts and misgivings before finally succumbing to the only conclusion that honesty would allow. It was not until after the sixth séance, so Feilding informs us, that he himself was ready to commit himself. It is worth quoting at some length from the note he wrote on December 6, following this séance:

> My own frame of mind when starting on this investigation was that, in view of the concurrent opinion of practically all the eminent men of science who have investigated Eusapia's phenomena, it was inconceivable that they could, in turn, be deceived by the few petty tricks that have, from time to time, been detected, and that it was therefore probable that the phenomena were real. All my own experiments in physical mediumship had resulted in the discovery of the most childish frauds. Failure had followed upon failure. While, therefore, I tended to accept the general hypothesis that the facts of the so-called spiritualistic physical manifestations, must on the evidence, be regarded as probably existent, my mental habit had become so profoundly sceptical, when it came to considering any given alleged instance of them, that I had ceased to have any expectation of finding it able to bear examination. The first seance with Eusapia, accordingly, provoked chiefly a feeling of surprise; the second, of irritation—irritation at finding oneself confronted with a foolish but apparently insoluble problem. The third seance, at which a trumpery trick was detected, came as a sort of relief. At the fourth, where the control of the medium was withdrawn from ourselves, my baffled intelligence sought to evade the responsibility of meeting facts by harbouring grotesque doubts as to the competency of the eminent professors who took our places, to observe things properly; while at the fifth, where this course was no longer possible, as I was constantly controlling the medium myself, the mental gymnastics involved in seriously facing the necessity of concluding in favor of what was manifestly absurd, produced a kind of intellectual fatigue.
>
> After the sixth, for the first time, I find that my mind, from which the stream of events has hitherto run off like rain from a macintosh, is at last beginning to be capable of absorbing them. For the first time I have the absolute conviction that our observation is not mistaken. I realize, as an appreciable fact in life, that, from an empty cabinet I have seen hands and heads come forth, that from behind the curtain of that empty cabinet I have been seized by living fingers, the existence and position of the very nails of which could be felt. I have seen this extraordinary

woman sitting visible outside the curtain, held hand and foot by my colleagues, immobile except for the occasional straining of a limb, while some entity within the curtain has over and over again pressed my hand in a position clearly beyond her reach. I refuse to entertain the possibility of a doubt that we were the victims of a hallucination. I appreciate exactly the fact that ninety-nine people out of a hundred will refuse to entertain the possibility of a doubt that it was anything else. And, remembering my own belief of a very short time ago, I shall not be able to complain, though I shall unquestionably be annoyed, when I find that to be the case [Feilding 1909, pp. 461–2].

I sometimes think that the Feilding Report should be made mandatory reading for any would-be member of CSICOP. Only those whose skepticism survived this ordeal intact would then need to apply! Yet, as this passage shows, Feilding knew only too well what to expect from his critics, and it could have come as no surprise when Frank Podmore, always the implacable enemy of the physical phenomena, wrote to the *Journal of the SPR* to attack the report. In his letter, published in the December 1909 issue, he reverts to the possibility of Eusapia's surreptitiously freeing a hand or foot and thereby accomplishing all the phenomena therein described (Podmore 1909). He was answered at length by Baggally (1910) in the following issue, February 1910, but alongside further letters supporting Podmore's criticisms. In his book *The Newer Spiritualism*, Podmore (1910, chapter 4) enlarges on this theme. He minutely dissects various séances in an effort to show where Eusapia might have been able to seize the advantage, but it is something of a tour de force and made no impact on the authors of the report. Podmore, we must remember, had never sat with Eusapia. In the end, he graciously admits that the job could not have been done more competently than it was by the Naples Committee, but he took his stand on his contention that no one, given the constraints within which they had to operate, could have got the better of Eusapia; and he urged that, unless she could produce effects inside sealed containers, the SPR would be well advised to leave her strictly alone.

Although many skeptics will sympathize with Podmore's attitude, Eusapia's reputation would have been safe after the publication of the Feilding Report had it not been for the subsequent debacle of her American tour. For, in the following year, 1909, Hereward Carrington, emboldened by the success of the Naples Committee, arranged for Eusapia to visit the United States. It was a decision he would live to regret. She arrived amid a blaze of publicity and was at once in demand from all quarters. According to Carrington (1913; 1954) some 31 sittings were held in all, including the four that took place at Columbia University in New York. She was, he alleges, tired, overworked, and ill at ease among investigators with no previous experience of dealing with mediums. Although her sittings were by no means unproductive, they were disappointing by previous standards and, as so often happened with her when things were not going well, she lapsed into her old bad habit of cheating in the usual fashion. This was all that was needed for the skeptics to raise the hue and cry. Eminent psychologists, like Hugo Münsterberg of Harvard and Joseph Jastrow of the University of Wisconsin, after just a few sittings, rushed into print in the popular magazines to denounce her and claim credit for exposing her, oblivious to the 20 years of patient work that had been done with her in Europe. Mark Hansel (1966) quotes at length from these outbursts as demonstrating the superior wisdom and discernment of the unbeliever and, today, if Palladino is still mentioned by psychologists, it was Münsterberg and Jastrow who said the last word on her, not Feilding, Baggally, or Carrington.[c]

Conclusions

Are we then justified in dismissing the career of "this extraordinary woman," as Feilding called her, with the one simple word "trickery"? Trickery is, of course, another of those convenient open-ended and slippery concepts that, no less than the concept of the paranormal itself, can be invoked to explain anything whatsoever. All the same, it is not unreasonable to ask what conjurer would agree to perform under the conditions to which Eusapia regularly submitted? These included (1) performing in a private room that was first searched and then locked and sealed against intruders who might act as accomplices; (2) undergoing a thorough body search before the sitting began,* (3) allowing one's arms and legs to be held by sitters whose one duty was never to let go; (4) producing sometimes phenomena in light sufficient, it was said, to read the small print in one's Baedeker. At all events, one leading American magician who observed her during her American tour was so impressed by her performances that he offered to donate $1,000 to charity if any of his fellow magicians could do as much under comparable conditions. There were no takers. (See Rogo 1975, p. 27.)

Apart from sleight-of-hand trickery, the only other counter-explanation that was occasionally invoked in connection with Palladino was hallucination, especially with reference to her materializations and pseudopods.† It is a somewhat desperate explanation, especially as there was always more than one sitter; but, in the nature of the case, it is very difficult to deny. However, skeptics can always rely on one supreme ally: the poverty of the human

---

* Hansel (1980, p. 61) suggests that Eusapia might have taken advantage of her female prerogative to refuse such a search. However, the task was usually given to female sitters, such as the two American ladies who were invited to attend the eighth séance of the Naples series, but Carrington mentions specifically that at the conclusion of the very successful sixth séance, Eusapia made no objections to letting the three men search her (Feilding 1950).

† Alice Johnson, at one time honorary secretary of the SPR, would occasionally advance this hypothesis when all else failed; but for a recent discussion of the "pseudopods" phenomenon, see Cassirer (1983b).

imagination. Some things go so far beyond our familiar experience and are so inherently hard to credit that even to contemplate them imposes a severe strain on our intellectual equanimity. It is not, therefore, suprising that people are content to clutch at any straw as an excuse for not having to take these things seriously and are pathetically grateful to critics like Hansel whom they can cite in self-justification. To such people Eusapia's mismanaged American tour came as a godsend.

But, for those who are willing to make the leap of the imagination that is required if we are to put ourselves in the shoes of those who came face to face with her phenomena, who, so to speak, had their noses rubbed in them, there are a number of useful lessons we can learn from her career. In the first place, it reminds us that fraud can go hand in hand with genuine psychic ability, so that it is always risky to generalize from the discovery that cheating has occurred. There may be all kinds of psychological reasons why certain persons in certain situations indulge in trickery. We can also learn from her case that the more fantastic phenomena are not necessarily any less real than those of lesser magnitude. In particular, we can no longer justify dismissing materialization as too preposterous to warrant serious consideration.

This last point, in turn, reopens a host of other controversial historical cases that now demand to be looked at with a fresh eye and the received opinion if necessary challenged. What about the young Florence Cook, for example? Must we ignore her because in middle age she took to cheating? Must we continue to defame the memory of one of Britain's most illustrious (not to say bravest) scientists by insisting that he was either the dupe of this 16-year-old girl or else her lover, who for the sake of sexual favors betrayed his fellow scientists and the cause of truth?* And what of those cases that flourished in the decade after Palladino? What about poor "Eva C," with her ectoplasmic faces that looked to all the world so suspiciously two-dimensional? The SPR investigators could prove nothing against her, though they were reluctant to authenticate her phenomena; but Gustave Geley, of the Institut Métapsychique in Paris, insists that he watched the faces taking shape and was able to produce a certain amount of photographic evidence to support his contention.† And must we still ignore the mountain of evidence that exists on the Margery mediumship because of one compromising incident late in her career? After all, did not the great Houdini stake his reputation on exposing her and

---

* *This was the thesis of Trevor Hall's (1962) book and is the one favored by Ruth Brandon (1983, chapter 4). Those who are not persuaded that Sir William Crookes, O.M., was either an imbecile or an unprincipled blackguard may wish to consult the analysis of the "Katie King" séances provided by Dr. G. Zorab (1980), a Dutch scholar, although his book has so far appeared only in Italian and Dutch.*

† *A reevaluation of the case of Eva C. (Marthe Béraud) is given by Brian Inglis (1984, chapter 4).* [d]

fail ignominiously?* To take one more example, the most fantastic of them all, what are we to make of the Brazilian medium Carlos Mirabelli? If the so-called Santos Report were to be credited, he would rank as by far the most powerful medium on record, surpassing D.D. Home.† Deceased individuals known to the sitters are said to have materialized in broad daylight while the medium was seated in full view strapped to a chair. These same entities conversed with the sitters, submitted to a medical examination on the basis of which they were pronounced anatomically perfect, allowed themselves to be photographed and later dissolved into nothingness while the sitters looked on incredulously. The witnesses, moreover, were mainly persons of professional standing, many of them physicians. The only objection one can raise in Mirabelli's case is that he was never tested outside Brazil. Plans to bring him to Europe fell through. It is, however, embarrassing to have to base one's counter-explanation on the assumption that what happens in Brazil need not be taken seriously and that Brazilians, even medically qualified ones, cannot be trusted to tell the truth. The point is, however, that even in such an extreme case as this, where we have every reason to query the evidence and to express suspicion, we cannot escape the responsibility of putting forward *some* counter-explanation.

When cornered, there is always one last trump-card that the skeptic can brandish in the face of the believer: *Where are all these marvels now?* The harsh fact of the matter is that there are no more Palladini. For all I know to the contrary, the phenomenon of materialization may be extinct and may never recur. Except in connection with poltergeist cases, we cannot even be sure that there are any more strong phenomena. Hence, since historical cases can never compete in credibility with cases that are still open to further investigation, the skeptic cannot be faulted if, like Podmore, he prefers to suspend judgment pending the advent of more compelling evidence, always provided he does not invoke spurious reasons for rejecting what evidence there is. But, equally, if the negative option is still valid, so is the positive option. It is no less rational, and it is certainly more adventurous, to adopt an attitude of basic belief as one's working hypothesis. If we remain entrenched in a rigidly conservative stance, we are apt to neglect phenomena that may be both real and important. Moreover, the basic believer is spared those intellectual contortions

---

* *Margery (Mrs. Mina Crandon) was one of the most controversial mediums of the 20th century. Inglis (1984, p. 167) reproduces a photograph of her encased in Houdini's fraud-proof box ("like an old-fashioned steam-bath with a hole for her neck and two for her arms"). Houdini is shown holding one of her hands. The séance had no sooner started when the lid burst open and the phenomena continued! Marian Nester, of the American SPR, a daughter of Dr. Mark Richardson, Margery's chief investigator, is preparing a book about this medium that should provide new grounds for reconsidering her case.*

† *See Dingwall (1930). I am indebted to Brian Inglis for drawing attention to this document in his discussion of Mirabelli's mediumship. See Inglis (1984, pp. 221–7). Further information on Mirabelli is provided in Playfair (1975, chapter 3).*

to which a skeptic is now driven when confronted with evidence for which there is no plausible counter-explanation. Lastly, if in the future new cases of a spectacular nature should arise, the basic believer will be in a better position and better prepared to deal with them.

Notes

a. I discussed the logical status of Hume's argument in my previous paper (see p. 142 and note f). See also the final paper of this volume.

b. For a recent reassessment of the Hodgson Report on Blavatsky, see Harrison (1986).

c. It is all the more ironical in that Carrington went to the trouble, prior to Palladino's arrival in the United States, of circulating prospective sitters details of her detected frauds and of the best methods of controlling for them. See Carrington (1954).

d. Since I wrote my paper, Adrian Parker (1988) has drawn my attention to an adverse report by a German researcher (Lambert 1954) who had originally been impressed by the Eva C. phenomenon but had been shown certain stereoscopic photos by Eugene Osty at the Institut Métapsychique after Geley's death that were strongly indicative of fraudulent constructions. Undoubtedly Lambert's disclosures detract from the case for Eva C. and, indeed, her reputation never recovered from them, but do they demolish it? Inglis himself discusses at length the Lambert evidence (1984, pp. 240–2) but comes to the conclusion, which I would endorse, that it cannot cancel out all the arguments for thinking that Eva C., like Palladino, was a genuine physical medium.

Parapsychology and Radical Dualism

Having in a previous paper in this volume (pages 123–132) given my reasons for doubting whether there could be a physical explanation for psi, I now take up the theme again in this paper and argue that, since this disposes of physicalism — i.e., the doctrine that every real event must have a physical explanation — the existence of psi, if it does exist, leaves us with no viable option other than radical dualism — i.e., the doctrine that the domain of mind is radically different from the domain of matter.

The paper was originally presented at the 26th Annual Convention of the Parapsychological Association held at the Fairleigh Dickinson University at Madison, New Jersey, in August 1983. An abstract duly appeared in Research in Parapsychology 1983 *but, in the course of the convention, I was approached by Frank Tribbe who asked if the paper could be published in full in the* Journal of Religion and Psychical Research *for which he is chairman of the publication committee. I duly consented and the article eventually appeared in their January 1985 issue. It was there followed by papers from Alan Anderson, Steven Rosen, Frank Tribbe and Evan Walker (in that order) each of whom had been invited to comment on my contribution. I was not asked in turn to reply to my distinguished critics but a final commentary was provided by the eminent philosopher-theologian Hywel D. Lewis who, as I knew, shared my dualistic standpoint. With the reprinting of this article in this context, I am taking advantage of the occasion to reply to my critics with an "Epilogue 1990."*

By "radical dualism" I mean the view that mind and matter denote separate domains of nature which, nevertheless, interact with one another at certain critical points. I use this term in preference to the more familiar "Cartesian Dualism" in order to avoid such criticisms or misunderstandings as may be attached to Descartes' own formulation of the problem. Radical dualism thus stands in opposition to the view that mind is no more than an aspect of, a function of, an attribute of, certain brain activity. On this latter view, while mental concepts may well be necessary if we are going to talk intelligibly about our own or others' experience or behavior, they can have no real explanatory force since everything we do or say or think is ultimately dependent on the state of the brain conceived as a purely physical system. We may call this the physicalist position since it is based on the idea that all explanation, in the last resort, rests on the laws of physics, and it is, unquestionably, the orthodox position on the mind-brain relationship at the present time in neurophysiology, psychiatry, experimental psychology and, even, philosophy of mind, at any rate in the English-speaking world. This position must be distinguished from pure materialism, that is the idea that there is no such thing as mind or that mental processes are reducible without remainder to physical processes or to behavior. Pure materialism is, I contend, a philosophical mistake and therefore not a genuine option at all. The choice, as I see it, is between radical dualism and the weaker forms of dualism which merely deny any autonomy to the mental component of the psychophysical organism. As for idealism, the idea that mind alone exists, which is the only other monistic option, while it is logically unassailable, it is so fantastic that there are today few explicit idealists although, as we shall see, it underlies a good deal in current thinking especially where this concerns the interpretation of modern physics.

The thesis that I shall try to defend in this paper is that if we admit the existence of psi phenomena, the orthodox-physicalist position becomes very hard to sustain and radical dualism then becomes the most plausible alternative. Conversely, if we reject or ignore the existence of psi phenomena, then, while there may still be good philosophical reasons for doubting the truth of physicalism, we lose the only empirical grounds we have for challenging the orthodox position. This is important because physicalism claims to represent the scientific standpoint and draws support from advances in brain physiology and artificial intelligence whereas radical dualism appears by contrast as old-fashioned, unscientific and barren. My thesis is not, of course, new. On the contrary, right from its inception, one of the strongest appeals of psychical research was precisely the prospect it afforded of vindicating the autonomy of mind against what then appeared to be the teachings of science. Nevertheless, it is a thesis that is constantly contested, not least by critics who are themselves active parapsychologists. I make no apology, therefore, for restating in my own way the case for radical dualism given the reality of psi. Obviously, in the space available, I cannot hope to rebut all the possible objections that could be brought against my thesis but I am hopeful that I can draw attention to the principal arguments in its favor.

The crux of the argument is this. For my thesis to be false we would have to show either (a) that physicalism could survive the acknowledgment of psi phenomena or (b) that such phenomena do not, after all, involve any special mental powers or functions, hence their existence, whatever else it implies, lends no support to the doctrine of radical dualism. Hence, if neither proposition (a) nor (b) can be upheld, my thesis stands. Let us start, then, with proposition (a).

Those who study the brain would, I take it, agree that nothing that we have so far learnt about the brain would lead us to think that the brain might be capable either of paranormal cognition (ESP) or of paranormal action (PK). For example, while many cognitive processes can already be simulated using a suitably programmed computer, we obviously would not even begin to know how to program the computer to exhibit ESP. Now it could, of course, be argued that this limitation is due entirely to the rudimentary state of existing brain science. However, I propose to show that it follows inevitably from more fundamental considerations. To make my point I shall discuss the case of telepathy since, of all the varieties of psi phenomena, it is widely believed that telepathy should be the most amenable to a physicalistic interpretation. At all events to discuss precognition or PK in this context would merely compound the difficulties which physicalism would face. If, then, we find that not even telepathy can be understood in terms of brain activity we can feel more confident that the same is true *a fortiori* of the other manifestations of psi.

Let us start, then, by asking how, in normal communication, an idea in the mind of A is conveyed to the mind of B? To this question the answer is not in doubt: it is done by means of language. The idea is first expressed in some linguistic form by A, using a language that is familiar both to A and B, the signals are then duly perceived by B who interprets them as expressing the original idea. Let us next ask what would have to be the case if telepathic communication depended likewise on the transmission of physical signals of some sort? We might imagine that the idea, suitably encoded in A's brain, was somehow able to modulate radiation emanating from A's brain which in due course was picked up in B's brain where it was duly processed and decoded. But then the inescapable question presents itself: how did B manage to decode correctly the relevant telepathic signals? Was B, perhaps, born knowing the appropriate code or did he, at some stage of his development, learn the code? Either answer rapidly reduces to an absurdity. How could the brain be innately programmed to recognize the coded equivalent of any idea that might arise in another person's mind or brain? What if the idea in question was some human creation that does not exist in the natural environment, how, in that case, could evolution have equipped our brains to respond to such a concept? Obviously the telepathic code would have to be acquired just as we have to acquire knowledge of our native language. But then, when and where and how is this knowledge acquired? It is only necessary to pose this question to realize that such an acquisition, of which at no time are we ever aware, would be an absurd fiction. Moreover, even if we were to assume that, in telepathy, it is not ideas but words which are transmitted (which would imply, incidentally, that telepathy could never function across a language divide even then we get no nearer to an explanation. For the letters or phonemes as encoded in A's brain would still have to be transferred to B's brain and, once again, we would have to decide whether B's brain was innately programmed to recognize the coded equivalent of these linguistic signals or whether B's brain acquired the capacity to decode them in the course of its development and, either way, we reach an impasse.

An objection that could be raised at this point—and I am indebted to Michael Thalbourne for bringing it to my notice—is as follows. Let us suppose that what is involved in telepathic communication is not any kind of semantic operation but rather the transmission of an image, a form or may be a sensation. After all, many ESP experiments suggest that what is apprehended is not any sort of conceptual idea but rather some purely formal aspect of the target picture or scene. Let us suppose that A is thinking about, or looking at, an apple. As a result certain centers of A's sensory cortex are activated and this might set up some kind of a resonance which then served to activate corresponding centers in B's sensory cortex so that B became aware of something round and green in his imagery. We might perhaps invoke Sheldrake's morphic resonance as the mechanism responsible. This may not be the kind of physics that the physicalist would welcome but we can let that pass. Now, however, a different question presses down on us: how is B able to resonate with A's brain rather than with the brain of C or D or indeed any other living brain? Certainly nothing in Sheldrake's concept of morphic resonance suggests an answer. On the contrary, the whole point of Sheldrake's theory of learning is that the changes that take place in one brain automatically facilitate similar learning in all other brains of the same species and that irrespective of time and place. Unless, therefore, some mechanism could be suggested to explain the kind of selectivity that telepathy would require we do not have even a glimpse of a tenable physical theory. There is, for example, nothing in the situation that could correspond with the tuning mechanisms whereby a radio receiver picks up the signal from a specific transmitting channel and sheer proximity, the obvious factor on the analogy of sensory communication, would clearly be inapplicable in the case of telepathy.

Would the prospects of a physical theory be any better if we took clairvoyance as the critical phenomenon rather than telepathy? We would at least be dealing then with a single brain, one that presumably would have to be endowed with something like a radar system. The difficulties here are manifold. For, even if the requisite energy were available to operate such a system it could only work if the scanning beam could be suitably modulated by the target object in such a way that the reflected signal could then be decoded in the subject's brain. But one has only to spell out what would be involved if we took the radar analogy literally to realize how irrelevant it is to the case of the standard clairvoyant test situation where one is dealing with pictures or symbols inside envelopes.

Some of you may, at this point, feel that I have already spent too long belaboring a communication model of ESP considering how few parapsychologists still take it seriously. Those who are still intent on finding a physical theory of ESP tend nowadays to turn to quantum theory to point the way. At the subatomic level we encounter many strange phenomena that provide counterparts to phenomena which at the macroscopic level would be deemed paranormal, for example, the property known as "nonlocality" that is said to govern the behavior of two particles which, though no longer in contact, remain nevertheless in a correlated state. Could ESP exemplify this principle of nonlocality? But the most comprehensive and developed theory of psi to take quantum theory as its point of departure is the so-called observational theory. This is based on the assumption that every physical system persists in a state of indeterminacy up to the instant when it is observed and so becomes determinate. All that we can know about such a system prior to the intervention of an observer is the distribution of probabilities with respect to the possible values that it can assume when it is observed. If, then, we allow our observer the power to influence that distribution in a given direction, we have all that, in principle, we need to account for those nonrandom effects we identify as a psi effect. Such an observer is then said to represent a "psi source."

Whether observational theory is scientifically or even logically sound, whether, as some critics allege, it generates insoluble paradoxes, whether it derives from a misinterpretation of quantum theory stemming from an idealist metaphysic, these are all still matters of fierce controversy which are, perhaps best left to the experts to resolve. The question we have to consider for our present purposes is whether, granted that such a theory is legitimate, it would provide a physicalistic explanation of psi phenomena? To answer this question it should help if we first ask what exactly we are to understand by the key concept, "observation"? Does an observation necessarily imply conscious awareness? Or, can the observation be performed by any suitable recording instrument, by which term we may include in this context the brain itself? If consciousness *is* essential — and physicists, I may say, appear to be very much divided on this issue in quantum theory — then it follows that there is at least one mental function, i.e. conscious perception, which would possess a power that is not that of the brain itself, namely the power to produce retroactive PK. And this contradicts the thesis of physicalism. The attempt to assign a physical meaning to consciousness by calling it a hidden variable (whatever that may mean in this context) as E.H. Walker has done, seems to me to beg too many questions to save the situation for physicalism. If, on the other hand, consciousness is *not* essential, then we are left without any explanation as to what it is about brains that could make them potential psi sources. And without at least some vague indication as to how brain activity might produce retroactive PK nothing in observational theory would lend any support to the physicalist thesis.

The collapse of physicalism that must inevitably follow the recognition of psi phenomena would not, however, suffice to establish radical dualism unless we can show that such phenomena are definitely attributable to mind. At the present time there are various models of psi which challenge what has been called the "psychobiological paradigm." I have space here to consider only the two which I believe are the most influential. According to one school of thought, which I like to call Flewism, in honor of its most articulate exponent, the English philosopher Antony Flew, nothing of any philosophical import would follow from the mere existence of paranormal phenomena and, *a fortiori,* nothing of any relevance to the mind-body problem. The main argument to which it appeals is that paranormality can only be defined in negative terms, in other words it is, precisely, the inexplicability of the phenomena that makes them of interest to the parapsychologist. But, from such purely negative characteristics, we cannot hope to derive any positive conception such as would be implied in calling them manifestations of the mind. A secondary argument stresses the capriciousness and unpredictability of the phenomena which make them quite unlike the manifestations of any other known mental ability or skill.

Flewism has a superficial plausibility, especially for those of a positivistic turn of mind. Extrachance scoring, it is sometimes said, it just extrachance scoring and we have no right to capitalize on such statistical anomalies by dignifying them with concepts like ESP. This view, however, misses some crucial points. I will try to illustrate what I mean with the help of an analogy. From the bald fact that someone has been officially designated an "alien," it does not follow that that person is without ethnic identity of any kind. All that follows is that from the official scientific standpoint, it is necessary that paranormality be defined in negative terms in the first instance and treated as an anomaly *pending* discoveries concerning the basic nature of the phenomena in question. The subsidiary argument of the Flewists fares no better. It is true, of course, that those who are credited with psi ability seem to have precious little control over its manifestations. But psi is by no means unique in this respect among the known range of human abilities. We have very little control over our intuitions or our occasional creative inspirations and none whatever over our ability to dream. These are all vital aspects of our mental activity but they are largely at the mercy of our unconscious. It might indeed be less misleading if we were to refer to psi as a gift rather than an ability insofar as the latter may suggest skill and achievement, but that is very far from saying that it is not a property of mind. Moreover if we leave aside the fact that this putative ability is, in the existing state of knowledge, neither controllable nor trainable, we will find abundant evidence from the parapsychological literature that it behaves much like any other psychological variable. Thus we find that there are marked individual differences, that performance is highly sensitive to the prevailing psychological conditions and atmosphere and we find, above all, that it displays in some degree that unfailing sign of genuine mental activity, intelligence and purposefulness. This last point is true even of routine laboratory tests considered a somewhat degenerate manifestation of the psi faculty.

The other main school of thought which I shall discuss in this connection is that which takes an acausal view of psi phenomena. It urges us to reject the commonsense view that there must be a *causal* connection between, say, the choice of ESP target and the successful ESP response or between instructing the subject to aim at a certain PK effect and the production of that effect. Such causation, it insists, would have to be essentially magical. We should recognize, instead, that the relationship in question is strictly coincidental. But the coincidence, in this case, is not, as the skeptic would conclude, a mere accident, it is one imbued with profound psychological significance. Under the rubric of "synchronicity" psi phenomena are thus, at one stroke, taken out of the arena of mental activity and transferred to a realm of what one can only call "cosmic destiny." Astrology and the various rituals of divination involve similar significant but acausal correspondences which it is assumed are somehow embedded in the web of our personal lives.

As expounded by a Jung or a Koestler it is a seductive idea but does it yield a viable and comprehensive theory of psi? As Bob Brier remarked recently in reviewing a new book on precognition, synchronicity is not so much an explanation of phenomena as a redescription of the puzzlement which they provoke and Flew has rightly pointed out that we do not talk about something's being a coincidence unless the conjunction in question has some subjective psychological meaning for us. It is not, therefore, at all easy to say just what we add to an account of a given psi phenomenon by calling it an instance of synchronicity. The nearest that I can come to grasping this concept is to take a literary analogy. Coincidences are common enough in works of fiction because they are deliberately put there by the author for the sake of the plot. To talk of meaningful coincidences in real life is to treat life as a kind of cosmic drama with the implication that these incidents are prearranged by whatever agency we hold responsible. When Descartes first put forward the doctrine of radical dualism in the 17th century, many contemporary metaphysicians declared that it was inconceivable how two such disparate entities as mind and body could ever interact. Accordingly some, like Leibniz suggested the idea of a pre-established harmony, mind and body do not interact but events are beneficently prearranged so that whenever I perform an act of will my limbs move in the appropriate way and, similarly, whenever my sense organs are duly stimulated I experience the appropriate sensations. Synchronicity extends the idea of a pre-established harmony to the case of psi phenomena and it strikes me as no less unparsimonious in the assumptions that it has to make. In both cases, it is far simpler to suppose that a causal transaction is, indeed, involved.

This concludes my case so I will proceed to sum up. The thesis I put forward was that, if we accept the parapsychological evidence, we must abandon physicalism. Physicalism can be made compatible with normal mental activity but not with paranormal mental activity. The reason is that every attempt to account for psi phenomena in terms of brain activity inevitably breaks down. In the case of a physical communication model it breaks down, not as is often supposed because we do not know of any suitable radiation that could act as the carrier of the information but, rather, because there is no conceivable way in which the message could be encoded at the source and decoded at the receiving end. The attempt to overcome this objection by appealing to some kind of morphic resonance linking one brain with another is useless unless there is some principle that would account for the selectivity that is involved. Resort to quantum physics and the observational theory brought us no nearer to the goal of a physical explanation for either we have to invoke consciousness, which is not a physical variable at all, or we have simply to attribute psi capacity to the brain without any indication as to why brain activity should have this consequence. Having thus shown that physicalism cannot work, once psi phenomena are admitted, the question then arose as to whether such phenomena must necessarily be ascribed to the mind. We discussed two alternative positions: (a) that such phenomena might turn out to be pure unattached anomalies of nature, trivial hiccups in an otherwise orderly cosmos or (b) that they could be due to an acausal matching of events as implied by the idea of "synchronicity" as some basic cosmic principle over and above space, time, and causation. Since neither of these positions could offer a plausible account of psi we conclude that radical dualism is the obvious alternative to physicalism granted the existence of psi.

Epilogue 1990: Reply to My Critics

In a lengthy paper "Pragmatic Dualism and Bifurcated Idealism," Evan Walker takes me to task for saying that psi phenomena afford the only empirical evidence for challenging the physicalist position. He insists that, whatever some physicists may have said to the contrary, QM (quantum mechanics) does require the introduction of a conscious observer in a way that treats consciousness as a nonphysical variable. I am in no position to dispute what Walker may say about QM, one way or another, but I find him an uncomfortable ally. He says, for example, "But things have now proceeded beyond the point of an arguable issue. The tests of Bell's theorem now show factually that the physicalistic interpretation of an outside independent reality apart from observation is specious." Does this mean, I wonder, that there just was no universe until conscious observers came on the scene? But, if so, whence came these conscious observers? This, indeed, would be idealism with a vengeance and I must repudiate it.

Hywel Lewis likewise objects to my saying that parapsychology alone affords the empirical basis for challenging physicalism. If we reflect carefully enough, he insists, on the nature of our consciousness, for example on our experience of pain, it becomes intuitively self-evident that such experiences cannot be equated with any set of physical conditions. I agree with Lewis and I share his intuitions. Unfortunately, so many neuroscientists and "neurophilosophers" that I come across evidently lack such intuitions. On the other hand, if psi were to be demonstrated beyond cavil, they would be truly stymied.

Frank Tribbe is also of the opinion that "apart from psi there are a number of areas where empirical data support mind supremacy." He discusses certain fringe developments in the life sciences by way of illustration including the work of the late Harold Burr and the more recent theories of Rupert Sheldrake which have been widely publicized. I can make no comment with regard to Burr, but, with regard to Sheldrake, who interests me very much, I would agree that, if he were to be vindicated, this would indeed necessitate a radical revision of the prevailing scientific world view that has hitherto provided the justification of physicalism. For example, the Sheldrake effect is supposed to apply even to certain inanimate systems such as the crystalization of new organic compounds. However, all this is still very speculative, at present Sheldrakean science is even more controversial than parapsychology itself.

Both Alan Anderson and Steve Rosen raise yet again the problem that baffled Descartes himself, namely how, on a radically dualist position, mind and matter could ever interact in the first instance. Anderson declares that I set myself "the impossible task of defending a universe divided against itself," while Rosen complains that I fail "to provide the smallest affirmative clue as to how mind — radically disparate from body as it is purported to be — can enter into causal interaction with the body." Their respective remedies, however, are very different. Thus, Anderson, in his brief commentary, defends the idealist option which I had the temerity to dismiss as too fanciful. He, on the contrary, can make no sense of matter conceived as an "independently existing, lifeless, meaningless, purposeless something." Rosen, on the other hand, in his much lengthier critique, takes his stand on a monistic or holistic conception of the universe inspired, as he tells us, by Spinoza rather than Descartes and by such modern thinkers as Alfred Whitehead.

What, then, can I say except that we must agree to differ? I can only reiterate what I have said elsewhere that I know of no logical argument that would exclude the possibility that a cause might be of a radically different nature from its effect. I would side, here, with Hume who argued that, in principle, anything could be the cause of anything else and only observation can establish what causes what. As to whether I have been too harsh on idealism, it may be that I have a blind spot in this connection. I would concede that idealism does make some kind of sense given a theistic frame of reference and where I and Anderson part company is precisely that I lack his religious commitment. Hence I have no problem in accepting the stuff of the universe as "lifeless, meaningless and purposeless" as science appears to indicate. On the contrary, my problem is why, under some divine dispensation, the world should have the semblance that it does.

Rosen's universe, on the other hand, insofar as I can make anything of it and insofar as it may be relevant to psi, strikes me as a reversion to the animistic universe of the hermeticists, neoplatonists and other practitioners of natural magic who flourished so vigorously during the Renaissance before the mechanistic universe of Galileo and Descartes had yet established its supremacy. Understandably, Rosen, too, clasps Sheldrake to his bosom. I have some sympathy with this approach inasmuch as I believe that psi is more at home in the context of traditional magic than it is in the context of science. Where I would take issue with Rosen is in his attempts to enlist modern physics to his aid.

Extreme Phenomena and
the Problem of Credibility

In August 1987, the Parapsychological Association held their annual convention at the University of Edinburgh. Robert Morris, the newly appointed Koestler Professor of Parapsychology, had been appointed chair of the program committee and it was he who invited me to give a talk on a topic of my own choosing. What follows is based on that talk. The present version is the result of the revisions I made after I had been invited, by a group of Australian academics, to contribute a chapter to a book they were editing to be called Exploring the Paranormal: Different Perspectives on Belief and Experience *(Zollschan et al. 1989).*

Here I take further the ideas I put forward in the chapter I had contributed to the Skeptic's Handbook of Parapsychology *(Kurtz 1985) (see pages 147–64). While I have no quarrel with those who, for reasons of caution or conservatism, prefer to suspend judgment as to the reality of the paranormal, I wanted to challenge those who, like Antony Flew, claim on general principles the right to dismiss all evidence purporting to demonstrate the existence of the paranormal no matter how strong it may otherwise appear. Here I have selected five historical cases for which no credible counter-explanation has ever been offered which are not merely paranormal but outrageously so, thus making it all the more imperative for the skeptic to try demolishing them. I conclude by discussing what we are to do with such cases if we do decide to "take them on board with us as part of our intellectual baggage."*

The Problem of Credibility

From time to time one comes across a claim about which one can say only that it makes one gasp. It goes so far beyond anything in one's experience, it makes such a mockery of all one's presumptions about what sort of a world it is that one is living in, one is at a loss for words. At the same time one can see no easy way of dismissing it as mere fantasy. Our ancestors might have called it a miracle or, if they disapproved of it, witchcraft or sorcery; I prefer a less loaded word so I shall call such cases "extreme phenomena."

The problem of deciding what is to be regarded as credible and what as incredible is a problem that has exercised philosophers since antiquity. The Greek skeptics were preoccupied with it and were able to find reasons for doubting everything. But, as with a number of perennial problems in philosophy—e.g., the problem of causation or the problem of personal identity—it is in the writings of the great 18th century Scottish philosopher, David Hume, that we find its classic formulation. Hume, moreover, brought it to bear directly on the question of extreme phenomena. His solution to the problem has been discussed at some length by Antony Flew (see Zollschan et al. (eds.) 1989, pp. 317–19). There he quotes Hume as saying: "A miracle is a violation of the laws of nature; and, as a firm and unalterable experience has established these laws, the proof against a miracle, from the very nature of the fact, is as entire as any argument from experience can possibly be imagined."

Hume could hardly be more positive and yet we must understand that he is not denying that a miracle might occur. Indeed, it was he, after all, who pointed out that we can have no proof that the laws of nature will hold from one day to the next! What he does insist on is that we could never be *justified* in accepting a miracle at its face value—not, at any rate, unless we could first be sure that it would be an even greater miracle if those who vouched for it were telling a lie. But, given the unrealiability of human testimony, such would never be the case. And, to drive home his point, he imagines what he would do if he were to find that all the competent authorities agreed that Queen Elizabeth of England, a month after she had been buried, returned to life, reascended the throne and reigned for a further three years. Would he then, as a conscientious historian (and, in his day, as Flew reminds us, he was esteemed more as an historian than as a philosopher) be forced to admit that here, at any rate, was one genuine miracle? By no means, "I would still reply," he tells us, "that the knavery and folly of men are such common phenomena, that I should rather believe the most extraordinary events to arise from their concurrence, than to admit so signal a violation of the laws of nature" (Hume 1748).

Although Hume's essay "Of Miracles" did not go unanswered by critics, who seized upon various weaknesses and inconsistencies in his argument, by and large most self-styled rationalists since then have been content to follow Hume's line. Hence we find Antony Flew reiterating the Humean position when he now declares, "Confronted, therefore, with any story about the occurrence of a miracle, or anything else which he knows to be impossible, the critical historian is, by his cloth, *required* to reject it as a fiction" (*idem,* my italics).

In what follows, I shall try to show, first, that Hume—much as we revere him in Edinburgh—was mistaken and that it is not necessarily any more rational to disbelieve than to believe in a given extreme phenomenon. I shall then consider whether there are, in fact, any actual instances of extreme phenomena to which one could justifiably lend credence and I will describe in this connection a number of notable historical cases that have so far resisted demolition. Finally, I shall discuss some of the consequences of taking such cases on board as part of our intellectual baggage if we were to do so.

Let us start, then, with the Humean argument. Obviously, to acknowledge a claim that runs counter to so much that we normally take for granted is a much riskier proposition than to dismiss it from one's thoughts without more ado. At the same time, if the facts *demand* that we acknowledge it, it would be sheer intellectual cowardice and evasiveness to refuse to do so. Now Hume argued, for the reasons we have mentioned, that the facts are *never* such as to make assent obligatory. To do justice to Hume's argument would require a paper on its own. Here I shall confine myself to what I would regard as its most serious defect. It is an argument which, whatever else may be said in its defense, *cannot* carry any weight with someone who has actually witnessed an extreme phenomenon—if, indeed, there are any such! Needless to say, I am not in this privileged position and that probably goes for most of my readers. Nevertheless, it would not be difficult for any of us to think up a scenario in which we not only witnessed an extreme phenomenon but were in a position to satisfy ourselves, to our heart's content, that we were not the victim of any kind of trick or illusion. As an empiricist, Hume could hardly deny us the right to trust the evidence of our own senses. Hence, since he does not deny that miracles *might* occur, and, hence, that some people *might* have direct experience of them, he would have to say that such people *must*, nevertheless, be disbelieved no matter how impeccable their previous reputation or credentials! Yet, if a rule is valid, it should be valid for all cases, real or hypothetical. It should not lead us to opposite conclusions depending on whether our knowledge of the event in question is at first or at second hand. Hume's argument amounts to an epistemological solipsism whereby only one's *own* experience is allowed to count. Such a prescription cannot, I submit, be regarded as rational.

Extreme Phenomena

Before we proceed to discuss some concrete examples, I want to make a few general points about how one might deal with them. There are, it seems to me, three pertinent questions that we should always ask and in the following order: (1) Could there be some normal explanation for what is alleged to have happened? If the answer to this first question is "yes" we need proceed no further, but if the answer is definitely "no" then (2) Could the witness have been deceived or mistaken about what they thought they had observed? If the answer to this second question is still "no" then (3) Could the witnesses, or those who report their testimony, be lying? Only if the answer to this third question is a firm "no" do we reach what I shall hereafter refer to as a "credibility impasse." The only escape from such an impasse is to plead that the evidence is incomplete and that if we had all the facts at our disposal the situation would appear in a very different light. The plea of ignorance can always be invoked to sustain any position which appears to contradict the facts but it should be recognized for what it is, a desperate expedient. It is certainly one way of escaping from a credibility impasse but we would do well to remember that dodging a problem is not the same as getting rid of it.

So far, all I have done is to argue that *if* we had good evidence for an extreme phenomenon, we would not need to discount that evidence on *a priori* grounds, be they Humean or otherwise. It is now time to turn to the more exciting question as to whether history supplies us with any cases that bring us to the brink of a credibility impasse. Like the good philosopher that he was, Hume did not try to make things easy for himself, as an inferior polemicist might have been tempted to do, by dwelling only on miracles that were plainly risible. He was aware, for example, that, only shortly before the time he was writing, a whole clutch of miracles, mostly having to do with healing, had been taking place in Paris, of all places, the then undisputed cultural capital of Europe. They were all connected with the tomb of François de Pâris, the revered and saintly Jansenist priest who had been buried in the cemetery of St. Médard.

Now the fact that Pâris had been a Jansenist, and thus a heretic in the eyes of the Church, made such claims a test case since the authorities, egged on by the Jesuits, did everything in their power to suppress or discredit them, even going so far, eventually, as to close down the cemetery, thereby provoking Voltaire's jibe that it had now become a case of no miracles by order! We must remember, therefore, that anyone testifying to such a miracle was risking persecution. Yet, in spite of this, scores of people came forward to add their own testimony. No wonder Hume was driven to exclaim: "Where shall we find such a number of circumstances agreeing to the corroboration of one fact? And what have we to oppose to such a cloud of witnesses?" But then, immediately, he answers his own rhetorical question in the way with which we are familiar. "The miraculous nature of such claims," he asserts, "is sufficient reason to dismiss them" since "when men are heated by zeal and enthusiasm, there is no degree of human testimony so strong as may not be procured for the greatest absurdity."

So long as we are content, like Hume, to stick to generalities, we may feel secure. Let us focus, therefore, on one specific case and see whether it, too, can be dismissed as the product of an overheated imagination.

1. The Case of Louise Coirin

The case in point is that of a Mlle. Louise Coirin, not one, incidentally that Hume mentions in his essay. Her story, as it has come down to us, is, briefly, as follows: She lived with her mother and stepfather (the mother having remarried after her father died) at Nanterre on the outskirts of Paris. Her two brothers, like their father before them, were officers in the Royal household. In 1716, at the age of 31, she developed a cancer of the left breast which gradually destroyed the nipple and flesh, leaving her with a suppurating wound whose odor was said to have rendered her almost unapproachable. In 1718, to compound her misery, she became completely paralyzed down her left side. The following year two local surgeons recommended a mastectomy, as the last slender chance of saving her life, but she declined. By 1731 — she was now 47 — she had reached the brink of death and had already received the last sacraments on several occasions. It was only then — on August 9th to be precise — that she decided to seek supernatural aid. As she was too ill herself to make the pilgrimage to St. Médard, she persuaded a pious woman of the neighborhood to undertake the mission for her. The woman was to bring back a clod of earth from around the tomb and her chemise after it had been in contact with the tomb. The following day, after annointing herself with the clod of earth and after putting on the chemise her recovery commenced. Before the end of the month she had again regained perfect health and, more to the point, her breast was whole again.

The Jesuits lost no time in putting out rumors that a relapse had occurred and that her cancer and paralysis had returned. To scotch these slanders, Mlle. Coirin went in person to Paris to make a deposition before a notary stating the full facts of her case. More important for us is the fact that one of the royal surgeons, risking the displeasure of the court, went in person to the same notary and testified that no trace of the cancer remained and he laid special stress on the fact that her left nipple was now so perfectly formed as to be indistinguishable from her right nipple.

Let us apply now to this case our three key questions. Could the phenomenon have a normal explanation? Spontaneous remissions in cases of cancer are, after all, not unknown to the medical literature. Indeed, they complicate the evaluation of some of the Lourdes cases. However, though I speak as a layman, I would suppose that the complete regeneration of a breast and its nipple must be unique. Could the witnesses, including a number of medical practitioners who are mentioned by name, have been mistaken about what they saw? Only, presumably, if some other woman, some lookalike, had impersonated Mlle. Coirin during the medical examinations. However, the fact that Louise Coirin was then able to resume her normal life among her family and friends makes such an hypothesis not only far-fetched but quite untenable. There remains, then, only one last possibility, namely that the entire story is a fabrication on the part of the writer on whose authority the case is known to us. This is by far the most attractive hypothesis from the standpoint of a skeptic since, so far as I know, there is only one extant source for this story, as for so many other of the St. Médard cases, namely the three-volume 1745 work by Carré de Montgeron.[a] Who, then, was this Montgeron?

Even Hume had to admit that Montgeron was no ignorant fanatic but a man of substance and repute. He was, in fact, a nobleman, a magistrate and a member of the Paris Parliament. Prior to his encounter with these events he had had the reputation of being something of a skeptic in matters of religion. But there are at least two facts that make it extremely unlikely that he had invented this case. In the first place he mentions by name in this connection a number of notabilities and public figures including churchmen and physicians — some of the royal doctors are mentioned by name. Secondly, even if he could have got away with such a fabrication, he had nothing to gain by it. On the contrary, in the event he had to pay dearly for his audacity in publishing a work of such a controversial nature so that, although he took the precaution of dedicating the book to the King (Louis XV), he was promptly interned in the Bastille. Even this, however, did not teach him a lesson since he managed to bring out two further volumes of cases while in prison. This is hardly what one would expect from a writer of fiction!

(2) The Case of Joseph of Copertino

For our next exhibit we must go back another century to a case that still ranks as among the most remarkable of all time. This is the case of the levitating friar, Joseph of Copertino (Cupertino). The late Eric Dingwall devoted a chapter to him in his *Human Oddities* (Dingwall 1947) from which I have freely drawn and, more recently, Stephen Braude has again drawn attention to this case in his *The Limits of Influence* (Braude 1986). Here are the main incidents of his life as far as we know them:

Giuseppe Desa was born in 1603 to an impoverished family of Copertino near Brindisi. He was resented by his mother who was soon widowed but she had him apprenticed to a shoemaker. By the age of 17, however, he had made up his mind to devote his life to religion. He was then taken on as a lay Capuchin but was dismissed again after only eight months for clumsiness and stupidity. However, the Franciscans took him in first as a servant but he was admitted as a novice in 1625 and, despite his lack of scholarship, was duly ordained in 1628 (Delaney 1980). As a monk he became notorious for his extreme asceticism and for the severity of the mortifications he would inflict on himself. What alone makes him of interest to us, however, was his habit of going into raptures and then levitating, sometimes to a considerable height, sometimes remaining suspended in midair for a considerable period. These levitations took place in broad daylight, sometimes in a church, sometimes in the open air. In all there are some 70 recorded instances of such levitations. His most spectacular feats were his flights to images placed high above the altar and the assistance he gave to workmen attempting to erect a Calvary Cross 36 feet high. It was said that he would lift it into place in midair after ten men had failed to lift it (Farmer 1987). There is even a story that, on one occasion, he carried a fellow monk up with him into the rafters of a church (Haynes 1970).[b]

I shall now describe one incident which strikes me as more evidential than most if only because it occurred during his final illness when two named doctors were in constant attendance. A certain Dr. Pierpaoli was in the process of cauterizing Joseph's left leg when he noticed that Joseph had gone into a trance and was sitting a few inches *above* the seat of his chair. To make absolutely sure that this was not an illusion, both doctors went down on their knees to get a better look. When this had gone on for about 15 minutes, Joseph's superior,. Fr. Evangelista, entered the room and was able to bring Joseph back to his senses—and to terra firma!—by calling out his name.

Joseph died in 1663 at the age of 60. Within three years of his death an official inquiry was instituted with the aim of establishing the true facts of his career and, in particular, obtaining sworn depositions from those who had witnessed the levitations. On this basis an official biography was eventually published in 1722 by one, Domenico Bernino. This, in turn, led to Joseph becoming a candidate for beatification and a process was duly set in train by the Congregation of Rites, the body responsible for such matters. What is noteworthy from our point of view is that the person in charge of this process, the so-called *promotor fidei,* was Cardinal Prospero Lambertini who was noted for his enlightened views—he even once corresponded amicably with Voltaire! (Haynes 1970)—and was the author of what became the standard work on canonization. Lambertini, whose role here was to play devil's advocate, does not seem to have raised any serious doubts about the levitations. He was more concerned about some of the more outrageous aspects of Joseph's life style, for he had little sympathy with such extreme asceticism. Nevertheless, in 1753, by which time Lambertini had become Pope Benedict XIV, beatification was duly decreed. Canonization then followed in 1767—just over a century after Joseph's death—and so it was that Giuseppe Desa became, for all the world, St. Joseph of Copertino.

Now let us ourselves play devil's advocate and see whether, from our sophisticated vantage point, we can puncture this pious tale. The first thing that will strike us, now that some three centuries have elapsed, is that nothing remotely like this has ever happened again. Of course, in every generation, there have been claims that someone, somewhere, has levitated. Most of the best known physical mediums are credited with occasional self-levitations— one thinks, inevitably, of Daniel Home—but, still, nothing on this scale or of this magnitude.

One's first impulse may be to regard this as another particularly glaring example of the natural human tendency to exaggerate. One is reminded of the stories that used to circulate about the dancer Nijinsky. It was said that he must have been able momentarily to defy gravity and he even seems to have believed this himself. So, perhaps, Joseph was in the habit of leaping up and down when he became excited and the legend took off from there and eventually got out of hand? I am afraid such speculations cannot get us very far. There would have had to be massive collusion to have produced this amount of documentary evidence.

More promising, from the skeptical standpoint, is that Joseph was the stooge or puppet in a fiendish Counter-Reformation plot to bring heretics back into the fold of the one true Church. This might account for what happened to Johann Friedrich, the Duke of Brunswick, a Lutheran, who is now remembered only as the patron of the philosopher Leibniz. The Duke visited Assissi in 1651 and, while there, expressed a wish to meet Joseph. With his two companions he was conducted to a chapel where, without being aware that he was being observed, Joseph was saying mass. After a while he was heard to utter a loud cry and was seen to rise into the air in a kneeling position. The Duke was so intrigued that he begged permission to go again next day. This time Joseph was seen to rise just a few inches but then to remain floating above the altar steps for about a quarter of an hour. This was too much for the poor Duke who then and there decided to become a Catholic.

Had he been ensnared by some adroit piece of conjuring or illusionism? Contrary to what some people imagine, the Catholic Church has always been extremely wary of exploiting miracles associated with living individuals—the treatment of the late Padre Pio wold be a case in point. So far from lending himself to such machinations, Joseph was all his life an embarrassment to his superiors. On no less than three occasions he was summoned to defend himself before the Inquisition[c] and, for much of his life, he was under strict orders to remain in his cell where he could least attract attention.[d] Of course we are heavily dependent on his biographer, Bernino, for our knowledge of his career—Dingwall relied mainly on this source—but Bernino names so many eminent personages that there would have been a limit to what he would have dared to invent or embroider. He cites, for example, three cardinals each of whom was willing to testify to having seen Joseph levitate. Then there is the incident when the father general of the order of St. Francis arranged for Joseph to kiss the feet of the then Pope, Urban VIII. As often happened when Joseph got too excited, he rose into the air and remained suspended there for some time until the Father General recalled him to his senses—to the amazement of the Pope (New Catholic Encyclopedia 1967). How easy would it be, one wonders, to invent an incident like this about a named pope? I do not know but, all things considered, I am inclined to agree with Dingwall when he says: "For my part I do not find it easy to believe that Cardinals, Bishops, Superiors, monastic physicians and lay visitors were all lying or engaged in a system of deceit for the apparent purpose of bolstering up the reputation of a fraudulent friar or the Order to which he was attached" (Dingwall 1947).

(3) The Case of "Margery"

From the middle of the 19th century onwards, the Spiritualist movement provided the powerhouse for generating paranormal claims. My remaining three exhibits are all drawn from the careers of physical mediums who flourished during the present century. My choice was partly dictated by the fact that each has recently been the subject of biographical studies which have come to my attention. Now, physical mediums, unlike saints, have a murky reputation and, to the uninitiated, this alone is sufficient reason for dismissing, or at least playing down, any claims that are made on their behalf. One could argue, with perhaps more logic, that the more suspicious a medium the more vigilant will be the investigators—no one, after all, enjoys being taken for a ride! Fortunately, both arguments are irrelevant when one understands that the critical question in such cases is *never* whether the individual involved *would* cheat but, only, whether he or she *could have* cheated in the conditions specified. It is their ability, never their morals, that are on trial.

These remarks are specially pertinent because my next exhibit concerns a medium who was, surely, one of the most tempestuous and controversial characters in the whole stormy history of psychical research. I allude to Mrs. Mina Crandon, née Stinson, known to the literature, and to all the world, simply as "Margery." Few mediums can have caused quite as much havoc in their time as did Margery. The American Society for Psychical Research split in two on her account (Tietze 1985) causing W.F. Prince to set up a rival organization, The Boston S.P.R. J.B. Rhine was so quickly disillusioned with her after only a single sitting (Brian 1984, Matlock 1987) that he never again wanted to have any further dealings with mediums, not, at any rate, unless, like Mrs. Garrett, they were willing to play it his way and guess cards. Hence one could say that Margery was instrumental in launching the new experimental parapsychology. Yet, in fairness, despite the revulsion which many decent people felt towards her, it must be said that she submitted meekly and indefatigably to the tedious and strenuous tests that were imposed upon her, perhaps, in the end, at the cost of her sanity. Ostensibly, she put up with it all for the sake of her deceased brother Walter, who had been killed as a young man in a railroad accident, and whose passive vehicle she had now become. At all events, whatever was really going on, she undoubtedly produced phenomena that still remain baffling.[e]

I shall here confine myself to a single phenomenon of Margery's multifarious mediumship, namely her "rings." A seamless linkage of solid rings—

a manifest topological miracle—is one of the rarest of extreme phenomena. Yet it appears that, during the 1930s, Margery produced a whole series of such linkages. Since none has survived it may seem a waste of time discussing them but we still have to make sense of the documentary and photographic evidence. Some of the component rings have survived—I have examined one such pair—they are substantial wooden objects. Care was taken that each ring in a linkage should be made from different timber so as to preclude the possibility that the entire linkage might have been carved from a single block of wood. According to the records of the séances at which "Walter" engineered these linkages, some dematerialization and rematerialization of the wooden rings seem to have been involved. We have a photograph of one intact linkage that is said to have been on display at one time at the offices of the American S.P.R. in New York and we have the text of a letter from an outside expert affirming that the linkage had been X-rayed but that "nothing resembling an artificially concealed cut or break could be detected" (Nester 1985). Unfortunately, with the perversity that is so typical of extreme phenomena Margery's linkages regularly (but paranormally) became unlinked. It is as if "Walter" could get no further than creating a semipermanent paranormal object.[f] The whole case, as you will note, bristles with these absurdities but who are we, after all, to deny that reality may at times come to resemble a theatre of the absurd?

(4) The Case of Indridason

My next exhibit may strike the reader as even more absurd. It is certainly more obscure. In this case, the protagonist, far from being world famous (or infamous), is someone whose very name was unknown to me until just recently and is unlikely to be known to my readers unless, that is, they happen to be Icelanders! Indridi Indridason was rescued from obscurity when, at the instigation of Erlendur Haraldsson, of the University of Iceland, his student, Loftur Gissurarson, wrote a monograph on him for his bachelor's degree. A new version of this monograph now appeared as an issue of the *Proceedings* of the Society for Psychical Research (Gissurarson and Haraldsson 1988). Indridason's mediumship first manifested in 1905—there had been no previous mediums in Iceland—but he died from tuberculosis in 1912 at the early age of 29. He never left Iceland and thus never came to the attention of those who were most experienced at dealing with physical mediums.

In some respects the investigation of his mediumship compares unfavorably with the best work of this kind being done in Europe. Except on rare occasions the sittings were conducted in darkness apart from the occasional striking of matches when permission was given. No attempts were made to use flashlight photography as had been done in the case of Palladino and others.

Assessment of the case is further hampered by the fact that all the contemporary séance notes in possession of the so-called Experimental Society have been lost. On the other hand, the case has some very positive aspects in its favor. In the first place the group who undertook the investigation were prominent persons in the community, writers, academics, scientists. They were not militant spiritualists seeking to propagate a creed; they concentrated throughout on the one key issue, namely whether the effects they observed were truly paranormal or just trickery. The most distinguished member of the group who, after 1908, took charge of the investigation, was Gudmundur Hannesson, who was professor of medicine at the University of Iceland from 1911 to 1946 as well as being twice president of the University and, for a time, a member of parliament. Gissurarson and Haraldsson say of him that "he had a greater reputation as a scientist in Iceland than any of his contemporaries and was known for his integrity and impartiality." He was, furthermore, a man of a markedly skeptical outlook. Most of the sittings took place in a small building specially built for this purpose by the Experimental Society but many were also held in Hannesson's own house where the medium was obliged to wear Hannesson's clothes. In the end, all the investigators without dissent, not least Hannesson himself, came round to the view that fraud was not involved and that the phenomena they had witnessed were, indeed, inexplicable.

During the four years, 1905–1909, during which Indridason was the subject of intensive study, he produced virtually all the classic phenomena associated with physical mediumship: raps, levitation of objects, self-levitations, strong breezes, luminous phenomena, unaccountable odors, direct voices, apports, the remote playing of musical instruments and even, on a few occasions, full form materializations. However, the particular incident that I want to discuss, although not one of the best attested — it pertains to the period before Hannesson took charge — is one that, just because of its bizarre and almost farcical character, raises the problem of credibility in its acutest and most uncomfortable form. It involves nothing less than the temporary disappearance of Indridason's left arm!

It happened for the first time at a sitting on December 19, 1905, and then on two subsequent occasions in the course of that winter. On the third occasion, we are informed, no less than seven witnesses were present each of whom signed a document at the end stating that they had not been able to feel or to find Indridason's left arm and were willing to certify this under oath. We are further informed that, at one point, Indridason stood in full light but still no arm was visible until it as suddenly reappeared half an hour later. The ostensible reason for this strange incident, as provided by Indridason's control personality speaking through the medium, was that the powers on the other side were getting ready to bring about a full form materialization. This was, in fact, a reported feature of his later séances.

So what are we to make of this story? An obvious ground for suspicion is that the investigators were never allowed to undress the medium. From the published account we cannot even be sure whether the medium wore his jacket throughout or was in his shirt-sleeves. Even so, it is not easy to fathom how anyone, however crafty, could manage to conceal an arm from seven inquisitive individuals whose one and only aim was to find it! No doubt the disciples of Batcheldor will see in this a further confirmation of the Batcheldorian doctrine that, unless some element of ambiguity is allowed, nothing paranormal can ever happen (Batcheldor 1984).

(5) The Case of Helen Duncan

All paranormal phenomena are, by definition, "impossible" but some, one is tempted to say, are more impossible than others. Nothing, I think, in all the literature of psychical research taxes one's credulity so severely as the phantoms of the séance chamber. There one has, at one moment, creatures that, for all the world, resemble living, talking human beings; at the next they have ceased to exist! It is fitting, therefore, that, for my last exhibit, we take a look at this ultimate extreme phenomenon and the example I shall discuss is one associated with the Scottish medium, Helen Duncan, who died in 1956 at the age of 58. In making this choice I may appear to be putting my own credibility at risk for there is no disguising the fact that she had an unsavory reputation. If miracles were the prerogative of persons of saintly character—or even of moderate refinement—poor Helen Duncan would be nowhere in the running. To be blunt, she was an uneducated woman of gross appearance whose manners and language were anything but ladylike. More seriously, both she and her husband-manager were almost certainly implicated in fraud. Nevertheless, she has two important advantages from my point of view. First, whereas we can no longer interrogate those who witnessed St. Joseph's levitations, Mrs. Duncan's phenomena are close enough to us in time for me to have met and corresponded with a fair number of those who *did* witness them. Secondly, my friend Manfred Cassirer has done his homework on her case and has produced a hefty monograph which he has lodged with the Society for Psychical Research (Cassirer 1984; 1985). If there were others like her at the present time I would not need to bother with such a tarnished case but alas, as with all my previous exhibits, there simply is nothing comparable at the present time.

The witnesses with whom I have spoken or corresponded, all persons whose sanity I have no reason to doubt—indeed two of them are good friends of mine and prominent members of the S.P.R.—all tell much the same story. They all speak of watching figures emerging from the cabinet or sometimes taking shape out of swirling masses of amorphous ectoplasm, sometimes they are of recognizable individuals whom the sitter had known in life, sometimes they engage in conversation, but, invariably, they soon disappear by sinking through the solid floor. On this last point there is, according to Cassirer, virtual unanimity. It must be said, however, that these spectacular phenomena were reserved for her clients who attended her séances. The phenomena she produced for psychical researchers, such as Harry Price or Mollie Goldney, were much less impressive, mainly copious quantities of ectoplasm whose paranormal origin remained problematical.

Eventually, Mrs. Duncan made legal history by becoming the last person ever to be tried under the "Witchcraft Act." This was an archaic statute, introduced in the reign of George II, which stated that "anyone pretending to exercise or use any kind of witchcraft, sorcery, enchantment or conjuration could be committed to prison for one year." Her trial at the Old Bailey, in March 1944, became something of a *cause célèbre* in wartime London (Becchofer Roberts 1945; West 1946). It lasted seven days, capturing the headlines in the daily press, at the end of which the jury of seven men and one woman, with little hesitation, found her guilty and she was duly sentenced to nine months in prison. Her defense counsel, during the trial, made a bold offer to stage a séance for the benefit of the jury who, after all, knew nothing about such matters, but, although the judge was willing to give his permission, the jury turned down the offer. That, too, might have made legal history but it was not to be. Perhaps the jury thought it would be less confusing to condemn the wretched woman without first seeing what it was she *claimed* to be able to do!

The defense did, however, produce a long string of witnesses. One of these who made a specially good impression on the court because she seemed to be a sensible, matter-of-fact sort of a woman, was Janet Rust, a retired municipal midwife and a widow who described, at length, her experiences at a sitting with Helen Duncan at Portsmouth only some two months before the trial on January 17, 1944. She told the court how she had there met and embraced her deceased husband and how she had felt the knobbly knuckles of his rheumatic hands, how she was able to identify her deceased mother by two moles on her face, the one in the hollow of her chin, the other above her left eyebrow and, finally, how her Aunt Mary appeared and spoke to her in Spanish with a Gibraltarian accent saying, "I would have come sooner but they did not understand."

Was all of this just a pack of lies? But, then, why should a professional woman of unblemished reputation want to perjure herself to no purpose? Was she, perhaps, deeply hallucinated during that séance? That is more plausible and yet the only way I know whereby such hallucinations could be induced is by hypnotizing someone and making the appropriate verbal suggestions. If Helen Duncan could do this without speaking or leaving her cabinet this, in itself, would suggest paranormal ability, albeit not of a physical nature. Of one thing, only, we can be certain. This could not have been the result of Mrs. Duncan producing her "ectoplasm" by regurgitating cheesecloth, a common accusation.

Conclusions

This concludes my selection of extreme phenomena. To recapitulate, we have discussed Louise Coirin with her new breast, St. Joseph of Copertino sitting on his cushion of air, Margery's impossible object, Indridason's missing left arm and, finally Helen Duncan with her troupe of phantoms. The literature of psychical research affords an endless variety of such cases and readers may enjoy compiling their own list of favorites. The common factor in all such cases is that they serve as intellectual irritants or conundrums. They contrive to disturb us and make us feel giddy but we can see no easy way of getting rid of them. I cannot go along with Flew who urges us to dismiss them, in principle, as fictions. To disbelieve on principle is not a mark of rationality but of an immutable conservatism.

Readers may feel cheated, however, that I did not select a topical or ongoing example. I can only plead that, looking around the world today, no obvious candidates presented themselves. Ted Serios who achieved fame with his psychic photographs has long been inactive. Uri Geller has taken a terrible battering while the "mini-gellers" have become ever scarcer. The so-called SORRAT group in Missouri has never won the confidence of the parapsychological community. Batcheldor's set-up in Exeter is fun for participants but is not easily translated into the public domain and moreover Batcheldor himself now says he makes no firm claims.[g] There is, of course, Sai Baba in India. He has his admirers among Western parapsychologists and I was certainly impressed reading Haraldsson's new book (Haraldsson 1987). All the same I cannot overlook the fact that Sai Baba has never permitted Haraldsson, or any other investigator for that matter, to test him directly.[h] If I had to choose a contemporary example of an extreme phenomenon, I think I would plump for the Chinese children. The are credited with clairvoyant powers far surpassing anything we have known in the West. I have now read three separate accounts about them; each was written by a Western scientist of Chinese extraction who knew the language, after a visit to the People's Republic. Each was allowed complete freedom to devise his own targets—pictures or inscriptions were used. Each was allowed to administer the test in his own preferred way. In each case the results were phenomenally successful and each scientist returned to the West satisfied that the children could not have tricked him (Jen 1982; Kiang 1982; Teng 1981). But, of course, this is no more than an appetizer and, until better communication is possible between the People's Republic and the West, it would be rash, indeed, to draw any conclusions.

Finally, what lessons am I asking the reader to take away from this recital of the incredible? While I am, I must admit, fascinated by such extreme phenomena, I do not wish to gloat about them. On the contrary, I am fearful about what might happen if such phenomena ever became more frequent or widely credited. Indeed, the irony of my position is that I am still, ideologically speaking, on the side of David Hume. I consider that excessive credulity does far more harm than excessive incredulity. Perhaps the greatest menace that confronts us at the present time is still, as it was for Hume, superstition, irrationality and fanaticism. The recent worldwide resurgence of religious fundamentalism underscores my point. Survivalists will, no doubt, find in some of these extreme phenomena a vindication of their position as they are, no doubt, entitled to do. For my part, however, it puzzles me why those on the other side should seek to communicate with us in quite such a queer and unseemly fashion. And yet I am bound to confess that I find it no less puzzling that such cataclysmic disturbances of the natural order should be a product of a medium's private unconscious. So we may have to entertain the notion that something like a transpersonal force or cosmic mind is being harnessed in these exceptional situations.

To be a rationalist does not mean agreeing that everything will, in the end, be susceptible to rational analysis even though we may hope that this will prove to the case. There may be some things that the human intellect will never understand and some phenomena that will never be explained. All that is demanded of a rationalist is that reason should never be abandoned in favor of some supposed shortcut to truth, whether we call this faith, intuition or whatever. At first blush these extreme phenomena that I have been discussing may appear to take us right away from the orderly world of science and plunge us back into the dark chaotic world of magic. On further reflection, on the other hand, the situation may not be quite so bleak. If you accept, as I do, that parapsychology, alone among the sciences, studies the influence of mind on matter, then, perhaps, it is no longer so unthinkable that every once in a while, mind overreaches itself with the consequences we have been discussing.

Notes

a. *I am much indebted to Dr. Ian Stevenson for procuring a photocopy of the relevant chapter from the Bibliothèque Nationale in Paris. As a medical man, Dr. Stevenson queried the diagnosis of cancer since, ordinarily, a young woman afflicted with a breast cancer would not be expected to survive more than a few years if it went untreated. He therefore consulted a colleague of the Department of Pathology of the University of Virginia who suggested that this might have been a case of tuberculosis. None of this, of course, goes any way to explaining the subsequent regeneration of the affected breast which is the phenomenon in question. More recently, Stevenson has alerted me to the fact that Charcot regarded Louise Coirin as an hysteric (see A.R.G. Owen Hysteria, Hypnosis and Healing: The Work of J.M. Charcot, London: D. Dobson, 1971, pp. 144–45). However, while hysteria might account for her paralysis, if it was responsible for the decay and regeneration of her breast, that would in itself, surely, be paranormal.*

b. Stories such as these earned him the nickname "the flying friar" and he is today revered as the patron saint of air travellers!

c. The Neapolitan Inquisition accused him of "drawing crowds after him like a new Messiah through prodigies accomplished on the ignorant who are ready to believe anything" (Farmer 1987). This may suggest a skeptical attitude on the part of the Neapolitan inquisitors but it certainly contradicts the idea that he was being exploited by his superiors.

d. Joseph constantly apologized for his levitations, calling them his fits of giddiness. They were, indeed, so disturbing to his superiors that for some 35 years he was not allowed to celebrate mass or attend choir and refectory within his own community (Farmer 1987). In 1653 the Inquisition of Perugia sent him to an isolated Capuchin friary where he was completely cut off from the outside world for the next four years, when he was allowed to rejoin his own order at Orismo near Assissi (Delaney 1980).

e. We shall be in a better position to evaluate her mediumship when Marian Nester has completed her book on Margery. Nester is the daughter of Dr. Mark Richardson, one of the principal investigators, and was a young woman when these events were taking place (Nester 1985).

f. It is tantalizing to speculate on the consequences if such an object had survived. For, the special virtue of such a "permanent paranormal object," from the credibility angle, is that it transfers the onus of proof from the claimant to the critic. It is then up to those who wish to challenge its paranormality to show how it could have been faked.

g. Batcheldor died subsequently in March 1988; see obituaries in the April and July issues of the Journal of the S.P.R.

h. While nearly all of Sai Baba's "miracles" look just like stage magic, there are, as Haraldsson makes plain, some formidable problems in supposing that this is what in fact they are. For one thing, Baba's life style is such that he is virtually never alone, not even when having a bath! He would thus almost certainly require accomplices. But, for a man with so many enemies, they would represent a high risk as he would be laying himself open to blackmail. Curiously his enemies have never even tried to pin a charge of fraud on him.

What Is to Count as Good Evidence for the Paranormal?

For a finale, we return again to the basic question—the relentless question—that has dogged our footsteps throughout this journey: are there any truly paranormal phenomena and, if so, can we set any limits on the form that they may take? The paper is based on a talk I was invited to give, in December 1988, first in Glasgow, to the newly formed Scottish Society for Psychical Research, initiated by Professor Archie Roy, and, later that month, to the Society for Psychical Research, in Kensington, London. It was published in the Parapsychology Review *(Beloff 1988).*

I doubt whether there is anything one can say at the present time about paranormal phenomena more important than the bald assertion that they exist. For, officially they do *not* exist. By this I mean that, although anyone is free at any time to assert their existence, and may even do so without putting one's credibility at risk, equally anyone is free to deny their existence without thereby exposing oneself to a charge of ignorance or prejudice. In this respect such phenomena are very different from those that have the sanction of official science which one can deny only on pain of being regarded as a fool or an ignoramus. In short, in our culture, belief in the paranormal is strictly our own private affair, like our religious affiliation.

This is surely a curious and disconcerting situation when we reflect that serious research on the paranormal has now been going on for at least a hundred years. But does it matter, you may ask. Is it necessary that everyone should agree about the reality of such phenomena? Some psychical researchers, at any rate, wearied by their vain efforts to impress the skeptics, try to bypass the question of proof. The important question, they insist, is no longer whether such phenomena *exist* but rather what they *mean*. They point out, not implausibly, that once the phenomena could be shown to exhibit certain meaningful characteristics that would make sense in relation to the rest of our knowledge, the problem of proof could be left to look after itself.

While I have some sympathy with this approach, I do not think it is realistic. All the evidence to date suggests that the phenomena are too anarchic to be brought under some acceptable scientific or philosophical rubric. Meanwhile the problem of proof does not go away and we ignore it at our peril. Thus, those in command of national scientific policy simply will not give us the funding we would need to pursue the process-oriented research we would like to do because they are not yet satisfied that we have any genuine phenomena to investigate. In any case, quite apart from trying to convince outsiders, I would myself dearly like to know whether the phenomena that I have now been pondering for a lifetime are indeed real or just illusory. Of course some privileged individuals claim certain knowledge of such phenomena based on their own personal and indubitable experiences. But this cannot help, it can only tantalize, the great majority who, like me, have never been vouchsafed such revelations.

It would be foolish, I think, to underestimate the strength of the skepticism that still prevails in scientific circles. No one, perhaps, in recent years has done more than R.A. McConnell, himself a physicist, to try to interest elite scientists in parapsychology. He has even published some of his correspondence with Nobel Laureates and others of that caliber (McConnell 1987, chapter 3). His efforts, however, as he ruefully confesses, have been largely unavailing. What little these scientists knew about parapsychology did not impress them and they showed no willingness to learn more. Like McConnell, I personally think they are mistaken but, unlike McConnell, I recognize that I occupy a minority position and I do not therefore accuse them of self-deception. Nor do I want to adopt a sour-grapes attitude such as was expressed by Jule Eisenbud (Pilkington 1987, p. 15), when he said: "Real progress in parapsychology will be made, I feel, only when its practitioners unfetter themselves completely from science and scientific institutions in order to work their own garden in their own way." So much, after all, is here at stake. Our entire culture could be transformed—whether for good or ill—if paranormal phenomena were universally recognized as factual. It is frivolous, therefore, to adopt a take-it-or-leave-it attitude. We should persevere in the hope that the truth—whatever it may turn out to be—will ultimately prevail. It is with these thoughts in mind that I have raised the question: what is to count as *good* evidence for the paranormal?

Let me say at once, to avoid misunderstanding, that, whatever the answer may be, even if we had to conclude that there was *no* evidence for the paranormal that one could call *good*, no such conclusion could compel anyone either to believe or to disbelieve if only because belief does not lie within our control. Confronted with the evidence we either do or do not draw certain conclusions and, in either case, we may be right or we may be wrong. It may be very useful in various contingencies to have explicit criteria for assessing the worth of the evidence but no such criteria can ever guarantee that we believe only what is true and disbelieve only what is false for, in the end, it comes down to a question of judgment, of weighing one criterion against another. Nevertheless, rules, precepts and criteria are not to be despised, they may be all we have to go by in a bewildering world. We might even define *good* evidence as that which satisfies *reasonable* criteria.

Let us take a look, now, at some of the criteria that prevail in different walks of life. The first point to notice is that what counts as *good* evidence in a given case is always relative to the *best* evidence that is available *in the circumstances*. In experimental science we are in the fortunate position of being able to apply the most stringent criterion of all, namely that no claim shall be considered as established until it has been corroborated by independent and qualified authorities. In the field of history, on the other hand, very different considerations come into play for the obvious reason that we are here concerned with past events which can never recur. Historians are thrown back on plausible inferences and, inevitably, the more remote the events and the sparser the evidence, the harder it will be to command a consensus. Yet other factors enter into the evaluation of evidence that comes before a court of law. A lawyer has the advantage, normally denied to the historian, or cross-examining the key witnesses who are even under oath to tell the truth. Furthermore the lawyer can nowadays use the findings of forensic science to support his case.

Parapsychology spans all three types of evidence. There is, first, the data from the parapsychological laboratory to which the same rules will apply as to any other experimental science. There is, secondly, the records of past experiments and investigations to which the same rules will apply as for historical evidence in general. And there is, thirdly, reports of spontaneous cases by living individuals which can be dealt with in much the same way as we deal with legal evidence.

Why, then, have we made so little progress towards satisfying our critics? The answer hinges on the fact that our critics are able to appeal to the Humean objections as a reason for dismissing all but the experimental evidence and, as we have already noted, the criterion for acceptability for such evidence is nothing less than repeatability on demand. And, since that criterion has not yet been met, not, at any rate, to the satisfaction of our critics, *all* paranormal claims are, accordingly, rejected as unfounded.

Since David Hume's essay "Of Miracles" still serves as the seminal text for contemporary skeptics, let us reconsider the classic Humean argument.[b] Hume never underestimated the value of testimony in all the *ordinary* affairs of life. On the contrary, he insists that "there is no species of reasoning more common, more useful and even necessary to human life than that which is derived from the testimony of men and the reports of eye-witnesses and spectators" (Hume

John Beloff, 1976 (photo by Bruno Beloff, age 13).

1777, section 10). Why, then, was Hume ready to set at nought such evidence when it came to the reporting or miracles? The argument is very neat. A miracle confronts us with a dilemma. If we accept the miracle at face value we fly in the face of everything we have learned to expect about the ways of nature and of the world that we know. If, on the other hand, we deny the miracle, we may impugning the good faith of witnesses who may well be persons of unblemished reputation. In the event Hume could only weigh one improbability against another but, given, as he called it, "the folly and knavery of mankind," he had no doubt that the latter alternative must always win the day.

To many this may sound the counsel of a cynic but it could be argued that the sheer success of the scientific enterprise since Hume's day has further strengthened Hume's argument. For nowadays, a miracle (read: paranormal phenomenon) not only runs counter to all our previous *everyday* experience, more importantly it appears to threaten the entire closely woven fabric of modern science. For it presents us with a new class of phenomena which science not only never led us to expect but appears powerless to assimilate. Of course, Hume himself and his subsequent followers are anxious to rebut a charge of dogmatism in this connection and would concede that science might, after all, have misled us. Certainly it would not be the first time that a new discovery has taken the learned world by surprise. But, nothing short of a repeatable demonstration would convince them that such was the case. Moreover Hume insisted that a miracle that was regularly repeated would cease to be a miracle, though we would say that it could still be an anomaly.

Is there any answer that a rational believer can make in the face of such reasoning? We may start by noting one very awkward consequence of any such blanket rejection of the paranormal. For there is one situation, at least, where it would be impossible for us to sustain the Humean stance, namely the situation in which we ourselves became the witness to a paranormal event in conditions where we could satisfy ourselves completely that we were not the victims of any trick or illusion. Such an eventuality must be granted by the Humean, if only for the sake of argument, if a charge of dogmatism is to be avoided. Yet, in such a situation, the Humean would have to agree that everyone else in the world would be justified in denouncing us, and our cowitnesses, as liars no matter how reputable or numerous we might be!

Leaving aside this paradox, however, what are we to say to the wider appeal to the authority of science and/or of commonsense? The latter, conceived as a set of basic limiting principles may already be said to have a much reduced authority if only because science itself constantly undermines it. On the other hand it would surely be a mark of flippancy or ignorance to belittle the authority of modern science which has a good claim to represent the most powerful and coherent body of knowledge there has ever been. Nevertheless, there are two options open to us which would allow us to acknowledge paranormal phenomena without repudiating the achievements of science. The first, which currently appeals to many parapsychologists, especially to those with a scientific background, is to argue that science as we know it is incomplete. That, in the fullness of time, a reconciliation will be found between the normal and the so-called "paranormal" within some higher synthesis, even if we can now only dimly envisage what form this will take. A few hardy theorists go even further and argue that the paradoxes of quantum mechanics already provides us with all the basic moves we require to achieve such a synthesis.

The second option, which appeals more to those of my philosophical cast, is to argue that, however accurate or comprehensive modern science may become within its own terms of reference, in the end it can never provide more than a partial picture of reality. It has enabled us to understand the physical universe as never before but it stops short of throwing any light on the domain of mind or spirit. If, therefore, we are correct in thinking that it is precisely at the intersection of mind and matter that psi phenomena arise, it is no longer surprising that science should have failed either to predict such phenomena or to explain them when challenged to do so.

Once parapsychology is no longer viewed exclusively from the angle of physics a much broader conception of what constitutes good evidence opens up. We may now have to forego the goal of *conclusive* evidence but *good* evidence can be recognized within a humanistic framework. A working rule that I have found useful in this connection is the following: a given paranormal claim may be regarded as evidential *to the extent that all alternative normal explanations remain implausible*. This Beloff rule is not infallible and it will therefore sometimes let you down. Like so many others, I once regarded the work of S.G. Soal as evidential simply because I thought it incredible that such a one as he would have cheated in his own experiments. But, alas, the incredible sometimes happens and we are all now sadder and wiser with respect to S.G. Soal; some believers, indeed, never recovered from the shock and thereafter became outspoken skeptics.

Someone might object to my rule on the grounds that one can never enumerate *all* alternative normal explanations so that, in a given case, there might always be *some* explanation which no one had ever considered. In practice, however, this objection is not as serious as it sounds. For the fact is that the different *types* of normal explanation are severely limited. One could even say that they boil down to only three basic categories. There is, first, the possibility that what is *perceived* as being paranormal is not paranormal at all but has some perfectly normal and mundane explanation. Examples are the artifacts that arise in experimental work or the coincidences that occur in spontaneous cases. Secondly, there is the ever present possibility that what the witnesses honestly thought they had observed was not what really happened. The shortcomings of unaided observation and unaided memory are all too familiar, not only to psychologists but to sleight-of-hand artists whose business it is to exploit them. This is a special hazard in the case of investigations of exceptional individuals. Thirdly, and finally, there always remains the possibility that, somewhere along the chain of testimony someone is not telling the truth (at any rate so long as we are not ourselves responsible for the claim in question).

Now, I would maintain that if, in a given case, we can exclude each of these three types of counter-explanation as too implausible to bear consideration then we have, by definition, good evidence for the paranormal. *Good* evidence, I repeat, is not *conclusive* evidence. We could still find that we have erred. But, granted that it is the *best* evidence possible in the circumstances, then it is *good evidence*. By this token, I do not think that anyone reasonably well acquainted with the literature of psychical research would have too much trouble compiling a list of cases that one could regard as good evidence.

The trouble is that the sophisticated modern critic no longer considers it his or her business to think up plausible counter-explanations. Until we can supply a repeatable experiment which they can try for themselves then there is nothing, they insist, that demands an explanation. Indeed, Ray Hyman (1985) in his lengthy chapter in *A Skeptic's Handbook of Parapsychology*, regrets the wasted efforts of earlier critics like Mark Hansel who went to great lengths to devise elaborate scenarios to explain away some well known case in the literature. Such scenarios are likely to be wide of the mark and are often virtually libellous, creating unnecessary resentment. The critic's job ends, according to Hyman, when he has pointed out all the possible pitfalls of a given experiment.

But, is there any reason why *we* should follow Hyman or Flew (1985) in writing off, as of no account, everything in the literature barring the experimental evidence? Supposing it *were* the case that psi was a rare or erratic intruder into the natural order? Or, supposing, as Braude (1986, p. 11) points out, psi ability was no different from the run of normal familiar psychological abilities ("the ability to be charismatic, whimsical, manipulative ... etc.") none of which could be elicited in a laboratory in any meaningful sense, it would still evade the test of repeatability, no matter how important or pervasive in everyday life.

However, even those who do not insist on restricting the argument to the experimental domain may yet feel dissatisfied with the definition I have offered as to what should count as good evidence. Such evidence, they may object, is all very well when we are dealing with the commonplaces of life but, as the saying goes: extraordinary claims demand extraordinary evidence. Thus, when we read a biography, we may entertain doubts about this or that detail but, if we find that the protagonist is being credited with miraculous powers our attitude changes abruptly, we begin to suspect that we have left the realm of history and moved into the realm of mythology or hagiography. For example, it does not surprise us that scholars should regard with suspicion the work of Philostratus when he writes about the Greek sage and thaumaturge, Apollonius of Tyana, who flourished during the first century of the Christian Era (Thalbourne 1985). Apollonius, I should explain, who is thought to have lived to be about 100, is credited not only with numerous miracles but shares with the prophet Elijah the rare distinction of never actually dying but, instead, of being teleported direct to heaven! For like reasons many modern Christians have acute problems as to how to interpret the miracles of the New Testament. The answer, however, is not simply to reject all miracles on principle but to insist on very cogent reasons for accepting what I prefer to call "extreme phenomena."

I have spoken so far of the situation that now obtains. What of the future? What prospect is there of providing the proof that has so far eluded us? There are, broadly, I would suggest, two directions where we may seek such an outcome. Further experimental research may yet hit upon some psi effect that is *so* robust that it can stand up to any amount of laboratory testing. Alternatively we may yet discover some special case so overwhelming in its evidentiality that it would silence all doubts.

One's assessment of the prospect must inevitably depend on one's theoretical orientation. Thus, if one happens to be a disciple of the late Kenneth Batcheldor, one will dismiss any such prospect as hopeless. Now, whatever else one may say about Batcheldor, one must admit that he is one of the few theorists who have attempted to explain what every experimental parapsychologist knows from experience, namely, that the phenomena we pursue are not just elusive—we could learn to live with that—they are actively evasive! The more one strives to pin them down the more they elude capture! Batcheldor, a clinical psychologist, developed a psychodynamics of the paranormal and devoted a lifetime of empirical research to substantiate it (Batcheldor 1984). Briefly, he believed that we all, whether we know it or not, suffer from a deep seated fear of psi and of the idea of exercising paranormal powers. Hence, the harder we strive to demonstrate psi, the harder will our unconscious strive to sabotage our efforts. To mitigate this frustrating predicament, Batcheldor suggested that we deliberately create loose and ambiguous conditions. Then, if anything paranormal *should* transpire, we could always appease our unconscious by pretending that it might, after all, be due to some trick or artifact. Hence "sitter-groups" that are run on strict Batcheldorian lines operate in the dark and refrain from taking the usual safeguards and precautions. They are often, it seems, rewarded with very striking phenomena but, of course, must resign themselves to letting a question mark hang forever over their findings.

To the skeptic, of course, all this is risible—the ultimate cop-out of the self-deceiver. To a Batcheldorian, on the other hand, it makes perfectly good sense. Thus, if you want the unusual privilege of witnessing extreme phenomena, the price you must be prepared to pay is to live with permanent ambiguity. Fortunately, Batcheldor, no less than all other mortals, may have been wrong. At any rate it may be worth speculating about strategies that would enable us to escape from his dilemma.

One such strategy which still has its advocates is the so-called "definitive experiment." Something along the following lines is envisaged. A team of top-ranking scientists, reinforced with some expert magicians, would supervise an experiment designed by certain leading parapsychologists. If, under these conditions, positive results were forthcoming then, whether or not we knew any more about the nature of the phenomena, at least we would thereafter know for sure that they exist. I doubt, however, whether such a "definitive experiment" is anything more than a mirage. Even in the unlikely event of positive results being forthcoming under such conditions their impact would soon fade. For a time, perhaps, the event would capture the headlines and give parapsychology a much needed boost, but as it receded into the past, doubts would be raised, commentators would start being wise after the event and, bit by bit, the whole episode would be swallowed up in a wave of what Brian Inglis has aptly called "retrocognitive dissonance" and so rendered null and void.

A more promising strategy would be to scour the population for another Daniel Home. By this I mean an individual whose psi ability was so pronounced as to be self-evident. Home, after all, could do what few other physical mediums have ever been able to accomplish, namely to perform in good illumination, that is, in defiance of one of the cardinal Batcheldorian constraints. Unfortunately few scientists paid any attention to Home when he was alive, despite Crookes' earnest entreaties, but it does not require much imagination to reckon what effect a latter-day Home would have in this era of the mass media and mass communication! When, in the early 1970s, Uri Geller first arrived on the international scene, it looked as if he might fill this role. It soon became apparent, however, that, for whatever reason, he was perfectly content with his ambiguous status and new found wealth and had no intention to submit his powers to a rigorous examination. Perhaps next time we shall be more fortunate. In the meanwhile another fantasy I like to play with is the idea of rearing a child psychic prodigy much as we now nurture our musical, chess or athletic child prodigies. Parapsychologists have always been hopeful about the idea of developing a training procedure for psi ability and it happens to be a special interest of our new Koestler professor, Robert Morris. Unfortunately, the only such children to come to my attention in recent years all live in the People's Republic of China and it is hard for us to know what truth there may be in the reports that reach us.

A more realistic approach is to exploit the relentless advance of modern technology. One need only compare contemporary methods of testing for PK, using computers and random-event-generators, with the methods used by J.B. Rhine when he first began testing for PK in the laboratory. At the 1985 convention of the Parapsychological Association, in Boston, three members of the prestigious SRI International (Radin, May & Thomson 1986) reported the results of their meta-analysis which they had carried out on no less than 332 published studies that had appeared in the literature since Helmut Schmidt first introduced the technique in 1969. On a conservative estimate, which involved adding a further 95 *putative* nonpublished and nonsignificant studies, their meta-analysis still yielded astronomical odds against chance in the order of 10^{18} to one. R.A. McConnell who, many years ago, carried out the most careful series of PK tests using dice ever to have been conducted, cites this particular report as, to quote his own words, "conclusively proving the occurrence of psi" (McConnell 1987, p. 193).

McConnell (not for the first time) overstates his case. It is, indeed, valuable to have such a meta-analysis but, in the nature of the case, it can offer no assurance to the next experimenter who comes along that he or she can confidently expect positive results, if only because the experimenters involved in the sample in question are to some extent a self-selected group. However, it is an indication of what might be done by an intelligent use of technology. I like to imagine that every amusement arcade in the country had been equipped with one machine designed by a parapsychologist and incorporating a REG. While awaiting a human operator it could run a simulated play that could serve as an empirical chance baseline against which to compare the human performance. If there is anything at all in the widely held supposition that micro–PK sometimes enters a gambling situation we should soon have massive data to prove it.

I come lastly to a strategy which would certainly be decisive if only it could be realized. It is one I have discussed before and it concerns the production of a permanent paranormal object or PPO for short. The classic case is that of the linkage of two seamless rings — a topological miracle. There can be no question that there *is* evidence, for what it may be worth, that the controversial medium, Margery, produced a whole series of such linkages during the 1930s using substantial wooden rings. One such linkage is even said to have been X-rayed before being put on exhibition at the offices of the American S.P.R. in New York (Nester 1985).

The peculiar advantages of the PPO are obvious. Its paranormality does not depend on any particular person's testimony nor on the conditions under which it was produced. It can be examined at leisure, using as many devices as necessary, by as many experts as one may care to nominate. With any other kind of evidence, strong or weak, the onus of proof is always on those who claim paranormality; in the case of a PPO the onus lies with the skeptic to show, if he can, that the object in question is a normal artifact. There is one snag, however, before we are home and dry. If two rings can become paranormally linked there is no reason why they might not equally become paranormally *un*linked. And that, indeed, is precisely what is supposed to have happened in the case of Margery's linkages, none of which, alas, have survived intact.

A nice illustration of a PPO of a rather different sort is to be found in Erlendur Haraldsson's new book about the Indian religious leader Sai Baba (Haraldsson 1987). Here is the relevant passage:

> Ms. Leelemma, a botanist in Guindy outside Madras, who has known Sai Baba since the 1940s, related to me in an interview in November 1977 that Sai Baba once told her to pick an apple from a tamarind tree in Puttaparti. She found the apple on the tree and, with Baba's permission, cut off the part of the branch on which both the apple and tamarind leaves were attached. She preserved this specimen for some time in formaldehyde in the college at which she teaches. Eventually the

apple became detached from the branch. Later people would not believe that the two pieces had ever been joined and she finally threw the specimen away.

One is naturally tempted to suppose that Ms. Leelemma made up the whole story. Indians have a reputation for being polite and may be tempted to tell gullible foreigners what they would like to hear (especially if they have come all the way from Iceland to hear it!) although her account, be it noted, tallies with those of another witness, the Raja of Venkatigiri, who also recalls plucking diverse fruits from a tamarind tree. Alternatively, she might have been either so shortsighted or so stupid as not to have noticed that the apple had just been tied to the tree by a fine thread. But, having said all that, one has just about exhausted the possibilities of a normal counter-explanation. Meanwhile, all one can say for sure is that if we now had that specimen, as she describes it, what a flood of light this would throw, retrospectively, not only on the claims made for Sai Baba but on so many episodes in the history of psychical research where the only reason for doubting their phenomena is their inherent incredibility! Nothing, after all, could be more incredible than a PPO.ᶜ

I recall, in this connection, that when my former doctoral student, Michael Thalbourne, was about to leave Edinburgh to join Haraldsson in India, I gave him a pair of black leather rings and begged him, if he were to be lucky enough to gain an audience with Sai Baba, to ask him to link them. This did not, after all, seem too much to ask of someone who claims divine powers! Alas, as Thalbourne and Haraldsson were soon to discover, Sai Baba never had the slightest intention to submit himself to be tested by scientists and other interfering busybodies. Either you became a disciple and accepted the miracles at face value or you remained an outsider and gleaned what information you could by interrogating the disciples. Haraldsson, right in my view, decided that even this was better than nothing.

Let me now summarize briefly what I have been trying to say. My main point was that what constitutes good evidence in psychical research is not in principle any different from what constitutes good evidence in any other field of inquiry. It is simply that, because of the suspicion and incredulity that inevitably surrounds all paranormal claims, the evidence has to be that much stronger than is necessary in a less contentious area. Unhappily, the one test on which the scientific community insists—repeatability on demand—is not one that we have yet been able to satisfy and I gave my reasons for doubting whether it could ever be satisfied. I concluded by describing three strategies that could conceivably serve to vindicate the paranormal, culminating in the production of a permanent paranormal object. I could offer no assurance that any of these strategies would succeed but, having already amassed so much *good* evidence, I feel that we would be failing in our duty if we did not continue to pursue the goal—or should I say the grail?—of *conclusive* evidence.

Notes

a. To my surprise, McConnell took strong exception to my paper when it appeared in the Parapsychology Review. His objections are given in a letter to the editor which were published in the Sept.-Oct. 1989 issue of the Review, pp. 13–4, followed by my own brief reply. I am taken to task for toying with the "titillating possibility that psi phenomena may occur without having to bear the burden of the certainty of their reality" instead of boldly parading our best experimental evidence in a frontal assault on the scientific Establishment. I share McConnell's desire to convert scientists to our view but I see no sign that anything short of a phenomenon that could be demonstrated in demand is likely to shake their complacency. In the meanwhile we must decide what we mean by "good evidence."

b. I must crave the reader's indulgence for reverting yet again to the case of the great Scottish Skeptic. There is no getting away from the fact, however, that it was Hume who propounded what still constitutes the bedrock of the case against the paranormal, i.e. that, if the antecedent probability of a paranormal event is zero, no evidence can count in its favor and, hence, no evidence can be good evidence. Thus Hume provides a natural point of departure in this context as he does for arguments about the causal nexus or the continuity of the self.

c. Since these words were written, Haraldsson drew my attention to an article by Bernard Wälti in the Zeitschrift fur Parapsychologie 30, 1988, 236–42. I thought this sufficiently important to be worth bringing to the attention of the English-speaking world and so, with the blessing of its author and editor, it is now scheduled to appear in the January 1990 issue of the Journal of the S.P.R. under the title: "A permanent paranormal object? Preliminary report on an unusual experiment with Silvio."

References

JOURNAL ABBREVIATIONS

Amer. J. Psych.	American Journal of Psychology
Brit. J. Phil. Sci.	British Journal for the Philosophy of Science
Brit. J. Psych.	British Journal of Psychology
Bull. Brit. Psychol. Soc.	Bulletin of the British Psychological Society
EJP	European Journal of Parapsychology
Internat. J. Parapsych.	International Journal of Parapsychology
J. Abn. & Soc. Psych.	Journal of Abnormal and Social Psychology
JASPR	Journal of the American Society for Psychical Research
J. Gen. Psych.	Journal of General Psychology
JP	Journal of Parapsychology
JSPR	Journal of the Society for Psychical Research
Parapsych. Rev.	Parapsychology Review
Phil. Rev.	Philosophical Review
ProcSPR	Proceedings of the Society for Psychical Research
Psychol. Rev.	Psychological Review
RIP 19—	Research in Parapsychology 19— (annual)

Alcock, James E. (1981). *Parapsychology: Science or Magic?* Oxford & New York: Pergamon.
Baggally, W.W. (1910). Discussion of the Naples Report on Eusapia Palladino. *JSPR* 14, 213–28.
Balanovski, E., & Taylor, J.G. (1978). Can electromagnetism account for extra-sensory phenomena? *Nature* 275, 67–7.
Barber, T.X. (ed.) (1976). *Advances in Altered States of Consciousness and Human Potentialities.* New York: Psychological Dimensions.

Basmajian, J. (1972). Electromyography comes of age. *Science* 176, 603–9.

Batcheldor, K.J. (1984). Contributions to the theory of PK induction from a sitter-group work. *JASPR* 78, 105–22.

Becchover Roberts, C.E. (ed.) (1945). *The Trial of Mrs. Duncan.* London: Jarrolds.

Beloff, Halla (1986). *Camera Culture.* Oxford: Blackwell.

Bergson, Henri (1911). *Matter and Memory.* London: Routledge & Kegan Paul (transl. from *La Matière et la Mémoire*, 1908).

Besterman, T. (1933). An experiment in "clairvoyance" with M. Stefan Ossowiecki. *ProcSPR* 41, 345–51.

Blackmore, Susan (1980). *Extrasensory Perception as a Cognitive Process.* Ph.D. Thesis. University of Surrey (unpubl.).

Blackmore, Susan (1986). *Adventures of a Parapsychologist.* Buffalo, N.Y.: Prometheus.

Brandon, Ruth (1983). *The Spiritualists: The Passion for the Occult in the 19th and 20th Centuries.* Buffalo, N.Y.: Prometheus.

Braud, Lendell, & Braud, W. (1978). PK effects upon a random number generator under conditions of limited feedback to volunteer and experimenter. *RIP 1977* 135–43 (abstract).

Braud, W. (1978). Allobiofeedback: immediate feedback for a PK influence upon another person's physiology. *RIP 1977* 123–34 (abstract).

Braud, W., & Schlitz, M. (1983). Psychokinetic influence on electrodermal activity. *JP* 47, 95–119.

Braude, S.E. (1978). Telepathy. *Nous* 12, 267–301.

Braude, S.E. (1979). The Observational theories in parapsychology: A critique. *JASPR* 73, 349–66.

Braude, Stephen E. (1979a). *ESP and Psychokinesis: A Philosophical Examination.* Philadelphia: Temple University Press.

Braude, Stephen E. (1986). *The Limits of Influence: Psychokinesis and the Philosophy of Science.* New York: Routledge.

Braude, S.E. (1988) Death by Observation: a reply to Millar. *JASPR* 82, 273–80.

Brian, Denis (1982). *The Enchanted Voyager: The Life of J.B. Rhine.* Englewood Cliffs, N.J.: Prentice Hall.

Brier, Bob (1974). *Precognition and the Philosophy of Science: An Essay on Backward Causation.* New York: Humanities Press.

Broad, C.D. (1967). The Notion of Precognition. In Smythies (1967).

Broughton, R. (1976). Possible brain hemisphere laterality effect on ESP performance. *JASPR* 48, 384–400.

Broughton, R. (1977). An exploratory study of psi-based experimenter and subject expectancy effects. *RIP 1976* 173–77 (abstract).

Broughton, Richard S. (1977a). *Brain Hemisphere Differences in Paranormal Abilities: With Special Reference to the Influence of Experimenter Expectancies.* University of Edinburgh: Ph.D. dissertation (unpubl.).

Brown, W.P. (1961). *Conception of Perceptual Defence.* Brit. J. Psych. Monogr. Suppl. No. 35.

Bursen, Howard A. (1978). *Dismantling the Memory Machine.* Dordrecht, Holland: R. Reidel.

Carrington, Hereward (1909). *Eusapia Palladino and Her Phenomena.* London: Werner Laurie.

Carrington, Hereward (1913). *Personal Experiences in Spiritualism.* London: Werner Laurie.

Carrington, Hereward (1954). *The American Seances with Eusapia Palladino.* New York: Garrett.

Cassirer, M. (1983). Palladino at Cambridge. *JSPR* 52, 52–8.

Cassirer, M. (1983a). The fluid hands of Eusapia Palladino. *JSPR* 52, 105–12.

Cassirer, Manfred (1984). *Witchcraft at Portsmouth: A Reassessment of the Mediumship of Mrs. Duncan.* London: Library of Society for Psychical Research (unpubl.).

Cassirer, M. (1985). Helen Victoria Duncan: A Reassessment. *JSPR* 53, 138–44.

Cupitt, Don (1984). *The Sea of Faith.* London: BBC Publications.

Delaney, J.J. (1980). *Dictionary of Saints.* Tadworth, Surrey: Laye & Ward.

Delanoy, Deborah L. (1986). *The Training of ESP in the Ganzfeld.* University of Edinburgh: Ph.D. dissertation (unpubl.).

Deutsch, J.A. (ed.) (1973). *The Physiological Basis of Memory.* New York: Academic Press.

Dingwall, E.J. (1924). An experiment with the Polish medium Stephan Ossowiecki. *JASPR* 21, 259–63.

Dingwall, E.J. (1930). An amazing case: the mediumship of Carlos Mirabelli. *JASPR* 24, 296–306.

Dingwall, E.J. (1947). *Human Oddities.* London: Home & Van Thal.

Dingwall, E.J. (1950). *Very Peculiar People.* London: Rider.

Dixon, Norman F. (1971). *Subliminal Perception the Nature of a Controversy.* New York: McGraw-Hill.

Dixon, N.F. (1979). Subliminal perception and Parapsychology: points of contact. In Parapsychology Foundation (1979).

Dixon, N.F. (1987). The J.B. Rhine Address. 30th Annual Convention, Parapsychological Association, Edinburgh.

Ducasse, C.J. (1924). *Causation and the Types of Necessity.* New York: Dover, 1969.

Dummett, M.A.E. (1964). Bringing about the past. *Phil. Rev.* 23, 338–59 [reprinted in Gale, R.M. (ed.) (1967)].

Eccles, J.C. (1953). *The Neurophysiological Basis of Mind.* Oxford: Clarendon Press.

Eccles, J.C. (1970). *Facing Reality.* New York: Springer; London: English Universities Press.

Eccles, J.C. (1977). The human person in its two-way relationship with the brain. *RIP 1976* 251–62.

Eisenbud, J. (1965). Perception of subliminal visual stimuli in relation to ESP. *Internat. J. Parapsych.* 7, 161–83.

Eisenbud, Jule (1982). *Paranormal Foreknowledge: Problems and Perplexities.* New York: Human Sciences Press.

Farmer, D.H. (1987). *Oxford Book of Saints.* Oxford: Oxford University Press.

Flew, Antony (1953). *A New Approach to Psychical Research.* London: C.A. Watts.

Flew, A. (1985). Parapsychology: Science or Pseudoscience? In P. Kurtz (ed.) (1985).

Flew, A. (1989). Evidencing the improbable and the impossible. In Zollschan, Schumaker & Walsh (eds.) (1989).

Flournoy (1911). *Spiritism and Psychology* New York: Harper [transl. from *Mélange de Métapsychique et de Psychologie,* Geneva: 1911].

Fodor, Nandor (1934/1966). *An Encyclopaedia of Psychic Science.* New Hyde Park, N.Y.: University Books.

Forwald, Haakon (1969). *Mind, Matter and Gravitation.* New York: Parapsychology Foundation.

Gale, R.M. (ed.) (1967). *The Philosophy of Time.* New York: Macmillan.

Gauld, A. (1977). Discarnate survival. In B. Wolman (ed.) (1977).

Gissurarson, L.R., & Haraldsson, E. (1988). The Icelandic medium Indridi Indridason. *ProcSPR* 57 No. 214.

Grattan-Guinness, Ivor (ed.) (1982). *Psychical Research: Its History, Principles and Practices.* Wellingborough, Northants: Aquarian Press.

Green, E.E., Green, A.M., & Walters, E.D. (1976). Biofeedback for mind-body self-regulation, healing and creativity. In T.X. Barber (ed.) (1976).

Gregor, P. (1972). "Perceptual Defense." University of Edinburgh: B.Sc. dissertation (unpubl.).

Gregory, Anita K. (1968). *The Ghost in the Machine: Rudi Schneider and His Investigators.* Library of S.P.R. (unpubl.).

Gregory, Anita (1985). *The Strange Case of Rudi Schneider.* Metuchen, N.J.: Scarecrow.

Gregory, Richard L. (ed.) (1987). *The Oxford Companion to Mind.* Oxford: Oxford University Press.

Hall, Trevor H. (1963). *The Spiritualists: The Story of Florence Cook and William Crookes.* New York: Garrett (reprinted as *The Medium and the Scientist: The Story of . . .,* Buffalo, N.Y.: Prometheus).

Hall, Trevor H. (1984). *The Enigma of Daniel Home: Medium or Fraud?* Buffalo, N.Y.: Prometheus.

Hansel, C.E.M. (1966). *ESP: A Scientific Evaluation* New York: Scribner's.

Hansel, C.E.M. (1980). *ESP and Parapsychology.* Buffalo, N.Y.: Prometheus.

Haraldsson, Erlendur (1987). *Miracles Are My Visiting Cards: An Investigative Report on the Psychic Phenomena Associated with Sathya Sai Baba.* London: Century Hutchinson.

Hardy, Alister (1965). *The Living Stream.* London: Collins.

Hardy, Alister (1966). *The Divine Flame.* London: Collins.

Hardy, Alister (1975). *The Biology of God.* London: Cape.

Harris, Harold (ed.) (1976). *Astride the Two Cultures: Arthur Koestler at 70.* London: Hutchinson.

Harrison, V. (1986). J'accuse: an examination of the Hodgson Report of 1985. *JSPR* 53, 286–310.

Haynes, Renée (1961). *The Hidden Springs: An Enquiry into Extra-Sensory Perception.* London: Hutchinson.

Haynes, Renée (1970). *The Philosopher King: The Humanist Pope Benedict XIV.* London: Weidenfeld & Nicolson.

Hebb, D.O. (1949). *The Organization of Behavior: A Neuropsychological Theory.* New York: Wiley.

Hickey, Des, & Smith, Gus (1978). *Miracle.* London: Hodder & Stoughton.

Hoebens, P.H. (1985). Reflections on Psychic Sleuths (edited by M. Truzzi). In P. Kurtz (ed.) (1985).

Hyman, R. (1985). A critical historical overview of parapsychology. In P. Kurtz (ed.) (1985).

Inglis, Brian (1984). *Science and Parascience: A History of the Paranormal 1914–1939.* London: Hodder & Stoughton.

Jahn, Robert, & Dunne, Brenda (1988). *Margins of Reality.* New York: Harcourt Brace Jovanovich.

James, William (1890). *The Principle of Psychology.* (2 vols.). New York: Holt.

Janin, P. (1974). PK into the past: an exploratory experiment (unpubl. paper).

Jen, C.K. (1982). Some demonstrations on extraocular image in China. In R.A. McConnell (ed.) (1982).

Johnson, M. (1973). A new technique of testing ESP in real life high motivation context. *JP* 37, 210–18.

Johnson, M., & Kanthamani, B.K. (1967). The defence mechanism test as a predictor of ESP scoring direction. *JP* 31, 99–111.

Jung, C.G. (1955). Synchronicity: An Acausal Connection Principle. Part I of C.G. Jung & W. Pauli *The Interpretation of Nature and the Psyche* (transl. by R.F.C. Hull). London: Routledge & Kegan Paul.

Kiang, T. (1982). Report on investigations into "Exceptional Human Body Function" in the People's Republic of China. *JSPR* 51, 304–7.

Koestler, Arthur (1960). *The Lotus and the Robot.* London: Hutchinson.

Koestler, Arthur (1964). *The Act of Creation.* London: Hutchinson.

Koestler, Arthur (1972). *The Roots of Coincidence.* London: Hutchinson.

Koestler, Arthur (1978). *Janus: A Summing-up.* London: Hutchinson.

Koestler, Arthur, & Koestler, Cynthia (1984). *Stranger in the Square.* London: Hutchinson.

Kogan, I.M. (1969). The informational aspect of telepathy. Paper presented to the U.C.L.A. symposium "A New Look at ESP" (unpubl.).

Kreitler, H., & Kreitler, S. (1972). Does extrasensory perception affect psychological experiments? *JP* 36, 1–45.

Krippner, S. (1968). Experimentally induced telepathic effect in hypnosis and non-hypnosis groups. *JASPR* 387–99.

Krippner, Stanley (1975). *The Song of the Siren: A Parapsychological Odyssey.* New York: Harper & Row.

Kurtz, Paul (ed.) (1985). *A Skeptic's Handbook of Parapsychology.* Buffalo, N.Y.: Prometheus.

Lambert R. (1954). Dr. Geley's reports on the medium Eva C. *JSPR* 37, 380–86.

LeShan, Lawrence (1974). *The Medium, the Mystic and the Physicist.* London: Turnstone.

Lloyd, D.H. (1973). Objective events in the brain correlating with psychic phenomena. *New Horizons* 1, 69–75.

Lodge, O. (1894). Experience of unusual physical phenomena occurring in the presence of an entranced person (Eusapia Palladino). *JSPR* 6 306–60.

Lodge, O. (1931). *Past Years.* London: Hodder and Stoughton.

Ludwig, Jan (ed.) (1978). *Philosophy and Parapsychology.* Buffalo, N.Y.: Prometheus.

McConnell, R.A. (1982). *Parapsychology and Self-Deception in Science.* Pittsburgh, Pa.: R.A. McConnell.

McGinnies, E. (1949) Emotionality and perceptual defence. *Psychol. Rev.* 56 244–51.

Malcolm, Norman (1977). *Memory and Mind.* Ithaca, N.Y.: Cornell University Press.

Markwick, B. (1978). The Soal-Goldney experiments with Basil Shackleton: New evidence of data manipulation. *ProcSPR* 56, 250–77.

Matlock, J.G. (1987). Cat's-paw: Margery and the Rhines 1926. *JP* 51, 229–48.

Medhurst, R.G., Goldney, K.M., & Barrington, M.R. (eds.) (1972). *Crookes and the Spirit World.* London: Souvenir Press.

Millar, B. (1978). The Observational theories: a primer. *EJP* 2, 304–32.

Millar, B. (1985). St. George and the Dragon: in memory of Piet Hein Hoebens. *JSPR* 53, 127–8.

Millar, B. (1986). Cutting the Braudian loop. *SRU Bulletin* 11, 72–9.

Millar, B. (1988). Cutting the Braudian loop: in defense of the Observational Theories. *JASPR* 82, 253–72.

Miller, J.G. (1940). Discrimination without awareness. *Amer. J. Psych.* 53, 229–39.

Milton, Julie (1986). *Displacement Effects, Role of Agent and Mentation Categories in Relation to ESP Performance.* University of Edinburgh: Ph.D. dissertation (unpubl.).

Mitchell, Edgar et al. (1974). *Psychic Exploration* (edited by J. White). New York: Putnam's.

Monod, Jacques (1971). *Chance and Necessity.* New York: Knopf (transl. from *Le Hasard et la Necessité.* Paris: Du Seuil, 1970).

Morris, R.L. (1975). Tacit communication and experimental theology. *RIP 1974,* 179–98 (abstract).

Mundle, C.W.K. (1964). Does the concept of precognition make sense? *Internat. J. Parapsych.* 6, 179–98.

Mundle, C.W.K. (1973). Strange facts in search of a theory. *ProcSPR* 56, 1–19.

Murphy, Gardner (1961). *The Challenge of Psychical Research.* New York: Harper.

Musgrave, Dorothy A. (1965). *Dorothy Kerin: Called by Christ to Heal.* Tunbridge Wells, Surrey: K & SC Printers.

Nash, C.B. (1986). Comparison of subliminal and extrasensory perception. *JSPR* 53, 435–55.

Nester, M.L. (1985). The Margery mediumship: I was there. *Fate.* April, 78–89.

New Catholic Encyclopedia (1967). Entry: "Joseph of Cupertino, St." New York: McGraw-Hill.

Nicola, John (1974). *Demonic Possession and Exorcism.* Rockford, Ill.: Tan Books.

Orme, J.E. (1974). Precognition and time. *JSPR* 47, 351–66.

Parapsychology Foundation Inc. (New York):
> *Psi and Altered States of Consciousness* (1968), edited by R. Cavanna & M. Ullman.
> *Parapsychology and the Sciences* (1974), edited by A. Angoff & B. Shapin.
> *Quantum Physics and Parapsychology* (1975), edited by L. Oteri.
> *Education in Parapsychology* 1976), edited by B. Shapin & L. Coly.
> *The Philosophy of Parapsychology* (1977), edited by B. Shapin & L. Coly.
> *Brain/Mind and Parapsychology* (1979), edited by B. Shapin & L. Coly.
> *The Repeatability Problem in Parapsychology* (1985), edited by B. Shapin & L. Coly.

Parker, Adrian (1975). *States of Mind: ESP and Altered States of Consciousness.* London: Malaby Press.

Parker, Adrian (1977). *The Experimenter Effect in Parapsychology.* University of Edinburgh: Ph.D. dissertation (unpubl.).

Parker, Adrian (1988). A sceptical evaluation of *A Skeptic's Handbook. JSPR* 55, 90–7.

Penfield, W. (1958). *The Excitable Cortex in Conscious Man.* Liverpool: University of Liverpool Press.

Perry, Michael (1959). *The Easter Enigma.* London: Faber & Faber.

Perry, Michael (1984). *Psychic Studies: A Christian's View.* Wellingborough, Northants: Aquarian Press.

Persinger, Michael (1974). *The Paranormal, Part II.* New York: MSs Information Corporation.

Pilkington, Rosemarie (ed.) (1987). *Men and Women of Parapsychology: Personal Reflections.* Jefferson, N.C.: McFarland.

Playfair, Guy L. (1975). *The Flying Cow.* London: Souvenir Press.

Playfair, Guy L. (1985). *If This Be Magic.* London: Jonathan Cape.

Podmore, Frank (1909). The report on Eusapia Palladino. *JSPR* 14, 172–6.

Podmore, Frank (1910). *The Newer Spiritualism.* London: Fisher & Unwin.

Poetzl, O.; Allers, R., & Teler, J. (1960). *Preconscious Stimulation in Dreams, Associations and Images* (Psychological Issues Monograph No. 7). New York: International Universities Press.

Popper, Karl R., & Eccles, John C. (1977). *The Self and Its Brain: An Argument for Interactionism.* London: Springer.

Pratt, J.G.; Rhine, J.B., et al. (1940/1966). *Extra-Sensory Perception after Sixty Years.* Boston: Bruce Humphries.

Pratt, J. Gaither (1964). *Parapsychology: An Insider's View of ESP.* New York: Doubleday.

Pratt, J. Gaither (1987). *Gaither Pratt: A Life for Parapsychology,* ed. Jürgen Keil. Jefferson, N.C.: McFarland.

Price, H.H. (1940). Some philosophical questions about telepathy and clairvoyance. *Philosophy* 15, 363–85.

Radin, D.I.; May, E.C., & Thomson, M.J. (1986). Psi experiments with random number generators: Meta-analysis Part I. *RIP 1985* 14–7 (abstract).

Rao, K. Ramakrishna (ed.) (1982). *J.B. Rhine: On the Frontiers of Science.* Jefferson, N.C.: McFarland.

Rhine, J.B. (1954). *New World of Mind.* London: Faber & Faber.

Rhine, J.B. (1974). A new case of experimenter unrealiability. *JP* 38, 301–11.

Richet, Charles (1923). *Thirty Years of Psychical Research.* New York: Macmillan (transl. from *Traité de Métapsychique,* Paris: Alcan, 1922).

Riess, B.F. (1937). A case of high scores in card guessing at a distance. *JP* 1, 260–63.

Rogo, D.S. (1975). Eusapia Palladino and the structure of scientific controversy. *Parapsych. Rev.* 6, No. 2, 23–7.

Rogo, S. Scott (1982). *Miracles.* New York: The Dial Press.

Roll, W.G. (1966). ESP and memory. *Internat. J. Neuropsychiatry* 2, 505–21.

Roney-Dougal, S. (1986). Subliminal and psi perception: a review of the literature. *JSPR* 53, 405–34.

Roney-Dougal, S. (1987). A comparison of subliminal and psi perception: exploratory and follow-up studies. *JASPR* 81, 141–82.

Russell, Bertrand (1921). *The Analysis of Mind.* London: Allen & Unwin.

Ryle, Gilbert (1949). *The Concept of Mind.* London: Hutchinson.

Schmeidler, G.R. (1971). Parapsychologists' opinions about parapsychology 1971. *JP* 35, 208–18.

Schmidt, H. (1974). Comparison of PK action in two different random number generators. *JP* 38, 47–55.

Schmidt, H. (1974a). A new role of the experimenter in science suggested by parapsychological research. In Parapsychology Foundation (1974).

Schmidt, H. (1975). Towards a mathematical theory of psi. *JASPR* 69, 301–19.

Schmidt, H. (1975a). A logically consistent model of a world with psi interaction. In Parapsychology Foundation (1975).

Schmidt, H. (1976). PK effect on prerecorded targets. *JASPR* 70, 267–93.

Schmidt, H. (1978). Can an effect precede its cause? A model of a noncausal world. *Foundations of Physics* 8, 463–80.

Scott, C. (1980). Comments on Beloff's "Seven Evidential Experiments" *Zetetic Scholar* 6, 110–12.

Schouten, S. (1977). Testing some implications of a PK Observational theory. *EJP* 1, 21–3.

Sheldrake, Rupert (1981). *A New Science of Life: The Hypothesis of Formative Causation.* London: Blond & Briggs.

Sheldrake, Rupert (1988). *The Presence of the Past: Morphic Resonance and the Habits of Nature.* London: Collins.

Smythies, J.R. (ed.) (1965). *Brain and Mind.* London: Routledge & Kegan Paul.

Smythies, J.R. (ed.) (1967). *Science and ESP.* London: Routledge & Kegan Paul.

Stanford, R.G. (1970). Extrasensory effects upon "memory." *JASPR* 64, 161–86.

Stanford, R.G. (1974). An experimentally testable model for spontaneous psi events.

Part I Extrasensory events; Part II Psychokinetic events. *JASPR* 68, 34–58; & 321–57.

Stanford, R.G., & Fox, C. (1975). An effect of release of effort in a psychokinetic task. *RIP 1974* 61–9.

Stevenson, I. (1977). Reincarnation: Field studies and theoretical issues. In B. Wolman (ed.) (1977).

Taylor, John (1975). *Superminds.* London: Macmillan.

Taylor, John (1980). *Science and the Supernatural.* New York: Dutton.

Teng, L.C. (1981). Letter to the editor. *JASPR* 51, 181–3.

Thakur, S.C. (1979). Hidden variables, bootstraps and Brahman. *JASPR* 50, 135–40.

Thalbourne, Michael A. (1981). *Some Experiments on the Paranormal Cognition of Drawings.* University of Edinburgh: Ph.D. dissertation (unpubl.).

Thalbourne, Michael A. (1982). *A Glossary of Terms Used in Parapsychology.* London: Heinemann.

Thalbourne, M.A. (1985). Apollonius of Tyana (unpubl. paper).

Thouless, R.H. (1951). A report on an experiment in psychokinesis with dice and a discussion on psychological factors favoring success. *JP* 15, 89–102.

Thouless, Robert H. (1972). *From Anecdote to Experiment in Psychical Research.* London: Routledge & Kegan Paul.

Thurston, Herbert (1952). *The Physical Phenomena of Mysticism.* Edited by J.H. Crehan. London: Burns Oates.

Tietze, T.R. (1985). The "Margery" affair. *JASPR* 79, 339–79.

Ullman, M., & Krippner, S. (1970). *Dream Studies and Telepathy: An Experimental Approach* (Parapsychological Monographs No. 12). New York: Parapsychology Foundation.

Valenstein, E.S. (1973). *Brain Control.* New York: Wiley.

Van Over, Raymond (ed.) (1972). *Psychology and Extrasensory Perception.* New York: New American Library.

Walker, E.H. (1974). Consciousness and quantum theory. In E. Mitchell (1974).

Walker, E.H. (1975). Foundations of paraphysical and parapsychological phenomena. In Parapsychology Foundation (1975).

West, D.J. (1946). The trial of Mrs. Duncan. *ProcSPR* 48, 32–64.

West, D.J. (1957) *Eleven Lourdes Miracles.* London: Duckworth.

Wheatley, J.M.O., & Edge, R.L. (eds.) (1976). *Philosophical Dimensions of Parapsychology.* Springfield, Ill.: C C Thomas.

Wittgenstein, Ludwig (1967). *Zettel.* Oxford: Blackwell.

Wolman, B.B. (ed.) (1977). *Handbook of Parapsychology.* New York: Van Nostrand Reinhold.

Wood, Ernest (1959). *Yoga.* Harmondsworth, Middlesex: Penguin.

Yates, Frances (1972). *The Rosicrucian Enlightenment.* London: Routledge & Kegan Paul.

Zanstra, H. (1962). *The Construction of Reality.* London: Pergamon.

Zollschan, G.K.; Schumaker, J.F., & Walsh, G.F. (eds.) (1989). *Exploring the Paranormal: Different Perspectives on Belief and Experience.* Dorset, England: Prism Press; Lindfield NSW, Australia: Unity Press.

Zorab, George (1980). *Katie King: Donna o Fantasma?* Milan: Armenia Editore.

Bibliography of Works
by the Author

Unless otherwise stated, John Beloff is the sole author.

I. Books

1962   *The Existence of Mind.* London: McGibbon & Kee; New York: Citadel (paperback).

1973   *Psychological Sciences: A Review of Modern Psychology.* London: Crosby Lockwood Staples; New York: Barnes & Noble, 1974; Utrecht: Het Spectrum, 1976 (Dutch); Mexico City: El Manual Moderno, 1979 (Spanish).

II. Books Edited

1974   *New Directions in Parapsychology,* with Afterword by Arthur Koestler. London: Elek Science; Metuchen, N.J.: Scarecrow, 1975; Rotterdam: Lemniscaat, 1975 (Dutch); Olten: Walter, 1980 (German), with a new introduction by E. Bauer & K. Kornwachs; Tokyo: Nagagami, 1986 (Japanese).

1989   John R. Smythies and John Beloff, *The Case for Dualism.* Charlottesville: University Press of Virginia.

III. Articles etc. *

1955   R.B. Cattell, D. Blewett & John Beloff. The Inheritance of Personality. *Amer. J. Human Genetics* 7, 122–46.

1956   R.B. Cattell & John Beloff. The factorial structure of the personality of 11 year old children across three techniques [in French]. *Revue de Psychologie Appliquée* 6, 65–89.

        Facts, values and moral solipsism. *J. Phil.* 53, 541–8.

1957   Method of serial extrapolation. *Quart. J. Exper. Psych.* 9, 155–68.

* *These do not include ordinary book reviews, letters to journals, etc.*

1959   H. Beloff & J. Beloff. Unconscious self-evaluation using a stereoscope. *J. Abnormal & Social Psych.* 59, 275–8.

1961   J. Beloff & H. Beloff. The influence of valence of distance judgments of human faces. *J. Abnormal & Social Psych.* 62, 720–22.

The stripe paradox. *Brit. J. Psych.* 52, 323–31.

J. Beloff & L. Evans. A radioactive test of psychokinesis. *JASPR* 41, 41–5.

Some comments on the Gombrich problem. *Brit. J. Aesthetics* 1, 62–70.

1962   Ratio judgment and the psychophysics of rectangles. *J. General Psych.* 66, 71–83.

1963   The mind-body relationship. *Modern Churchman* 7, 33–41.

Explaining the paranormal. *JASPR* 42, 101–14 [reprinted with an epilogue in Ludwig (1978)].

1964   Matter and manner [invited commentary on E. Girden's "A review of psychokinesis"]. *Internat. J. Parapsych.* 6, 93–9.

What are we up to? *J. Parapsych.* 28, 302–10.

1965   J. Smythies & J. Beloff. The influence of stereotactic surgery on ESP. *JSPR* 43, 20–4.

M. Ryzl & J. Beloff. Loss of stability of ESP performance in a high-scoring subject. *JP* 29, 1–12.

The Identity Hypothesis: a critique. In Smythies (1965).

Humanism and the paranormal. *The Humanist* 80, 176–80.

1966   J. Beloff & I. Mandleberg. An attempted validation of the "Ryzl technique" for training ESP subjects. *JSPR* 46, 229–49.

1967   Parapsychology as science. *Internat. J. Parapsych.* 9, 91–8.

Report on the Maimonides Dream Laboratory. *JSPR* 44, 24–7.

A guide to the experimental evidence for ESP. Appendix to Smythies (1967).

J. Beloff & I. Mandleberg. An attempted validation of the "waiting technique." *JSPR* 44, 82–87.

Can paranormal abilities be learned? *JASPR* 61, 120–9.

1968   ESP: proof from Prague? *New Scientist* 10 (Oct.) 76–7.

Summary of Conference. Parapsych. Foundat. (1968).

God and parapsychology: reflections on Sir Alister Hardy's *The Divine Flame*. *JASPR* 62, 217–22.

1969   The "sweethearts" experiment. *JASPR* 45, 1–6.

Current problems in parapsychology. *Synapse* 20, 21–8 [journal of the Edinburgh Medical School].

J. Beloff & T. Regan. The Edinburgh Electronic ESP Tester (E.E.E.T.) *JSPR* 45, 7–13.

1970   Creative thinking in art and science. *Brit. J. Aesthetics* 10, 58–70.

Parapsychology and its neighbours. *JP* 34, 129–42. [reprinted in Wheatley & Edge (1976)].

A. Parker & J. Beloff. Hypnotically induced clairvoyant dreams: a partial replication and attempted confirmation. *JASPR* 64, 432–42.

J. Beloff & D. Bate. Research report for the year 1968/69. *JSPR* 45, 297–301.

J. Beloff, M. Cowles & D. Bate. Autonomic reactions to emotive stimuli under sensory and extrasensory conditions of presentation. *JASPR* 64, 313–19.

1971   J. Beloff & D. Bate. An attempt to replicate the Schmidt findings. *JSPR* 46, 21–30.

J. Beloff & D. Bate. Psi efficiency: a formal comparison of three different measures. *JP* 35, 273–89.

John Beloff (left) with Hans Bender, September 1972.

1972   The scientist as oracle (essay-review of Jacques Monod's *Chance and Neces-sity*). *Virginia Quarterly Review* 48, 289–92.
        Parapsychology. In H. Eysenck, R. Meili & W. Arnold (eds.). *Encyclopedia of Psychology*. London: Search Press.
        The place of theory in parapsychology. *Research Letter of the Parapsychology Laboratory, University of Utrecht*, 2–22 [reprinted in Van Over (1972)].

1973   A note on an ostensibly precognitive dream. *JSPR* 47, 217–21.
        The mind-body problem as it now stands. *Virginia Quarterly Review* 49, 251–64.
        Belief and doubt. *RIP 1972*, 189–200.

1974   ESP: The search for a physiological index. *JSPR* 47, 403–20.
        The subliminal and the extrasensory. In Parapsych. Foundat. (1974).

1975   I sogni che annunciano il futuro. *ESP* 1, 14–22.
        The study of the paranormal as an educative experience. In Parapsych. Foundat. (1975).
        Introduction to Parker (1975).

1976   Mind-body interactionism in the light of the parapsychological evidence. *Theoria to Theory* 10, 125–37.
        On trying to make sense of the paranormal. *ProcSPR* 56, 173–95.
        Koestler's philosophy of mind. In Harris (1976).

1977   Intervju med John Beloff. *Sökaren* No. 3, 20–22.
        The Geller controversy: the current state of play. *RIP 1976* 199–200 (symposium).

[a] Historical Overview; [b] Parapsychology and Philosophy. In Wolman (1977).

Backward Causation. *Parapsych. Rev.* 8, No. 1, 1–5 [reprinted in Parapsychology Foundation (1977)].

Psi phenomena: causal versus acausal interpretation. *JSPR* 49, 573–82.

1978   Is mind autonomous? (essay review of Popper & Eccles [1977]). *Brit. J. Phil. Sc.* 29, 265–83.

Why parapsychology is still on trial. *Human Nature* 1, 68–77.

R. Broughton, B. Millar, J. Beloff & K. Wilson. A PK investigation of the experimenter effect and its psi based component. *RIP 1977*, 41–8 (abstract).

The limits of parapsychology. *EJP* 2, 291–302.

The inevitability of dualism [invited commentary on Puccetti & Dykes' "Sensory cortex and the mind-brain problem"] *Behavioral & Brain Sciences* 3, p. 347.

1979   Current directions in European parapsychology: Great Britain. *RIP 1978*, 1–2 (symposium).

Changing concepts of mind and matter: in defense of the psychobiological paradigm. *RIP 1978*, 11–12 (symposium).

Parapsicologia. In *Dizionario Enciclopedico*. Milan: Unedi.

The categories of psi: the case for retention. *EJP* 3, 69–78.

Voluntary movement, biofeedback and PK. In Parapsychology Foundation (1979).

The importance of parapsychology: a reply to H.B. Gibson. *Bull. Brit. Psychol. Soc.* 32, 244–6.

1980   I. Stevenson & J. Beloff. An analysis of some suspect drop-in communications. *JSPR* 50, 427–48.

Parapsychology. In *Colliers Encyclopedia*. New York: Macmillan.

Dr. J.G. Pratt: An obituary. *JSPR* 50, 294–6.

Coming to terms with parapsychology. *Encounter* 54, (Jan.) 86–91.

Is normal memory a "paranormal" phenomenon? *Theoria to Theory* 14, 145–61.

Intervista con John Beloff. *Parapsicologia* (Feb.) 55–7.

Could there be a physical explanation of psi? *JSPR* 50, 263–72.

Seven evidential experiments [with invited commentaries from 13 contributors and a reply by the author]. *Zetetic Scholar* 6, 91–120.

1981   Das Paranormale: kan die Kontroversie beiglegt werden? [transl.] In H.P. Duerr (ed.) *Der Wissenschaftler und das Irrationale*. Frankfurt: Syndikat. Vol. 2.

J.B. Rhine on the nature of psi. *JP* 45, 41–54 [reprinted in Rao (1982)].

J. Beloff, D. Emmet, M. Morgan, R. Sheldrake, I. Thompson. Discussion on memory. *Theoria to Theory* 14, 187–203.

1982   Foreword to: Thalbourne (1982).

Why we need a commission of inquiry. *RIP 1981*, 129–31 (abstract).

M. Thalbourne, J. Beloff & D. Delanoy. A test for the "extraverted sheep versus introverted goat hypothesis" *RIP 1981*, 155–6 (abstract).

Die Fingerabdrücke von Psi [transl.]. *Zeitschrift für Parapsych etc.* 24, 13–23 [reprinted in E. Bauer & W. von Lucadou (eds.) *Spektrum der Parapsychologie: Hans Bender zum 75 Geburstag.* Freiburg: Auru. 1983].

Psychical research and psychology. In Grattan-Guinness (1982).

1983   B. Markwick & J. Beloff. Dream States and ESP: A distance experiment with a single subject. *RIP 1982,* 228–30 (abstract).

Arthur Koestler, Psychologist. *Encounter* 61 (July) 28–31.

Three open questions. *Parapsych. Rev.* 14, No. 1, 1–6; or *RIP 1982,* 317–27.

1984   The reality of psi. *New Ideas in Psych.* 2, 51–5.

Hypnotism and the paranormal. *Changes* 2, 45–7.

Research strategies for dealing with unstable phenomena. *Parapsych. Rev.* 15, No. 1, 1–7 [reprinted in Parapsychology Foundation (1985)].

1985   Science, religion and the paranormal. *Free Inquiry* 5, 36–41.

Parapsychology and radical dualism. *J. Relig. & Psychic. Res.* 8, 3–10.

The meaning of psi: the Western perspective. *J. Indian Psych.* 4, 1–12.

Parapsychology and the expectation of progress. *EJP* 6, 71–9.

Robert Henry Thouless: an appreciation. *JP* 49, 221–7.

1986   Retrodiction. *Parapsych. Rev.* 17, No. 1, 1–5.

What is your counter-explanation? A plea to skeptics to think again. In Kurtz (1986).

George Zorab and "Katie King." In F.W.J. Snel (ed.) *In Honour of G.A.M. Zorab.* Amsterdam: N.V.P.

Killing or letting die: Is there a valid moral distinction? *Euthanasia Review* 1, 208–12.

1987   Comments on J.G. Pratt's "Some notes for the future Einstein for parapsychology." In Pratt (1987).

Parapsychology and the mind-body problem. In R.L. Gregory (1987).

The Importance of Psychical Research. S.P.R. pamphlet.

Parapsychology. In A.V. Campbell (ed.) *A Dictionary of Pastoral Care.* London: SPCK.

Parapsychology: The continuing impasse. *J. Scientific Exploration* 1, 191–6.

Parapsychology and the mind-body problem. *Inquiry* 30, 215–25.

In what way is psi anomalous? [invited commentary on K. Rao & J. Palmer's "The anomaly called psi" and on J. Alcock's "Parapsychology: science of the anomalous or search for the soul?"] *Behavioral & Brain Sciences* 10, p. 570.

1988   The history of psychology in one lecture. *Edinburgh Review* 78/9, 65–74.

Parapsychology and Physics: Can they be reconciled? *Theoretical Parapsychology* 6, 23–9.

1989   Extreme Phenomena and the problem of credibility. In G.K. Zollschan, J.F. Schumaker, & G.F. Walsh (eds.) (1989).

The Rhine Legacy. *Philosophical Psychology* 2, 231–39.

Name Index